KICKING BACK

NEDUM ONUOHA

WITH HUGH FERRIS

KICKING BACK

Biteback Publishing

First published in Great Britain in 2022 by
Biteback Publishing Ltd, London
Copyright © Nedum Onuoha and Hugh Ferris 2022

ISBN 978-1-78590-747-0

10 9 8 7 6 5 4 3 2 1

A CIP catalogue record for this book is available from the British Library.

Set in Minion Pro

Printed and bound in Great Britain by
CPI Group (UK) Ltd, Croydon CR0 4YY

*This book is dedicated to my family and close friends
for supporting me through all of life's adventures*

Contents

Foreword

'**S**orry, what? You want stories about Nedum? Deary, deary, deary me. He's the most boring man in history!'

Then the cackle. The one that is contractually obliged to follow each sentence Micah Richards utters. Three minutes later, he's joined on the Zoom call by Joe Hart.

'Hart-dog! What's happening!'

'Sorry I'm late. Been at the butcher's getting my dinner.'

The laugh again.

'What's going on?' Joe seems equally unimpressed with the task ahead. 'Everyone's selling out! What's Nedum's book even about?'

'He'll be putting the world to rights, won't he.'

'Oh, he'll love it. Absolutely love the fact his opinion might poke people. But I guarantee it will also make them think.'

• • •

I played alongside Micah and Joe for both Manchester City and the England Under-21s. For reasons that immediately became questionable, I left them alone to have a conversation about me…

• • •

MR: I don't know why he's asked me to do this. When he was the main man at City and he got a little injury, I leapt in and took his place in the team!

JH: I think that speaks more about him, Meeks. He's not looking for a big-up. He's looking for honest people. I'd like to think we're not here to say he's an amazing guy or a great player.

MR: True. He was class, though. When we were growing up, he was playing two or three years higher than his age group at the City academy. We called him 'Chief', because he was the No. 1 guy, but back in the day he was a striker. He used to bang goals in left, right and centre. He was just quicker and stronger than everyone and actually had decent technique. I'm not even joking!

JH: That's kids' football, though, isn't it? He likes to think it didn't change, but it did. If he's being truthful, he knows that I could dominate him if he was going against me. With all the intellectual standing he had, when I was in goal against him, I could mess with him so bad. He was mine. He was a toy, and continues to be, because I know that he brings it up all the time. So, I can confirm that he couldn't score to save his life in training.

MR: But I don't understand, honestly, Harty, because when he was younger he used to just run past a defender, drop his shoulder and smash it into the top corner! I thought this guy was going to be ridiculous. Now, though, I play five-a-side with him and he's got one of the worst techniques in the history of shooting! On the ball, he's so awkward! All that talent for scoring goals he had at a young age; I don't know what happened to him. It just went!

JH: I did love playing with Nedum, though.

MR: Once he got a bit bigger and he was moved to the back, he was just so good. He was incredible, and I thought he was going to be the next Sol Campbell. He had it all: one-on-one defending, tactical nous, talking with his teammates and leadership. I'm telling you, the next Sol Campbell. I know it'll hurt him that it didn't work out that way, but the problem was he didn't actually do anything wrong. He was just injured at the wrong time and then Roberto Mancini didn't give him a chance at City. He was so unlucky, and that's really being honest about the situation. He was just really unlucky.

JH: The most important thing for me is that I trust those defensive players ahead of me as a footballer and as a person. I trusted him, and he trusted me. That's the best feeling ever for me as a goalkeeper. I knew nobody would get past him easily, and if they did sneak through he had the ability to deal with it. He was very honest in his communication, and I'm a big communicator too, so we worked well.

MR: He could have been better at jumping. I'm all arms everywhere when I'm going up for a header, but he was too nice!

JH: And sensible. He certainly wouldn't party like you and me, Meeks! His fun was different, but we always respected that because we saw his thought process. Whether he was on a night out or not, he had a real good balance. It's not easy to both play and party and it can leave people by the wayside, but it was really good for others to look at Nedum to realise you don't have to try to be a rockstar. I first met him when I was still at Shrewsbury

Town, but the sportswear company Umbro had taken a punt on me. Nedum was pretty much Mr Umbro at the time, and I found him quite intimidating with his big frame and deep voice. I was nervous because I was starting to roll in Premier League circles, but I was still a League Two player. I didn't really expect people to have any idea who I was, but Nedum immediately put me at ease. That strikes me about him, you know, that he has an ability that I really like in someone, and that's to dictate the mood of a room. He took the time to get to know me, and I saw that as a huge quality. I was being linked with Manchester City at that point, so maybe in a way he was just tapping me up! Then when I joined the club, I could tell that everyone kind of understood him. And he might have been the geeky one of the group, but you couldn't mess with Nedum!

MR: I think the turning point in Nedum's career was when he was playing brilliantly under Mark Hughes in 2009. All the fans were singing, 'Nedum for England!' I'd been in the team but got injured, and this time Nedum replaced me. He was incredible for the rest of that season. I started sweating, thinking I wouldn't get my place back! But I desperately hoped he would get an England call-up.

JH: We all wanted that for him.

MR: There are two ways of finding out when you've been picked for England. You sometimes get a text, but you always get a letter. We were going out to reception at Carrington, and he hadn't received a text but there was a letter waiting for him. His form had been so good he would have been excited to read it, but it was another call-up to the Under-21s, not to the senior team. I think that was demoralising for him because if he didn't get his England chance then, he was never going to get it, because he couldn't have done any more, or played any better. He was even playing ahead of me! But then Mancini came, and it was another case of bad timing.

JH: It's about managers, and sometimes it's about moments. When I met him, he was the kind of person who had it all figured out. The pathway was there. But when you get to the very top it doesn't really matter how good you are, because everyone's good. It can fall apart pretty quickly, and when it did for Nedum at City, it wasn't through any fault of his own. He had some big decisions to make about how he was going to behave as a person, and he took the high road. We expected it, because of the man that we knew, but it's not easy to do. It hardened him and left a lot less room for bulls**t.

MR: Joe, how many times have I rung you over the last fifteen years, whether I've been doing well or badly? I've opened up about certain things with you, and with Nedum too. But he never really does the same. I think he wants to be the one who can solve the problem, because honestly, he's like a brainiac.

JH: I get the impression he likes a crisis because it means that he can help people. There were countless difficult dressing rooms at QPR, for example, and I think it actually suited his character. Them making him captain was the best thing they ever did. He's good at dealing with carnage!

MR: It's interesting that he's written a book, because he normally doesn't like to reveal what's going on his life away from football. Even when he was going through what he did with his mum. How are you supposed to deal with that? I would text him and ask if he was all right, and he'd just say, yeah and that he wasn't worried. He can't have been OK, but he felt like he had to show that he was in control of every situation. Some people might think that's a positive thing, and I know men aren't great at talking to each other, but it can't have been good for his mental health.

JH: He was very forward with us about some things, like Joey Barton or Roberto Mancini, but I think he's been hurt more than he ever thought he would, and that's a heavy burden.

MR: I just feel like he took too much in, Joe. We're all human, no matter what. I like to think that he would have been able to reach out to us more if he had been genuinely struggling. What he's been through is tough. Like, the guy couldn't catch a break, and a lot of it is my fault! When we were fighting for the same position in the team, he went away with the England Under-21s and scored, but the following night I got my only goal for the senior team. I stole the glory only twenty-four hours later!

JH: Why didn't you just leave him alone!

MR: But then Pablo Zabaleta did it to me! The biggest game of all our careers – the last day of the season in 2012 – Pablo scored the first goal for Manchester City against QPR. It could have been anyone, but it was him. It was like a dagger to me as I sat on the bench, and it must have been a bit like how Nedum had felt with me. That's just life, isn't it? Wrong place, wrong time is somebody else's right place, right time.

JH: I'll never forget that Under-21s goal you mentioned. It was in Montenegro. That was the night, when he and I were together in the tunnel, that he was racially abused by armed guards. I just knew I had to stay with him and back him up whatever. I didn't know what to do, but I wanted Nedum to know I was 100 per cent behind him. It wasn't like we were on the street; we were grown men, so I'm not sure we'd start swinging, but we could at least have tried to reason with them. This was like a stand-off, but there were more of them and they had guns.

MR: He was so young at the time, still just trying to figure stuff out. He would have felt so powerless. I've changed now and my brain's programmed differently, but I would have probably got shot if I was there. I would have been aggressive.

JH: It was strange, and it still feels weird talking about it now. I'd love to have done something about it, though. Not in terms of fighting because you can't beat six guys up, but why didn't we even think to report it?

MR: There's only so much you can do. Those guards are gone. It's not that I don't care, but it doesn't affect me any more: they're the kind of people that if they're going to be racist then let them. They're doing that to Nedum for a reaction, so they can shoot him or baton him. I'm now more worried about the root of the problem. If someone's brought up in a racist family, can you blame them for being racist? I think you've got to look at the bigger picture and educate that son or daughter while they're still young. You can help the people who want to learn, but with those who don't you've got no chance. It doesn't matter what you say. And I know that sounds bad, but it's just the truth.

JH: Nedum would have a good go at convincing anyone, though.

MR: He's just so intelligent! Football people normally only care about football, but Nedum knows everything about everything.

JH: You'd go the whole hog if you got involved in an argument with him, especially if you were going to dare to challenge what he was saying. You'd be stuck there for hours as he subjected you to long words and his dedication of proving just how right he was!

MR: The thing with Nedum is that there's no point arguing because you're not going to win. You could have a valid point,

Harty, but he'd spin it on its head and make you see it from a completely different angle. By the end of it you're agreeing with what he's saying!

JH: He's a tough one to get into a chess match with.

MR: 'Shut up, Chief. We know you're a genius.'

JH: 'OK, you win.'

MR: 'Yeah. Well done.'

JH: He's a special character and a special guy, but he does love the sound of his own voice. And he pretends he doesn't! Is there going to be an audiobook? Because if there is, he'll have to read it.

MR: I'll always help Nedum out, but apart from *Biff and Chip* when I was younger, I've never read a book.

JH: Oh, come on, Meeks, you're better than that.

MR: Anyone from my old teams, I'll give them my full support. 100 per cent.

JH: So, are you going to read the book?

MR: I'll listen to the audiobook. But that's it.

Introduction:
neɪdjuːm ɒnuːəʊhə

'**W**hat's your name?'
    'Nedum Onuoha.'
There's a silence. I'm thinking, here we go.
'How would you spell that then?'
I then proceed to spell it out, always the same way. Every time.
'It's Nedum. That's N–E–D–U–M for *mother.*'
Then I pause, so that they know it's now time for my second name.
    'Onuoha. That's O–N for *November*–U–O–H–A. Onuoha.'
Then there's another silence, during which I start to think to myself, I wonder if they actually wrote that down? Many times before I've spelled it out to someone just like that, and then the correspondence arrives with my name split into three, or with extra letters put in. I've had Ohuoha, or Ohuona, or versions where the 'O' is swapped with the 'U', because it might feel more natural for them to say it like that.
This happens literally every time I'm on the phone. I've reached a point in my life where I now expect people not to

1

listen to me when I tell them how my name is said and how it is spelled. And that's a really weird position to be in. Every day I wonder if I should make a bigger deal of it. I've heard people be mocked for not being able to say Murphy or Jones or names like that. Yet, still, here I am. Instead of others being mocked for not being able to say my name, I'm being mocked for having a name people can't say. Nobody's around to fight that battle for me, so, as is the case with most things, you end up accepting it.

I always introduce myself as Nedum, but my full name is Chinedum. I was born in Nigeria to Nigerian parents, and all my direct bloodline is Nigerian. Amongst Nigerians, I would be called Chinedum, because it has meaning within the culture of the Igbo, the tribe I'm in. In their language, *Chi* means God. I'm Chinedum; my older sister is Chioma (we call her Diuto); and my younger sisters are Chidinma (Chidi) and Chiamaka. Chinedum means 'God guides me', so that's why they don't simplify it in Nigeria, where faith and family mean everything. I'm not embarrassed by my name. I never have been, even though in the past I didn't wear it like a badge of honour as I probably do now. I was always proud of it, but it's mattered more to me since I became a father in 2014, and my three kids all have Igbo middle names, which my dad helped me with, because it attaches them to their history. Our history.

My family moved to the UK when I was five. Even in Nigeria my parents had always called me Nedum, but they wanted to make it easier for people in their new home to understand, particularly as they wouldn't have realised the significance of the 'Chi' part anyway. I never asked them if I could change from Nedum, and I have no middle name to use instead, as my father had decided to when we arrived in the UK. I remember when I was in primary school there was a spell when I really wanted to be called Denzel. I'm not sure why, as I was too young to have watched anything with Denzel Washington in, but I was obsessed with the name, and I used to write Denzel on my schoolwork, even though I knew that I didn't really want to change it permanently. Neither my family nor the school were up for participating, so I wasn't able to do it for long. My identity was essentially wherever I was at any particular moment. If I was in school, I wanted to fit in at school; if I was at training, I'd want to fit in with people at training. Now I think being different is more a strength than a weakness.

However, I have on occasion during my adult life also changed my name by choice. In Starbucks, trying to tell a barista your name is Nedum is like talking to a brick wall. They're going to write whatever they want on my cup. So, I'll call myself Nathan. Surely everybody knows a Nathan, or at least recognises the name. The downside is when they shout for a Nathan and you've forgotten that's you. So, even when you try to change your name to fit in, you don't hold it in the same way you should because it's not your identity. I understand there might be a natural British embarrassment about not wanting to offend, but I live in Manchester, an incredibly diverse city. I don't see why people freak out when they see something different, when ultimately that sense of difference exists all around us in a multicultural society.

Or you could be waiting at the doctor's surgery, and you know it won't be long until you're called from the waiting room. Mrs Murphy and Mr Jones arrived just before you, and they've gone through. Then the intercom clicks, ready to call up the next patient. You can hear the intake of breath, and instead of saying your name they let the breath out. You can't see it, but you can sense the confusion. A few second later, they try again. 'Err... Mr...?' They don't need to finish, because that's the exact moment I realise I'm next. They're looking at a series of letters, and they don't know how to say them. They can continue in one of two ways. Some people try, and the ones I appreciate the most are those who do, fail, apologise, then ask me how they're supposed to say it. Then there are others who, when I point out they've said it wrong, assume it doesn't matter as I knew they were talking about me anyway. They might not care about getting it right, and I accept that people think my name is different, but it's my identity, so surely it does matter? Sometimes it stresses me out a bit, but what can you do? You can't start an argument with somebody to prove they're wrong when they don't care about being wrong in the first place. Getting into a debate with somebody who doesn't care doesn't work. If it happens to my father, he makes them care by flipping the tables on them, deliberately getting their name wrong and often finding that they struggle to deal with it. When it's you, you notice.

Some of the people who know me best have never called me Nedum, not once. When I started my career, I made every endeavour to introduce myself in a proper manner, but within the world of football you tend to be spoken about more times than you will introduce yourself. From the moment somebody says this is your name, it spreads, and that is your name. You never have control of it. So, until I went to play in the USA in 2018, I was known in football as Chief. Most people I played with would call me Chief over Nedum Onuoha, because it became clear that saying Nedum Onuoha was hard. I've never once introduced myself to anyone as Chief. The first person to call me that was Manchester City Academy coach Alex Gibson in my Under-17s year. One day at Platt Lane, I remember he had a huge smile on his face when he said, 'You know what, I'm going to call you Chief. Yeah, you're the Chief.' It felt like Alex had a great sense of pride in calling me that, and I don't think he did so with a racial or tribal mindset, and I didn't and still don't take it that way. He had no idea that it's a word that fits so well with my history and in Igbo culture is a compliment. It was a stroke of luck on his part, but for him mostly about convenience. He didn't want to have to look at the five letters in my first name and six in my surname and try to figure out how to say it. It made it easier for people to talk about me. Little did he know the impact it would have over the course of the next fourteen years. The people in the academy knew me as Chief: the reserve team manager, the first teamers, they all ended up calling me Chief. As did those at both Sunderland and QPR. I would be introduced as Chief, to the extent that there were probably people along the way who didn't know what my actual name was, and certainly not how to say it.

Hundreds of people throughout my career knew me as Chief, despite me never once using that name myself. I had no control over it and didn't choose it, but it stuck, and I only escaped it when I went to America. There, I could be whatever I wanted to be. In the US, players don't necessarily know every single Premier League player like those in the UK might do. They tend only to watch the bigger games from the bigger teams, so someone could have spent the whole season playing for a club in the bottom half of the table, for example, and then arrive at a Major League Soccer team to people not knowing who they are. I could shape my own identity, and I loved that. By the end of my time in America, a lot of the people I had met and worked with really looked up to me for the way I carried myself and the way I played; they trusted me. It was really exciting to go over there, and I walked with my shoulders back knowing that I could choose to be whoever I wanted to be. And I chose to be a good guy, so that helps!

• • •

When Alex Gibson first called me Chief, I was a striker and had already done my GCSEs. I'd got into Hulme Grammar School in Oldham after passing their 11+ exam a year early, so for me it was a 10+. I remember taking the Manchester Grammar School entrance exam too, but I didn't get in, so after Year 5 of primary school I went straight to Year 7 at Hulme. I didn't have the same background as most of the kids there; when I first joined there were only two black boys and we were both in the same class, so it's fair to say I was different. Although I stood out, there weren't any barriers to me fitting in or speaking to whoever I wanted. Because it was a private school, I wasn't the brainiest person there; I might have been in tier two, or at least middle of the range. So, even though I was at the Manchester City Academy and maybe in the top 1 per cent in the country in that way, at school I was the median.

There were certain days when I'd take the bus straight to the academy from school. While others might have been driven from home or had a chance to get changed, I turned up in my blazer, looking just that little bit different. But at least the academy was nothing like a school playground. I wasn't always the biggest guy, but I was one of the quickest; I was strong, and I've got tons of pictures from that time which show I was very athletic, but at that age everyone's skinny. I wasn't imposing, not visually stronger than everybody else, and when you're at a football academy there's no time to bully because you only train twice a week and play once at the weekend. It's nowhere near as hostile as when you see somebody every single day.

Also, I wasn't isolated as the only clever one. Two of the best players in that set-up were Nathan and Jonathan D'Laryea, who are still two of my closest friends to this day. They went to Stretford Grammar and both are teachers now. They were very intelligent, and therefore a bit different too, so I wasn't by myself. I was never a million miles away from fitting in because it was a good group of people, very honest and humble. We were mostly Mancunian kids, and everyone was happy to be there playing together.

I changed from being a striker to a defender when I was sixteen. It was becoming clear I had the physical attributes needed to be a centre back, but I think it was just as much my intelligence that helped me succeed in that position. There is an assumption made about young black football players – whether they're defenders or strikers – that they're fast and strong and that's it. It's a shame it's like that, because it's a stereotype that sticks. When you're a young player and people haven't seen you play 100 games, there's no real significant data on you, so in describing you people go for the things they can see straight away. Young and black equals fast and strong. But some of the things that make a really good defender, for example, won't be noticed unless someone has pointed them out first. How would you realise that a player you've never seen before reads the game well or has good positional awareness while they're also running fast? Making assumptions like this is reductive and often based on a player's ethnicity. The same happens if you're a black striker.

We've seen for years that if someone like me is playing up front and they score a lot by running through on goal, people will say, 'Look at the way he holds the ball up,' or 'Look at how quick he was running on to that pass.' They might be a really good finisher, but it'll be said that they're getting those chances because they're quick. The opposite is true of a No. 10: everyone wants to talk about their technique. For them, physical attributes are a bonus, not an expectation. But if you're a No. 9 or a centre back and you're black, the technical element isn't spoken about.

I was physically strong and could play men's football at the age of seventeen. I was quick too. I could do all that stuff, but one of my strengths was my ability to read the game. I used to think about the game in a different manner to other people because, like at school, I enjoyed taking in all the information that was available to me. That's why I didn't get many yellow cards for diving in during my career. I don't think other people took the time to consider the strengths of my game, but I did, and my teammates didn't just trust me to run fast, they trusted me to stop the ball going in the goal, which requires a bit of intelligence.

There are foundations of defending, which in its simplest form is about winning headers, making tackles and winning duels – but only after you prove you can do those things will someone say you're intelligent or can read the game well. It's a bonus, not an expectation, and when I was starting my career my good judgement was never mentioned. I think that was partly because of my race and partly because back then football wasn't viewed in the same manner – most of the opinions were coming from inside the stadium, where people didn't necessarily know the ins and outs of the game. There's the potential for a greater level of understanding today because the level of analysis is very different. It used to be that you'd get your feel for football just from *Match of the Day*. Now, you can seek it out wherever you want, from somewhere very in-depth like *The Athletic* to YouTube channels that say, 'Man kick ball down channel, was good ball...'

There was one player who escaped this institutional stereotype: Rio Ferdinand. He was always spoken about as somebody who reads the game really well, although he was the exception not the rule. Playing for Manchester United, he was able to display these qualities because at that time there wasn't as much defending to do as at almost every other club. But imagine any player like him, starting their career five years earlier and playing for a different team, being described as looking great because he reads the game well. They'd say someone looks great because he can head it and kick it.

People making assumptions about a player based on their race is something some footballers have to deal with, but the perceived lack of intelligence is a cliché all footballers have to deal with. My education helped me to read the game. Football can be simplified to being about taking instruction and learning. I was somebody who was trying to learn about the game, to learn how things work, and I felt like it was easy for me to do that because I'd spent pretty much the rest of my life being given tasks and trying to figure stuff out. I could recognise how a striker was going to shoot, recognise where the runs in behind would come from and understand where I needed to be to stop them. I wasn't just out there living in the moment, staring at a ball and chasing it around. Being somebody who would be described as a critical thinker did help me develop as a player. Having said that, the other side of that coin is that when things aren't going well you can overthink it. I would know if a goal was my fault, even if that was based on something I did two minutes earlier. That's when intelligence doesn't necessarily help you. Some players might not think about the game too deeply, and for them it's just a moment they're able to brush off. They carry on without realising how they might have negatively affected something; I find it hard to move on.

My identity is built on conflicts, and I'm proud of who I am. I understood I was different when I was younger, but even then I didn't necessarily want it to be seen as a weakness, and I tried to fit in wherever I could. Maybe I shouldn't have accepted certain things and certain names I was called. But I learned. I learned about football, and I learned at school. And once you figure something out, it's great. I'll have conversations with anybody about anything, and I'm more than happy to say, I don't know the answer, but next time we speak I guarantee you that I will. During my A-Levels at Xaverian College in Manchester, I was told by a teacher that whatever grade I got for my business studies AS-Level, I could expect to get a grade less for A2. I told them that couldn't be true, but they insisted. So, I dedicated the next year to really understanding how the subject worked, figuring out how people were awarded marks in exams and doing past papers. I'm somebody who does everything possible and reads everything possible to learn as much as possible. I got a B for AS-Level and an A for A2.

I don't go in half-hearted with anything. If I want to get better at something, I'm all-in. That was true of playing football but also of learning about my place in society. Growing up, I tried to balance my sense of identity with my desire to fit in. Now, though, I'm at a point where I feel my identity is my strength, in terms of both who I was as a footballer and who I am as a human. It means I can talk about different perspectives, and my education helps me to look at these things more objectively, taking in as much detail as possible. I've seen a lot of stuff – some good, some bad – and it's helped me mould who I am today. I think I'm a good person, and I value my life. All I want to do now is add more value by being myself, not someone else. Everything you're about to read about my upbringing, my family and friends and my football career in England and the US is from a person who feels like he can walk through the rest of his life with something to say.

So why not kickback with Nedum?* That's Nedum, N–E–D…

---

* *Kickback with Nedum* is available wherever you get your podcasts.

Chapter 1

Just like the end of every weekday, Chidi and I left Miles Platting Junior School and turned right down James Street. Then it was a left onto Varley Street, where the Degussa Mill was on your right-hand side. Next, we had a choice: we could have taken the slightly shorter route through the park – but we didn't want to run into Buster, the Alsatian that would *always* chase us (I don't like dogs even now). So, we kept to the main roads, crossing over the towpath and then taking a left onto Bradford Road. We lived at 391.

I'd taken two steps into the house, thinking Dad was home, when I heard voices. I walked upstairs: there were two strangers in my parents' room. I panicked and ran downstairs. 'Chidi! We're being robbed!'

Giving my younger sister no chance to respond, I ran out of the front door while she hid behind the sofa. The men must have been desperate, because when they heard us they escaped through the back door. They didn't take anything. Guided by more sinister intentions they could have taken my sister or me, but our arrival home had scared them off. They had run away from two children under the age of ten.

My heart was beating out of my chest when I walked back into the house and saw Chidi still inside. I was supposed to have taken her with me. For the next hour and a half the two of us waited for Mum and Dad to come home. It didn't occur to me that we should dial 999 because we were just kids and we didn't make phone calls, and I'm not sure I knew where the phone was anyway. And what would they have done? The police around there were used to that type of thing. We just had to wait for our dad to phone them when he got back. The next day, it was business as usual. It had to be. The same walk to school and back: James Street, Varley Street, avoid Buster, the towpath, Bradford Road all the way to 391.

This wasn't the first time someone had broken into our home. Even our neighbours had robbed us before. This, though, was the only occasion I'd walked in on it taking place. I was nine and Chidi was six, and maybe it's a good thing it happened when we were that young, because thinking about it now is terrifying. Once you've stepped inside your house to witness someone who is not welcome, it never feels the same again. It's the same building, and you can change the locks, strengthen the doors, even get 24-hour security if you want, but after you've been burgled you never get that sense of safety you once had. Every time you put the key in the door, you're almost expecting to see someone who shouldn't be there on the other side. Being nine, I turned the key without fear after a day or two, but as I got older and began to understand the world better, it started to return. What would have happened if those men had realised it was just two young children who were entering the house? Maybe next time they'll come a bit earlier or see the value in kidnapping or hurting one of us.

Today, I still feel the guilt I experienced when I saw Chidi hiding by the sofa. I was a child, but I was in charge of Chidi, and I had left her behind. It was a fight-or-flight situation, and because I had only my fear within me I didn't stay and fight for my sister. From that point and through lots of other events in my life, I've grown to realise there's more going on than just what you see through your own eyes. I was responsible for Chidi, and something could have gone seriously wrong because of my actions. If it had, I might have been too young to really understand the depth of it then, but now the thought of it is horrifying to me. So, nobody in a crisis gets left behind, and you do what you can to help everyone, not just yourself. Fight, not flight. 391 Bradford Road taught me that.

It was our first house in the UK, and it was not in great shape. It was the best we could do in that moment, but no family our size would ever have wanted to live there. It was a council house that required some work: there was mould on the walls and once even slugs crawling on the floor. Later, on our last night there, we slept just on mattresses because our beds had already been dismantled, and our heads were right next to the slugs. It wasn't great, but we made do.

We had moved there from Nigeria when I was five. Our previous home was in Warri, in the south of that country, on an estate for Delta Steel workers called 'Camp Extension Delta Steel Township'. Both my parents had jobs at the company; my mum, Anthonia, was a water microbiologist, and my dad, who was then using his first name – Enyinnaya – was a metallurgical engineer. I don't remember a lot about growing up in Nigeria and where we lived, but I do have the sense that we were reasonably comfortable. We had a maid, which was not something every family would have. I was born on 12 November 1986, just a year after my sister Diuto. I remember Diuto being taller than me for a significant part of my childhood, when she was basically my carer, both in Nigeria and then those first years in the UK. She was a very considerate sister who would try to look after me, even though there was so little difference between us in age, and Chidi too. She took on the role of mother when ours wasn't there, making food and making sure we didn't behave like demons. A figure in my mum's image.

Diuto needed to step up because my mother was the first of the family to leave Nigeria for the UK, to study for a PhD in environmental sciences at the University of Salford. Both my parents worked incredibly hard at their education, and even though I wouldn't claim they were gifted or that things came naturally to them, they were very successful. It wouldn't have surprised many people that in 1990, at the age of thirty-one, Mum moved to a different country to invest more time into her education. The next year, Diuto, Chidi and I all joined her in her new home just north-east of Manchester city centre, where Dad would join us nine months later. Five of us all in that little house in Miles Platting.

Adjusting to our new home was made easier by the fact we'd spoken English in Nigeria – it's the national language there, even though the Igbo tribe to which my family belongs has their own language too. There are about 300 ethnic tribes in Nigeria, a country with more than 200 million people, and each has their own language. The differences mean that one tribe doesn't necessarily understand another (which blows my mind when I think about it), so they are united by English. In Nigeria, your tribe is your backstory, your language the nuance to your identity, but being Nigerian of any tribe was enough to bring together those who'd moved to the UK. Even though they'd chosen to leave their home, my parents welcomed the familiarity that other Nigerians in Manchester provided, and they were drawn to one another, particularly as it helped them to get through some tough times.

My parents did bring a little bit of Igbo culture with them, retaining some of the simple words and phrases they'd used with us in Nigeria, but we didn't have any conversations using the Igbo language once we'd moved because it wasn't something that was going to benefit day-to-day life. It is likely that had I stayed in Nigeria I would have followed the same path as everyone else there in embracing the culture more, but it was more important for my parents to learn how it all worked in England. There was no back and forth, and I couldn't tell you the Igbo words for anything like 'knife' or 'dish' or whatever, but you'd often hear greetings and endearing terms in the tribe's language: '*Kedụ*' means hello. Dad might say '*oliạ*' as an alternative: how are you doing? Then you'd respond with '*Ọ di mu mma*': I'm well. They'd say '*ka chi foo*' for goodnight. '*Biko*' is please. Mum might use the nickname '*bobo*' for me, or '*nna-m*' or '*nna-nna*', which actually means father but in this context is given to a child. They'd also say '*biạ*': come here. And if you heard '*wahala*' you were in trouble. '*Wahala*' means stress, so one of your parents saying 'you give me "*wahala*"' was the last thing you needed.

My dad still uses some of it now as a little reminder, but I'm convinced that back then he'd speak in Igbo to others to make sure we didn't understand what he was saying. We might be at an aunt's house or someone was visiting us, and they'd either spend the whole time speaking in Igbo or a conversation that had started in English changed language part-way through, and we wouldn't have a clue. It would have been partly subconscious but partly deliberate, knowing my dad. He enjoyed throwing a spanner in the works. I don't mind that he did, either, because it's helped me retain a good sense of what the culture entails.

Those first few years in Manchester were difficult for both my parents. My dad joined us in 1992 and immediately went to study at the University of York before going on to spend two years at Manchester Metropolitan University training to be a teacher. His first proper job in the UK was teaching maths in a high school. My mum, who was now Dr Anthonia Onuoha, found that as a black woman in early 1990s England, getting a PhD had made things worse for her, not better. My mum had worked incredibly hard to get her doctorate, but now she was consistently told she was overqualified for jobs, and she suffered because of it. Looking back now, I seriously doubt that her main problem was being overqualified. It seems far more likely to me that prospective employers in early 1990s England were intimidated by the name that appeared on the application. To get a job she would have to overcome the stigma of being firstly a woman, then a foreigner. That's before you consider that 'Anthonia Onuoha' was preceded by 'Dr'. Even in 2020, some people in America were refusing to call the wife of then President-elect Biden 'Dr' Jill Biden. There was an infamous op-ed in the *Wall Street Times* claiming that because her doctorate wasn't anything to do with medicine, she shouldn't use the title. How many times has that standard been applied to men? You could be a doctor of something ridiculous like television screens, and because you're a male that's fine. My mum spent a large part of the first few years we lived in Manchester doing work like putting leaflets inside newspapers, because that was the only job people were willing to give a black woman who had a PhD in environmental sciences from Salford University.

• • •

This is how it began in the UK for Anthonia and Martin Onuoha (my father had decided to use his middle name after moving) and their three children. We were in east Manchester, a lot of which has been gentrified in the time since I lived there – just five minutes down the road there's a place called Ancoats, which looks swell now – but the same investment hasn't yet made its way to Miles Platting. It's exactly like it was all that time ago: poverty-stricken and affected by low-level crime. It wasn't a case of gangs being everywhere, but young people in particular would do illegal things just for a laugh. Every time my parents bought a new car – one that was new to them, not brand new – it would be burnt out or have its tyres and other parts removed. I remember one year around Bonfire Night, these guys were letting off rockets from the exhaust pipe of my dad's tan Nissan Sunny. It was just a group of lads who thought it was funny, but I'll never forget how my dad dealt with them, heading out of our front door to grip one of them by their collar, lifting him off the ground. Fight, not flight. They were in their late teens or early twenties, but the one my dad had in his grasp just started crying his eyes out as his friends skedaddled. This was the calibre of criminal: the kind who would run away, say if nine- and six-year-olds walked in on them trying to steal something from a house. I can understand why someone might have met their match with my dad, though.

He's just a bit smaller than me now, but he's a strong fella. He showed them aggression, and they wanted none of it. I watched it all while looking out of the window and thinking, yeah, good luck guys, good luck with that one. I always felt protected by my father, and he made sure we never felt vulnerable in what could at times be a threatening environment. And it wasn't just him: if it was a verbal confrontation, my mum would be the one mixing it with whoever dared to take her on!

Like my parents, I don't really take to being bullied, and like those guys firing rockets out of our car exhaust, there was someone who found that out the hard way. At school, as a five-year-old battling the cold of a new country by wearing what I can only describe as a ton of coats, I was a target. I was a black foreigner with an accent in a very white space, and even though I was a child some of the other pupils weren't familiar with diversity, certainly not in the way they might be now. You know what kids are like with someone who's different: they try to alienate them, and they'll joke around at the expense of the new, strange-looking boy, saying, 'Look at this guy,' and 'What's this?' One of them had said something to upset me, and when I went home and told my parents they said I should stand up for myself. The next day, when that same kid tried to poke fun at me again, I very much stood up for myself. I headbutted him. It's the most instinctive thing I've done in my life, and it's certainly the only headbutt I've ever delivered. The boy didn't bleed, but he did cry. I started to worry about being in trouble, which I was, but only at school, not at home. My parents understood all too well what would have led to that moment.

I think I had some sense of regret at the time, but ultimately people did treat me a bit differently afterwards. It was the first step on a long journey to discover the strength to speak up in the face of bullying, which is something I encourage my children to do now. Even though I was always one of the bigger kids for my age, I wouldn't necessarily have had the biggest presence because I've not always been somebody who is good with words or particularly outspoken. My eldest daughter, Amaia, is the sweetest girl in the world, and my biggest concern is that someone is going to be mean to her. She doesn't deserve that, but if it happens, I'm always going to try to get her to stand up for herself. Not through violence but through understanding her own value and speaking to the right people so that it can stop. I'll tell her to call the bullying out for what it is and never to let anybody push her down, because it's wrong. I've since come to appreciate the lessons I learned in those early days at Miles Platting Junior. When you're in the moment, you just take it day to day and you don't think too much about it. I didn't know how to react when I was being bullied, and I certainly didn't imagine I'd be headbutting anyone, but I can now look back and try to teach my children the same lessons I have come to learn about how important it is to speak up and seek help.

• • •

Our immediate experience of British culture was limited in Manchester, because most of the people my parents spent time with were originally from either Nigeria or other parts of Africa. You could have been anywhere in the world when you stepped into those houses, because once inside they all felt the same. My first window into what you might call traditional British life was provided by the Wyon family. Andrew Wyon had had a contract with Delta Steel in Nigeria and met my dad during the time he spent working in Warri. On Andrew's last day there, he invited my family to visit the Wyons at their home in Bath. That summer, and for many summers afterwards, we spent part of the holidays with Andrew and Linda Wyon at a house that felt like a whole other world to us. It was massive, old, very British (imagine late-'80s décor!) and bordered by a golf course. We didn't have a back garden in Miles Platting, so we would spend the days whizzing down the big water slide they had in theirs. There was so much space just to go wild. Then, we'd eat rhubarb crumble. Rhubarb! Just incredible. They'd grow it in the garden and make all sorts of puddings with it. This, I can guarantee you, was the first time I'd had rhubarb. It was also the first time outside my own house that I could be myself. I have a memory of one Christmas visit when I was doing a stupid dance, being silly and playing the joker, happy to try to entertain the adults with everyone laughing at me. It was so different from home. I always enjoyed spending time with the Wyons, who got on well with my parents, and as they had fostered kids from all kinds of backgrounds during their lives, the first time we visited them Diuto, Chidi and I became like three more for them to care for. My dad describes the Wyons as our first British 'family', and we'd call Linda and Andrew 'auntie' and 'uncle'. They were wonderful human beings and so welcoming. Although there was one thing I didn't like: their cat. It used to scare the life out of me, and I've got the heebie-jeebies just thinking about it. That's probably where my dislike of animals comes from. That and Buster.

Back home, the joys in my life came from football, and for a while netball too. Diuto and I would play together, and the netball coach at Miles Platting Junior encouraged me, despite it being taboo for boys to play the sport. The coach was called Maria Kennedy, and she is my favourite teacher of all time. We're still friends now. She was effervescent and made me really want to play netball, even though I was the only boy doing it. Her support was pivotal in me not being bullied, and so I was able to go to practice and have great fun doing it. Why wouldn't I? I was running and catching a ball. What more could I ask for? Well, maybe kicking it…

I used to play on the streets around my house during the summers in Miles Platting, but my first real football memories come from a park five minutes away, just off Alan Turing Way – not the one where Buster would chase me, but very close to it. We'd put jumpers down for goalposts and just play and play and play, for hours at a time. I loved it, partly because I considered myself lucky to be able to do it (I had to ask permission from two parents who didn't encourage me to have any social life for the rest of the year when I had schoolwork to concentrate on) and partly because I quickly realised I was good at it. Whether it was in a game of Wembley (pairing up with someone in a knock-out tournament) or five against five, I was one of the best players. Sometimes that was a problem. One of my neighbours would provide the ball for our games, and he once told me I was so good there was no point in him playing any more. He took his ball and went home. I didn't have a ball of my own, so that was the end of that.

Those who are familiar with this part of east Manchester will realise I've not yet mentioned a very significant landmark that has appeared in the years since I left: the Etihad Stadium. I've often had the chance to reflect on how fitting it is that my earliest football memories are from a field that is now in the shadow of Manchester City's ground. Every time I drove there as a City player, I passed the house where I first lived in the UK, thinking, 'I went from there to *there*,' from 391 Bradford Road to the Etihad. Even to this day, when I go to the stadium to work for the media, I pass the house and think of the memories it brings. It was an important part of my history and where my football journey started, but I'm so glad I don't live there any more. More than two decades on from when my family survived there just by making do, thousands of City fans walking to and from the stadium each matchday pass that house, completely unaware (until now, perhaps) that one of the players they cheered for – and who cheers for their team still – fought there to fit in to a new country and establish an identity that would end up being defined most by the blue of Manchester City.

Eventually, I started playing organised football, first for my school and then for a team called AFC Clayton. I was a year young for the Miles Platting Junior team, but I was still able to do well enough for the coach to say I should try out for a Sunday League side. I didn't even know what Sunday League was at this point, so he gave me a piece of paper with a whole load of teams, training schedules and phone numbers, and as AFC Clayton were only a few minutes up Ashton Old Road from where we lived, I chose them. I went for a training session, and just like that I was playing for the team. Well, teams. In my first season, which was 1996/97, I played for both my age group and the one above, one on Saturdays and the other on Sundays. By the end of that season, I'd won player of the year in both the Under-10s and the Under-11s, the trophy for most man-of-the-match awards (in both teams), and I was the Under-10s top goal-scorer too. I know all this because I still have most of the trophies on display in my house! That's not to say both teams were successful, though. At that same end-of-season awards ceremony, the Under-11s celebrated their biggest win (7–6) and biggest away win (4–3), which were both against the same team, Ashton Moss. They were the only two victories we had the whole year, and we got absolutely battered in every other game.

One of my man-of-the-match awards came in the Divisional Cup final, which we won and celebrated by going on an open-top bus ride. I was buzzing! But that wasn't the only momentous thing to happen that day. I'll never forget the feeling when my dad came to me after the game and told me that someone from Manchester City had scouted me and wanted me to go for a trial. This was half the story: I found out much later that a Manchester United scout was also there and my dad had turned him down on my behalf. He claims he did it because I was a City fan and he figured out I'd probably not want to play for United, but at the time I didn't really support City. I liked them, which considering United was *the* team at the time was significant, but I really just liked football at that stage, so I don't know why my dad said that. I don't regret that he did, but it's interesting that he didn't even bring me into the thought process; he just decided for me. Maybe he'd realised something that's occurred to me since: playing for a team that didn't win all the time (which was certainly true of the City side of the mid-'90s) might have made me a better person. In the semi-final of the Divisional Cup, we'd beaten a team that hadn't lost in something like three years, and they were all crying after the game. 'Get over it,' I thought. 'Try playing for a team that loses every week and see how you feel!'

I remember my Manchester City trial as clear as day. I'd been scouted by Len Davies, who's since passed away but who was really good to me throughout my time at the academy. I turned up feeling pretty tense and wearing a full Euro 96 kit. Matching shorts, matching socks. And red. They didn't hold it against me, because after doing a little bit of skills training and then playing a match, I was immediately asked to sign for them. I was the first player to join what had just changed from being a School of Excellence to an academy. Nedum Onuoha, aged ten, a Manchester City player.

Chapter 2

When I was nine, the year before I joined the Manchester City Academy, our family of five became six. My youngest sister Lynda was born – her Igbo name is Chiamaka, but she became the only member of our family to be given, and use, an English name, which she took after Linda Wyon, her godmother – and so we needed a bigger house. Eventually, we managed to get a place up the road in Harpurhey. It wasn't brilliant, but compared to the slugs, the mould and the car exhaust rockets it felt like a palace. We had grass in the garden. There was a place to park a car. The living room was bigger. It just had a different vibe, and we were happier there. It still wasn't the best area in the world, and we couldn't afford much, but it had so much more than Bradford Road. Harpurhey is north of Miles Platting and is centred on Rochdale Road. We lived at 614. Being on Rochdale Road was important to me, because it was very well connected to the bus routes I would use for both the academy and my new school, Hulme Grammar in Oldham.

Mum and Dad had it all laid out, at least in theory. My parents hadn't moved our family to the UK just because of the possible furthering of their education; they also wanted their children to benefit from the kind of schooling that wasn't available in Nigeria. They liked the idea of Diuto becoming an engineer, Chidi a lawyer, Lynda a scientist and me a doctor. The plan was for all of us to do the relevant entrance exams for private schools in the area, and if we got in, we would seek help on the fees with, for example, a bursary. They were already making huge sacrifices to contribute financially themselves, working two jobs each, using up as many hours as possible in the day. At one point my dad was working as a teacher by day and at the Royal Mail sorting office by night. He'd come back from school at five or six in the evening and snatch a bit of sleep before heading off to the sorting office at nine. Then he'd be back home at five or six the next morning before getting ready to go to school again. All the money my parents made was for rent, bills and school. If they hadn't sent us to the schools they did, we might have had a better situation at home, but that was the trade-off: they wanted to give us the best education possible. It also didn't help the financial situation that I was eating my parents out of house and home. I would eat just about everything, all the time. On the weekends when I had football matches, my mum would go to a fruit market and get a full box of bananas, knowing full well I'd get through them before the Monday. Lo and behold, I always did.

These are the reasons why I say I was lucky to go to private school. Not because I was undeserving of it, because I worked hard at my education, but essentially because my parents couldn't afford it. All three of my sisters and I went to private school, funded by their sacrifices. It's also why my dad in particular demanded high standards when it came to how well we did at school. If we weren't interested, why should they go above and beyond?

I wouldn't necessarily describe my dad as strict, but there was certainly no socialising allowed on school nights, which became increasingly difficult to come to terms with as I got older. Early on in my time at Hulme, I had a chance to go on a double date to the cinema not too far from school. I liked one of the girls at the time and really wanted to go, but there was a problem: the film was at nine o'clock in the evening. In our house you weren't allowed out at that time on any night, let alone a school night. We had homework to complete.

• • •

Hulme was a very diverse school, and it reflected Oldham's thriving Asian community, but there were next to no black people. In the whole boys' school, it was me and Okey. I remember thinking, 'Where's everybody else?' Outside of my family and those Nigerian friends of my parents, I hadn't encountered that many black faces in Miles Platting, at AFC Clayton or even in the City academy, but now there were even fewer. Unlike in those first days at primary school, though, I wasn't a target at Hulme because something was different this time: I was the boy who played for Manchester City. This also helped me to overcome those restrictions on my social life which might have otherwise been embarrassing. Being relatively popular, though, did not mean being cool. I tended to hang out with the nerdy crowd. I spent time with Okey, and I still speak to him now, but my closest friends at Hulme were Liam Wright, Andrew Morgan and

Sebastian Coleman-Celis. Because I'd got into the school a year early, they were all older than me. I really enjoyed being around them, as they seemed a bit more genuine than those I had met in the football team, and we ended up forming a band. They encouraged me to learn bass guitar, introduced me to new styles of music and not once did we feel the need to worry about girls. With their help, I discovered a whole new side of myself I didn't know I had. The band didn't have a name, and we just played covers. It was me on bass, Liam and Andy on guitar (Liam was lead) and Seb on drums. Seb was like a Grade 8 drummer while the rest of us were a little less talented, but we could play. It was good, I wasn't bad, and to this day those are probably some of the most fun times I've ever had. We played in public once for a charity event at school, and we did 'She's Electric' by Oasis. By then I'd started to get used to playing football in front of a small crowd, but that was the first and only time I ever played music to one. I enjoyed both, but the hierarchy was clear in my mind. It was the band second, Manchester City first.

City had signed me to be a defender, but in my first game for the academy I played up front and scored five goals. It was against Blackpool at the Armitage Centre in Fallowfield. A lot of my early games were there, and after my dad had been the one to decide on my behalf that I should encourage City's advances and spurn United's, it was my mum who was the constant presence on the touchline. She was all-in, and from the moment I had games to go to, including for AFC Clayton, Mum was there. Dad was supportive too, as even though this wasn't part of the original plan I was at least still in school, so he didn't think it was too much of a deviation. I think of him as still being in the metaphorical car but in the passenger seat. Mum was definitely the driver.

City allowed to me to play for my school team, but after one more year at AFC Clayton (Under-12s player of the year, most man-of-the-match awards, both trophies in the cabinet) they asked me to stop. It was difficult to find the time to combine the two anyway, and there was certainly no comparison. In one I was sharing the facilities with Sunday League players, at the other I was in the same building as the Manchester City first team at Platt Lane. While we tended to be out on the pitches at different times, the first team used to train close enough for us to run to the nearby car park and stick autograph books through the fence as they walked off after training. I filled those books, and then when I became a ball boy I tried to collect all the match programmes to add to a growing compilation I'd started and that included some from as far back as the 1980s. I might not have thought of myself as a City fan before I started playing for them, but I found it fascinating learning about the history of the club.

The moment I realised City was *my* team was the first time I wore the same kit as those players from whom I'd been getting autographs. City fans will know exactly what I mean when I say it was the Kappa one. Brother was the sponsor. As a ball boy I wore that kit for games and saw the first team in the same one, and suddenly I sensed I had found an identity. I was only a ball boy and part of an academy team that wasn't brilliant, but there I was representing Manchester City. It occurred to me that up until that point I'd been lots of different people. My home life was real, and being with my parents had given me a feeling of security, but every time I left the comfort of my household I found myself submitting to other people's standards and not bringing who I was to that space. At school, playing football, seeing so few black faces at either, I didn't know how to be part of those environments. I had asked myself: 'What does it mean to be a pupil at Miles Platting Junior, or Hulme? What does it mean to be a player for AFC Clayton?' I didn't know and had to adapt. But after initially asking the same question about what it meant to be part of Manchester City's academy, now I had my answer.

A lightbulb was lit, and for the first time I could see a footballing future. Sunday League didn't give me the sense of progress I was looking for. Then, all of a sudden, I'm playing for City, we're all wearing the same kit (which rarely happened in Sunday League) and I had a potential path plotted out for me: I'm *here* now, and this is how I get *there*. I revelled in the fact I now understood what it would take and the stages I'd have to go through. First, you start playing seven-a-side, then you move up to a full-size ball. Next, it's onto the bigger pitches, and eventually you have to start wearing a shirt and tie to matches. After that it's training full-time, then with the first team. It was all there: a clear and obvious road ahead, even if there was no guarantee I would get to the end of it. I carried this new sense of identity with pride, particularly at school, where it carried a lot of weight. Wearing the tracksuit the club gave me was part of that, of course, but as far as my fellow pupils were concerned I didn't play for Manchester City's academy, I played for Manchester City.

Having the kit was one thing; trying to get it to fit was another thing entirely. There were only two sizes available, a minimum and a maximum, and if you were bigger than a maximum you were going to have problems. You would have to put it on and just hope it didn't split. When I was in the City Under-14s, we played in a tournament on the Isle of Man, and, as ever, my shorts were too small. Then I got a groin injury, which required treatment from a physio who on this occasion was female. Receiving treatment from a female physio when you're fourteen and your shorts are too small is a recipe for significant embarrassment. She did her absolute best, as did I, to try to act like nothing was happening, but it was very, very awkward. Certain unnecessary events are typical for boys of that age, and I'm convinced the tightness of my shorts was the principal reason for one of the most uncomfortable moments of my life. Thankfully the injury was serious enough for me to come off. Attempting to carry on playing would have been the only thing that could have made it more humiliating.

• • •

The chance to be a ball boy for first-team matches was one of the perks of being an academy player. There weren't that many spaces available, but because so many of my teammates didn't support the club not everyone wanted to do it. Well, I did. Firstly, to be in there, seeing professional football players in real life and of course wearing the same kit; and secondly, to get tickets to games at Maine Road, which meant my mum could come and watch. That was how I got to go to the 1999 Division Two playoff final.

The first season I was in the academy was 1997/98, and Manchester City's first team was relegated. They'd been one of the favourites to be promoted from what was then called the First Division to the Premier League, but after a campaign when

Frank Clark had been replaced as manager by Joe Royle, City finished twenty-second and went down to the Second Division. It was the first time in the club's history that they'd been in the third tier of English football, and getting out of it as quickly as possible was considered vital. For the whole of the next season I was a ball boy, and with each game I felt more of a connection with the club. The door of the ball boy room led out directly into the tunnel at Maine Road, so we'd stand with the players just before the match. Their dressing rooms were on either side a little further down the tunnel, so we could see when the players were coming and time our exit from our room to coincide with their arrival. These were the players who by the end of the season had dragged the club from mid-table into third place and a spot in the playoffs. After beating Wigan over two legs, they reached the playoff final at Wembley on 30 May 1999.

It was my first visit to Wembley, so my mum decided to make a trip of it. Her brother Emeka lived in Stockwell, south London, and the playoff final gave us an opportunity to stop by. In their house there was Uncle Emeka, Auntie Flo, my cousins Georgia, Jodie and eventually Josh. And a shower. I'd never in my life taken a shower until the first time we visited them after they moved over from Nigeria. We had a bath at home and so did they, but they'd adapted theirs to include a shower with a rubber attachment that you'd jam into the tap. I was fascinated by it but could never get the temperature right, always scalding or freezing myself – though that didn't stop it being a fun part of going to Stockwell.

After seeing our family, we departed for the game itself. I was wearing the yellow and navy-blue second kit that the team would have on that day. I remember walking to Wembley, seeing the twin towers, sensing the excitement in the streets and around the stadium. All of it helped twelve-year-old me understand that this was an important game. I would have the chance to go to the national stadium again in the future, but the first time is something you never forget. Maine Road is big, but Wembley is so much bigger. Because I hadn't had the chance to sit with other fans at City's ground and because I had no experiences in the famous Kippax stand, I was often prevented from feeling like a true fan. Until now. I was in amongst them at Wembley, from the walk up Wembley Way to taking our seats in the stands.

With a promotion place on the line, the game itself came to life in the last ten minutes of normal time. City's opponents Gillingham scored twice, in the eighty-second and eighty-seventh minutes. We were 2–0 down approaching the final whistle.

'We should probably go,' my mum said. 'To try to escape the traffic.'

I understood. 'OK, sure.'

We left our seats, walked out of the arena into the concourse and down some steps. There was a shout. Right there, behind us.

Someone had been following us out. 'We've scored! I'm going back in!'

I looked at Mum.

'Should we go back in too?'

'No, we don't need to. It won't make a difference.'

At 2–1, deep into injury time at the end of the game, we left. I didn't mind because I needed food. We started to walk towards McDonald's when there was another shout.

'Did you hear that?' I asked my mum.

'I heard it, but we're outside now. We can't go back in.'

I'd missed the moment. Paul Dickov had scored what was for

most City fans at the time the most celebrated goal in the club's history. The same Paul Dickov for whom I had been ball boy and would later play alongside when he returned for a second spell in the City team, had equalised to complete our remarkable comeback. It was the ninety-fifth minute, and the score was 2–2. There would be extra time, and I would be listening to it on my Sony Walkman radio in McDonald's, eating a big fat burger.

Manchester City won and were promoted in the most dramatic of circumstances. It would have been incredible to see the goals, to see the penalty shoot-out and be there for Nicky Weaver's famous wheeling-arm celebration. But by the time I got home and saw it for the first time on the replays, it didn't matter to me that I'd missed it. It was a very special day, and not necessarily just for those moments that took place after I left, or even the result itself. I had seen Wembley. I had seen a big game, one that was the culmination of all those the club had played up until that point. I missed the very last seconds of it, but we won. *We* won.

• • •

The Manchester City Academy of the late 1990s was very different to how it is now. Now, it operates with a massively higher budget and with similarly heightened expectations, but when I was there the academy's connection with the community was still something that gave the club and its fans great pride. Back in 1986, City had won the FA Youth Cup with a team that was almost exclusively made up of local boys, and that was still celebrated when I joined a decade later. My daily route in and out of Manchester and my experiences at City helped me begin to identify as a Mancunian. I was surrounded by boys who lived within the M60. We had a geographical bond and shared the same footballing experiences too. Before we'd become academy teammates, most of us had played in Sunday League. Nathan and Jonathan D'Laryea played for Medlock, and they destroyed my AFC Clayton team every time. I remember one game finishing 10–2. We were united by football, and unlike at school where you can be measured in a million and one different ways, we were all good at playing the very game that had brought us together, in a city we called home. We were Mancunians playing for Manchester City. It was a shared purpose, and for the first time I felt like I was a legitimate part of that. The little kid with an accent who'd been bullied at school when he arrived from Nigeria not knowing how to fit in was gone. *I* was a Mancunian playing for Manchester City.

The D'Laryea twins are still two of my closest friends to this day. Their dad's Ghanaian, although they were both born in England, and their mum is British. Like almost everybody of Nigerian or Ghanaian descent, we argued about which country has the better jollof rice (it's all about whether you use long grain or basmati and how spicy you want it; either way the answer's Nigeria) and bonded over football and our shared experiences of going to private school. The twins went to Stretford High and their dad had the same vision for them as mine did for me. The current academy recruits at City have their education provided for them. They all have a place guaranteed at St Bede's, a very highly rated, and expensive, Catholic private school in Manchester. How my parents would have loved me to have that opportunity. Most of the players during my time didn't want that education, let alone have access to it; they might have worked towards a qualification like a BTEC out of the classrooms at Platt Lane. Modern academies have realised the importance of education (even if it's true to say the attendance record of a lot of the players isn't great), and any academy that doesn't offer the kind of thing City does will fail to compete for the best young prospects. I think providing that option is important, as there's no guarantee they'll have a career in football. How many make it to play in a Premier League team? The number's tiny. What about just having a career in the game, at any level? It's bigger than tiny, but not massive. They might have to enter the real world at some point, and City has invested in something at no great relative expense to itself, which in turn covers its players' backs should that happen sooner than they'd planned. Who knows how far you'll get as a young person if you get the best training available both in football and at school?

Combining both helped my popularity at school, where being a City player was very significant. There were other people who were doing well at both football and other sports, but as time passed I think people understood the value of the fact I was at the academy. It helped even further that I was getting noticed for being a fast runner as well. In the winter I played football, and in the summer it was athletics. Throughout almost my entire five years at Hulme, they'd maybe overlap but never clash, so I could do both. I finished second in the English Schools' Athletic Association Junior 100 metres at Under-15 level, with a time of 11.09 seconds. The story that's told about that race is that I beat Craig Pickering, who went on to represent Great Britain at the Olympics. The part of that story that isn't told as often: the next year he took me to the cleaners – I finished fourth in what I think was my last competitive race. Football was starting to reduce the amount of time I had for anything else. I would have carried on if I could, but winter training was necessary if I was to progress as a sprinter, and that was the time for football. To go without would be the same as starting a football season without pre-season. I'll never know what fulfilling my potential in athletics would have brought, but it wasn't a case of me weighing up which sport to continue. The decision was made for me, because Manchester City had offered me a full-time contract.

Chapter 3

It was February 2002 and I was at Hulme studying for my GCSEs when I got a phone call.

'Nedum. You're in the squad for the FA Youth Cup game against Everton. We need you to get here.'

'When is it?'

'Tonight.'

As soon as school was finished I had to get to Platt Lane. From there, to Goodison Park. I was fifteen and didn't know any of the people in the Under-18s team. I hadn't had one training session with them. But there was a player in the opposition who was well-known enough to be the talk of the bus ride to Liverpool. He was pretty good by all accounts, older than me but younger than a lot of them, and really tearing it up. I wondered who they were going on about. Later that day I spent ninety minutes sitting on the bench watching Wayne Rooney dominate, just bully everyone. He got two in a 4–2 win for Everton just five months before he made his senior debut at the age of sixteen.

Players like Wayne Rooney and competitions like the FA Youth Cup were the difference between my early years at the

Manchester City Academy and going full-time. It was before I had expected, but the coaches had given me a little teaser of what my immediate future looked like. The logistical changes meant I had to leave school. I was going from training two days a week and playing on weekends to a new six-day-a-week schedule. The venue was the same, but the atmosphere was different. As a younger player, I'd come into Platt Lane in the evening, when it was a shared public facility housing more than just the City academy teams. While other people were milling about or going to the gym, I'd quickly get my gear on in the changing rooms and head out onto the AstroTurf. We wouldn't touch the grass pitches. Not until we were full-time, that is. Then it was made clear that this was our job: finish training today and prepare for training tomorrow; finish training tomorrow to get ready for the game on Saturday. Then you might get a text on Monday to say you have to be ready for another game midweek, maybe even a call from the manager to train with the first team. Now I was part of the bubble of professional football, and so there was to be no more Hulme Grammar.

I had taken my GCSEs and done well, so academically I knew I was capable of carrying on, and there was never any doubt in my mind that I would continue my education. It was just where I did it that would have to change. Training was now my priority, so I could either study for a BTEC in the canteen at Platt Lane or go to Xaverian College. The latter was my only real option, as it allowed me to do my A-Levels, and their relationship with the club meant my football and study schedules could work side by side. The D'Laryea twins and I would do the five-minute journey between Xaverian and the training ground, often in Jonathan's Peugeot 207, sometimes in Nathan's silver VW Golf, which I'm convinced he owned until he was at least thirty. They would also pick me up from home on their way to training, and we'd talk about absolutely everything on those many car rides: football, school and how we had completely contrasting views on girls, all to a constant soundtrack. This was the early 2000s, and we'd listen to 50 Cent and other hip-hop acts, some R&B and artists from the UK garage scene. We'd get hold of music one of two ways: from a shop in Affleck's Palace in Manchester city centre that stocked up with new stuff every Friday, perfect for us to go and raid after training; or on a mixtape provided by Jonathan and Nathan. The latter was not the cheaper option – illegal music sharing was becoming very popular, and the twins would use LimeWire to download songs, which they'd then burn onto CDs and charge you a tenner for. This was the D'Laryeas' side hustle.

This was where some of the first wages I received as a footballer went. After going full-time I was on £80 a week, and whatever didn't go on the twins' mixtapes went straight into my bank account. My strategy was just to stack it. I got to £1,000 relatively quickly because I wasn't really spending any money, and I felt a sense of pride when I hit that mark. I felt so rich: after just a few months my balance had hit four figures! When that £80 first landed I would treat my girlfriend Lucy: something from Pizza Hut – the all-you-can-eat buffets were *the* place to be – or a value meal. I would treat her so well!

The fact the D'Laryeas also went to Xaverian meant there were three outliers in the academy, not just one, and it's a lot harder to poke fun at three people who are doing things a bit differently. Strength in numbers to the extent that we were sort of looked up to as opposed to ridiculed. But that would only work if I was also good at football. When Manchester City's first team wasn't at the level it is now, the youth system was one of the things that helped the club retain its standing in the game, and even when money became tight in the lower divisions the budget for player development was famously never cut. It was a smart investment. City knew it would be cheaper trying to bring a youngster into the team than to sign expensive talent it couldn't guarantee would work out, particularly when it had to cut its cloth. Even before that there was the famous FA Youth Cup-winning team of 1986, featuring a host of local boys who went on to form a large part of the side that memorably beat Manchester United 5–1 at Maine Road in 1989. This was the reputation the club was trying to uphold when it established the academy.

Jim Cassell was in charge, and he was the one to make me the academy's first signing. He had a good relationship with my mum and always made sure everything was right with me – a really nice guy. Cassell helped to produce a new generation of young players, one that would stretch for around ten years before the Abu Dhabi takeover revolutionised the facilities and finances of the academy. He and the academy had many success stories, but the first big one was Shaun Wright-Phillips. Shaun provided a pathway that I could follow, one that others had already followed before me. Let go by Nottingham Forest for being 'too small', Shaun had been brought into City's youth system at sixteen and gave him his first-team debut a year later. By the time I became a full-time academy player, he was an established member of the first eleven, having helped City get promoted into the Premier League the season before. He would have only been twenty, and so he was still close enough in age to those like me, let alone to players like Joey Barton, Stephen Jordan, Paddy McCarthy and Willo Flood, who, because of Shaun's success, could see a clear path to the first team. There was never any guarantee that you'd reach that level, and some of those who'd been with me at the academy weren't able to, but there was definite progression. Each time I saw someone who had walked that same road play for the first team it gave me encouragement, as did each step along the way: training with the age above, playing a reserve game and maybe even joining a session with the first team. I even saw the evolution in what players wore at certain levels. The budget of today's academy means each new recruit gets flooded with new gear, but apart from what I had for being a ball boy on matchdays, we didn't get free tracksuits until we were much older. The dress code for Under-14s and 15s was a jumper over a collared shirt and tie, and before I got to that age those were the clothes I wanted to wear. Then the year I got there they changed it, so I never got the chance!

The quality of the football was improving as well. When I first started at the academy, the teams I was in weren't great. Probably 50/50 in terms of wins and losses. The results got better as I progressed, and by the time I'd reached Under-15s our team was very good. Then my Under-16s team only lost one or two games all year, with similar form the next season too. At Under-18s level we were one of the best teams in the whole country and amongst the favourites for the FA Youth Cup. Up until that point I'd heard about Manchester United, Aston Villa, Leeds, Blackburn and Middlesbrough: these teams were always far and away better than we were. After 2001, though, you could see the academy was changing, buoyed by the success of Shaun Wright-Phillips and others, and it brought a different level of expectation at training and in matches. It also inspired some of the local boys to join City instead of all heading to Manchester United!

• • •

Coming to the academy full-time meant a change in position. City wanted me to be a centre back, and there was a moment in pre-season which made me realise my days as a striker were numbered. It was at Platt Lane in the last game before the season started. I was played through with just the goalkeeper to beat, with all the time in the world. I tried to open up my body and knock it to the keeper's left, but it went just past the post. There was silence. Complete silence. I never started as a striker for City again. If they'd been thinking about switching me, that was the final nail in the coffin. I'd been scoring tons of goals in the younger age groups, but this was a sign the standards were higher and perhaps why they had a different long-term future in mind for me. At least as a centre back I'd still be in the team, and seeing that I'd played in defence at school it wasn't a tough transition. The coaches also always retained the option of sending me up front when they needed a goal. At the beginning of that first full-time season in 2002/03, this happened a lot: at Christmas I was second top goal-scorer, with nine. There were two weeks in a row when I scored two and then – against Nottingham Forest – three, with a perfect hat-trick: one with the right foot, one with the left and a third with a header. I was like, I'm sizzling here. As a centre back this is unbelievable! One game against Everton, we were killing them. It was a 1–0 battering. But then they scored a late goal. With five minutes to go, our coach Alex Gibson moved me forward. Soon afterwards I was played in down one side of the defence; I pushed someone out of the way to go through one on one and slotted the ball into the bottom corner. Having put us ahead, I was immediately sent back into the back four to see out a 2–1 win. I'd been a striker for a couple of minutes, tops. Maybe if I'd done that in the pre-season game, I might have been one for longer.

I was playing well and enjoying my football, winning most of those early games. The talent level was special too because we had Kasper Schmeichel in goal; Paul Collins and Danny Warrender in defence with me and Nathan D'Laryea; Marc Laird and Carlos Logan on either wing; Ian Bennett alongside Jonathan D'Laryea in central midfield; and Stevie Ireland as a No. 10 behind Karl Bermingham up top. We were good but still humble, which is much easier when you're only on £80 a week. Apart from those players who had come over from Ireland, who would be given extra money to put their parents up, we were all on the same amount, doing the same thing. We were also predominantly Mancunian, with only Stevie, Marc and Kasper from further afield. We represented Manchester City's academy, but at its core it felt like just another young team in Manchester.

Representing England, on the other hand, was elusive to me and my teammates, despite our success on the field. We had players in the Ireland, Scotland and Wales teams, but even though we were a good side in that age group not in England. It was strange, because it wasn't a case of the whole City youth set-up being ignored, as there were players older than us who were being selected. Shaun Cartwright and Dorryl Proffitt were two names you'd always hear being hyped up. They were the chosen ones, literally, because they'd been picked for England. It just felt weird how much attention they were getting from the national set-up compared to our team, which had lost only four games maximum in about three years – especially when you consider that neither of them went on to play any senior games of note for anyone.

This was my first experience of 'the system', a series of foot-balling bubbles that for reasons often nothing to do with your ability, you're either in or out of. At one point, Dorryl Proffitt was playing more games for England than he was for the acad-emy. He wasn't good enough for City, so he wasn't selected. But for England, things appeared to be different. You'd think you'd get recognised on merit, and sometimes you do. But sometimes you don't, particularly if you're not in the system. For England, rightly or wrongly, that was based around a core group of players they believed would turn into something. But the question was, how did you get into the core group, and were they watching any players outside it? Clearly they weren't at that time, because they seemed to be consistently picking one who couldn't even make his academy team. Those they wanted were those they were familiar with or had worked with for a number of years. Their progress didn't really seem to matter. It was a shame for all those people who were desperate to get the chance to play for England, and not just me but a few in my team: it didn't seem to matter how well we played, the opportunity wouldn't be there because somebody else had already got it, and they were in the system.

The first time I was recognised by England was after I'd al-ready broken through to the Manchester City first team. I was eighteen, and it was for an Under-20s game against Russia. The Under-20s isn't really an official age group as it usually gets built into the Under-21s, so it was a rare fixture for them, but it provided my first call-up. Lee Croft and Bradley Wright-Phillips had also been selected from City. The game was on a Tuesday at The Valley, Charlton Athletic's ground in south-east London. After arriving on matchday I was given a programme, so I took the opportunity to look for myself in it. As I read down the page talking about all the different players, I noticed one in particular: Stacy Long. Alongside his name, the programme detailed how Stacy had played for England a few times and just last week – by which point I'd been in a Premier League squad for three months – made his debut for the Charlton reserves. I'd first played for City's reserves around three years prior. But Stacy Long was in the system, so he'd been playing for England, and 'a few times' too.

The England Under-20s beat Russia 2–0, and I scored from a set-piece. I was so proud that it was the first shirt in my career I ever got framed, and my dad still has it up on the wall in his house. That summer there was to be an Under-19s European Championship. But when the squad was picked, I was only on standby. I thought, I'm really not part of the system at all, am I? I'm playing in the Premier League and scored on my debut for the older age group, but now I can't get into the squad for the younger group. It didn't add up. None of those players selected ahead of me had the same Premier League experience I had, but they had been involved in previous England games, and that appeared to be the only qualification necessary.

I was disheartened after missing out on the U-19s Euro but tried to reason why. It's not like I'd always been desperate to play for England, but my experiences up to that point had shown me that there was a path you could follow if you performed to the levels expected. Now all I was seeing was a pathway for some people but not others.

• • •

The path I'd started to follow at Manchester City appeared clearer to me. Every day was a new feeling: my first injury, my first start for a particular age group, my first time being left out, my first yellow card. When you're full-time and then a pro, the money changes but your routine doesn't. There are only so many days in the week. Within that routine, though, there was a sense of progress. I'd be playing for the Under-17s and every so often would get asked to step up to the Under-19s. That would mean training with them on a Friday and playing a game the next day. Often I'd be back with the Under-17s on Monday, but the next time I might get asked to play a match for the reserves on a Tuesday. If that happened I felt like I was cruising, but whether they were trying to manage my expectations or only picking me to fill a need due to injury, it was never a case of me being a regular for either the Under-19s or the reserves. Just a call-up now and again. I'd feel the progress, though, if one of those promotions was for a significant game. At the end of a season playing for the Under-17s, the Under-19s picked me for a playoff match against Blackburn – crucially, when everyone else was also available. It was their way of saying that if they really wanted to win a game, I was part of that plan. We lost, but I did well and felt like I had merited the decision for them to select me ahead of the regular centre backs. I'd been playing more for the Under-19s and the reserves, but appearing in a big game for which they would only pick their best team provided a benchmark for me. It was a launch point too, because the following summer Manchester City manager Kevin Keegan asked me to train with the first team.

Chapter 4

I've never felt so lost on the field in all my life. Ali Benarbia had played a through-ball past me, and I had no idea how. I didn't see it coming, and I didn't see where it was going. As I tried not to fall over, I just managed to look around and spot that someone was clean through on goal. It was Nicolas Anelka. He was Manchester City's record signing, and the mercurial Benarbia a club cult hero. These were players I'd only ever watched before, and now I was sharing a pitch with them. It was nuts. These were all the guys. Strictly speaking, my team was the Under-17s and occasionally the Under-19s; this was the Manchester City first team, and the standard had changed.

In the summer of 2003, just a year after I'd gone full-time at the academy, Kevin Keegan wanted me to be one of the younger players to train with the senior pros during pre-season. It wasn't a particularly dramatic moment, as it turns out; no case of a dream story or anything. It was just a text or a quick word with a coach to say either you're training with them or you're not. Every step up I'd taken had first been a temporary one, after which I'd returned to my age group, and those of us with the first team knew we were providing bodies to make up the numbers. We weren't even in the same category as those players in the reserves who more often than not tended to train with the first team. It was exciting but also surreal. Moving through the different stages at the club up until that point, my teammates had gone through the process with me so had been familiar throughout. But this was a whole new team, and it was an interesting experience trying to learn the flow of it. I didn't know anyone apart from the one or two who had been promoted from the academy before me, but even they were too old for me to have ever played or trained with them. So, I liked to watch – from afar, as we weren't in the same dressing room as the main first team anyway – and try to remain as silent as possible. I'd also try not to stare, because like any sixteen-year-old in a situation that's exciting, I wanted to try to play it cool, as if training with the Manchester City first team was something I did every day. At that point, of course, it wasn't. You'd hope to come back, but it felt very much out of your hands, regardless of whether you played well, badly, or had an Ali Benarbia through-ball almost land you on your backside.

'Ali's good, isn't he?' The other players would say to me, with a smile. Initially it appeared a bit condescending because I'd just had a nightmare in front of them all, but it was also reassuring that I hadn't been the only one over the years. I was able to understand straight away that there were special talents at this level, and Benarbia's teammates made it abundantly clear that what had happened to me had happened to everyone. That was certainly what I'd tell my friends, anyway. For those who had been with me since the Under-10s, it felt like I'd become prime time. I'd talk about the players I had been training alongside and say how good they all were. How you could tell that Nicolas

Anelka was the main man, turning up for training later than everyone else. They'd look up to you, but for the first time I started to see a separation between those who weren't being called up to occasionally play at a higher level and the likes of us who were now training not even just with the reserves but with the first team, while some were still with the Under-17s.

The most important person in helping me and others bridge this growing gap was Shaun Wright-Phillips. He was the pin-up for players who were coming through to the first team from the academy. He was also an incredibly nice person. Bear in mind I'd played with his brother Bradley as well, so there was a connection there too. Bradley was a musical influence, introducing me to UK grime and raves, while Shaun ended up giving me a set of his Pioneer turntables. They were worth about £500 each at the time, so I couldn't have afforded them. I didn't know much about vinyl or Sidewinder tape packs, but they both introduced me to the London lifestyle, and while the turntables were a gift from Shaun they were also his way of showing his approval. He couldn't hold my hand through my initial experiences of the first team, but he could make me feel as comfortable as possible. He had realised that if you were there, you were there for a reason. Whether you were showing your best on your days with the senior pros or not, he went about trying to put you at ease so you could be your normal self, performing the role of a chaperone to those who had followed him there from the academy. Shaun was aligned to the academy and understood his own importance to the club's youth system, and in turn the academy to the club. He would look back and see other people on the path he had walked and know what was required to get to each level. By the time I broke through, he was already one of the main people within the first team, and as a consequence his voice went far. He helped to bring young players into the fold, and if you were with Shaun, you'd be all right.

I tried not to get too far ahead of myself in that initial pre-season with the first team. I was still only sixteen and had no idea what was to come, so I took the chance to learn how to make the biggest step up I'd faced and deal with new players. It was exciting. I took all the information Kevin Keegan had to offer, and because it was pre-season he was happy to invest time in the young players he'd called upon to help out in training. I also had to adapt to new surroundings, because the first team didn't train at Platt Lane any more. They'd moved to a new complex in Carrington in 2001, and the first time Jonathan and Nathan D'Laryea and I went there we had to take four buses!

In fact, it wasn't just the training ground that had moved. In the summer of 2003 Manchester City started playing their home games at the new City of Manchester Stadium, which I had watched being built just yards from my first house in England. Its original use was for the Commonwealth Games in Manchester in 2002, which was great for a fifteen-year-old sports fan like me. I'd been to watch cycling at the Velodrome just across the road from the stadium and actually appeared at the stadium itself just before the Games began. There was an event for local athletics clubs, and because I'd joined Trafford AC when I was combining track and field with football at school, I was invited to run a 4x200 metres relay on the track that just days later would be used for the Commonwealth Games themselves. I ran the second leg, a bend and a straight. I was still massively into both sports at the time, and it felt crazy to be involved, even though I don't think we won the race. A year later, after a new tier had been built and two corners filled in, City were ready to move in, and their first game was against Barcelona. Some of my very first training sessions with the senior side were just before that match, which was also Ali Benarbia's last for City. I watched from the South Stand as we beat a team including Ronaldinho.

Manchester City's stadium move meant I never played a senior game at Maine Road, the club's home close to Platt Lane in the heart of Manchester. I had already played there a couple of times, including in the FA Youth Cup semi-final second leg defeat to Middlesbrough in 2003, which I think might have been the first time I appeared in a match on TV. For footballers my age, very few games were broadcast live: only those in the Youth Cup and the Victory Shield, which was an Under-16s international tournament for the home nations. This was when you'd learn about the new prospects if you hadn't already played against them yourself. We'd watch any televised games ourselves and would hear people raving about Wayne Rooney, or before him Joe Cole, and the Youth Cup was so exciting because of the extra exposure it would bring. It also gave us the opportunity to run out at a club's main stadium, which for normal academy games we wouldn't, and there was no guarantee we would make it as pros to get that chance later in our careers.

Playing at Maine Road provided a completely different experience to those I'd had across all those years as a ball boy. In academy matches you would just start the match after hanging around on the field waiting to kick off. We didn't walk out of a tunnel. But this was a big game. Proper referees, all that stuff. And at Maine Road. We would come out of the tunnel (from the dressing rooms this time, passing the ball boy room on one side) and see a completely empty Kippax Stand on the opposite side. The Kippax, named after the street it originally ran along-side, was a huge two-tier stand that had around 10,000 seats. When I was given tickets as an academy player I'd sometimes be sat high up in the Kippax, which despite being the length of a touchline rather than at one end of the ground was the loud-est and best stand to be in. Much better than the North Stand, which was a nightmare: I'd been in the North Stand twice, and on one of those occasions I remember chairs being thrown to-wards my head by Millwall fans. In front of the away supporters is also where I'd be positioned when I was a ball boy, and you can figure out why we didn't get any seats to sit on while the boys in front of the Kippax did!

Most of the time my mum and I would sit in the Main Stand, and on the night of the Middlesbrough game, this was the only part of the stadium open to the public. There were only a few hundred people there, and they were all behind us as we walked onto the pitch. Even that was more than I was used to, though, so it was special to have people cheering for us, and we could hear it as we came out. One player revelled in the unique atmosphere provided by having fans on only one side of the stadium. Lee Croft, the winger in our team that year, used to love stepovers and enjoyed playing to the crowd. Quite the funny character. It became a running joke that he'd play the first half on one wing, and then in the second half he'd switch to the other wing just so he could have the crowd alongside him for the whole match. He'd try everything to gee them up, entertaining them with all his flicks and tricks. It wasn't in front of a full house of 30,000 people, but just the mere fact we were playing in those sur-roundings with our families watching was incredible.

We lost that game against Middlesbrough. Andrew Davies

scored an extra-time winner from a set-piece. There was always more pressure in the Youth Cup, especially because we were a good side. The club hadn't won it since 1986 and wouldn't again until 2008. Being at home brought an extra significance to it as well. It mattered more, and there were more eyes on us. People would look to a Youth Cup run – more than, for example, the Under-17s or Under-19s games – for who might be the next guy to come through. There was almost a sense that we needed to put on a show, because that would help propel us to the next stage. We wanted to win the trophy, but we often felt more proud if someone online was saying how good we were after the game – this was the chat room era and fans were starting to gather on forums, so we might have a look to see what people thought about us. Not if we had played badly, though! If I'd had a good game, I'd be straight in there hunting around, but always at the risk of finding out that others disagreed and not seeing the praise I was expecting. That upset me, particularly if I wasn't being talked about elsewhere as the next prospect to come from the academy. It didn't have any real effect on my career, but as a youngster with nothing to do and nothing like the vast amounts of internet entertainment that's available now, that was the place to go.

Then, the next day, the paper would come out. Nobody in the media would bother covering academy games, certainly not back then, but the Youth Cup was different. Chris Bailey was the Manchester City correspondent for the *Manchester Evening News*, and that Middlesbrough game was the first time he gave me a rating. It was the beginning of an obsession, and not a good one. I used to read my ratings in the *MEN* all the time, and I'll be honest I hated Chris Bailey because of them. I always thought scoring players was an incredibly unfair thing to do, even though all the newspapers did it and most journalists see marking players out of ten as an unpleasant necessity. The ratings in the national press didn't really concern me, but on a local level they did.

Once I'd got into the first team and was able to see my ratings on a regular basis, it felt to me that certain players started the games at an eight before they'd even kicked the ball. There's a pitfall for defenders, as a lot of the good things we do don't get replays but do have an impact. It appeared to me that those playing at the back start from a five because they're not the fashionable members of the team. Then a team could lose 2–0 and the centre back could have been the best player, but they will always have a low number because of the scoreline. What kind of system is this? It had such a significant effect too, because if someone hadn't been to the game, they'd look at the ratings to find out how a particular player had done. It delivered so much power into the hands of just a few people, and if a journalist didn't like you, they could materially affect your value to those you lived amongst in the city itself. I hated that.

As a young player I would take my rating personally, and I would seek it out even knowing how angry it might make me. There came a point when I just cut Chris Bailey off, and it was because of the ratings. What Chris said about teenagers after a Youth Cup game would shape people's impressions of them, because opinions of a player in the early part of their career aren't set by fans watching them live but by what they are told. The player might be determined as a really good prospect for a club, but if you ask fans it's unlikely they'll remember what they saw to make them think that. It's what they heard or what they read.

• • •

The summer of 2003 brought not only my first taste of pre-season with the Manchester City first team but also the first of my AS-Level exams. I'd been studying maths, business studies and information communication technology at Xaverian College and was staggering the full A-Level courses over three years. Meanwhile, I continued to get closer and closer to the City first team. As they had for my entire time at the academy, the two went hand in hand. Summer 2003: two AS-Levels, and training with the first team. Summer 2004: one AS-Level, two A-Levels and playing with the first team.

My Manchester City debut was against Bury in a friendly on 21 July 2004, and I don't really remember it. As it was the first game of pre-season, the whole team was changed at half-time, and I came on for the second forty-five minutes. I think I'd been given a squad number, which was a thrill (even if it was up in the forties somewhere), and the match finished goal-less, so I must have played well enough for us not to concede. What I do remember is how I felt afterwards. I felt like I had just played for Manchester City, and that it really mattered. Nothing had been guaranteed up until this point, and I had no idea what was to come, but I'd played for City's first team. This was special, and the first step on a whole new path. I never expected it to happen, but that's where I was, at the age of seventeen, and it was exciting.

I also noticed that I hadn't been with the first team that pre-season just to make up the numbers. Kevin Keegan was always nice to me, but he had started to take more time to develop my game. In that match against Bury, there is one moment that sticks in my mind. I was at right back, and the ball was played down the channel on my side. I raced to get there before the attacker, looked around to see what I could do. My back was to goal and I was facing the touchline with the opposition player right on top of me. I just rolled it out of play. They had a throw-in and played on, but at the end Kevin pulled me over and said, 'You did really well, but remember when you passed the ball out of play? I don't want you to do that. I want you to roll it to the keeper so we can start the next attack.' Putting the ball out hadn't been a problem before because it was something I'd been doing in the academy. It was no-risk, and we were encouraged not to overplay. Now, the first-team manager was pulling me to one side telling me I had more in my locker than what I'd displayed and encouraging me to show more personality. The right thing to do is to try to keep the ball for your team, even if there's a sense of danger, trusting the players around you and yourself to deal with the situation in the right manner.

Kevin didn't need to say that, but he chose to at that moment and it immediately changed my perception of how to play in that position. From that day on I'd always look to see if I could keep the ball first before making sure I put it out of danger if there were no other options. The manager didn't just make that point to me either; he spoke to the press a couple of months later, saying I was 'very quick and strong', but his 'one possible weakness is his use of the ball. He doesn't give it away, he just doesn't do much with it.' Being quick and strong with a lack of finesse in possession might be the ultimate cliché when describing a young black footballer, but at least Kevin was basing it on some first-hand evidence. As a youngster I wasn't the best ball-playing defender in the world, but it hadn't been asked of me by that stage of my career and at that time City didn't have an expansive team that required its defenders to hit pinpoint diagonal passes. You defended, then you rolled it to a teammate. I was very solid at that. In terms of attacking from the back: unremarkable. I could have got better on the ball, so he was right. I had to learn that being more progressive in possession took character and personality, and as long as I didn't take any unnecessary risks I could play the way Kevin Keegan wanted. It's one of the reasons Kevin was perfect for me. He also had Stuart Pearce alongside him as a first-team coach, and he would give the youngsters bits of individual training (I remember working with him on hitting half-volley clearances high into a net – not exactly Total Football), but Kevin was the one who encouraged the youngsters not only to come into the team but to play the game in the right way.

Despite making the breakthrough during the pre-season of 2004, I was by no means a regular at first-team training and had to bide my time. Then, that October, I was at college one Wednesday and my phone went.

'What number do you want?'

It was Les Chapman, the City kit man.

'Er...'

Before I could answer Chappy snapped back.

'What number do you want?'

'What do you mean, what nu...'

'I'll give you 16. How does that sound?'

It didn't appear like I had much choice. 'Er... sounds great.'

'Good. You're in the squad for the weekend.'

Chapter 5

Les Chapman chose my first squad number. That was on the Wednesday. The night before, Kevin Keegan had watched me play for the reserves in a derby against Manchester United and told the kit man he wanted me to train with the first team on the Thursday and be part of the squad for the weekend's Premier League home game against Chelsea. The reserves match took place at the athletics arena next to the City of Manchester Stadium and was a sell-out with more than 6,000 fans watching – a rare thing for a game at that level – and Kevin was one of them. In fact, the manager always attended reserve team matches, and so we saw them as auditions, or more accurately as opportunities to make sure we didn't mess up. Eleven players just hoping to keep treading water. I was playing right back for Manchester City, and Manchester United's left winger was Kieran Richardson. It was a huge battle, a head-to-head that nearly had us fighting during the game. But the biggest crowd that arena has seen went home happy after a City win, and I had played really well. I trained with the first team for two days, and when the squad list went up for the Chelsea game I was on the substitutes' bench.

It was my first call-up for a competitive senior match, and up until that point the only official word I'd had was from Chappy. I was stunned he'd given me No. 16, as that was a really low number for a seventeen-year-old kid from the academy. I thought, that's a first-team number. I sat on the bench on 16 October 2004, watching Nicolas Anelka score the only goal from the penalty spot in a 1–0 win. That would be Chelsea's only league defeat of the entire season, which they'd end as champions in José Mourinho's first year in charge.

I wasn't devastated I hadn't come on, I was just astonished by the fact I was there. I'd woken up on the Wednesday before, tired from the match on Tuesday night, without a first-team squad number or any inkling that I'd be given a chance to step up any-time soon. Three days later I was sitting pitch-side in front of 40,000 people as José prowled the touchline in front of me. I'd warmed up alongside all those big stars out on the field. Players whom I wasn't even training with regularly because my team was the reserves. If I'd been asked to go on, I imagine I would have been a wreck. Probably crying my eyes out, knees shaking. I tried to take every single bit of it in, but even just being on the bench it all happened too quickly. I hadn't had much time to get my head around it. It was very, very exciting. As was the money. By that time my £80 a week had gone up slightly to £85, plus a £20 reserve-team win bonus, before tax. For watching City's first-team win as a substitute, without coming close to kicking a ball, I was paid an extra £3,750. Insane. I'd have to wait to get hold of that money, though, as it was still a little under a month until my eighteenth birthday, when I could officially turn professional.

I was still seventeen when I made my competitive debut for

Manchester City. I didn't have to wait long after that Chelsea game, but it was still longer than I anticipated. The next match was the following weekend, an away game at Newcastle, and during the journey to the north-east the day before I saw my name mentioned on the notorious yellow breaking-news ticker on Sky Sports News. Nedum Onuoha is set to keep his place in the squad for Sunday's game at St James' Park, it said. But when the team for the match was named, there was no place for No. 16. My experience against Chelsea had raised my expectations, and I'd had my head turned by a clearly incorrect news story, so sitting in the stands alongside Jonathan D'Laryea watching City lose 4–3 to Newcastle was an instant reminder that football never goes the way you expect.

The next day I got another surprise. The team that had played against Newcastle had a recovery session, but there was another game on Wednesday, against Arsenal in the League Cup. So, the rest of the squad gathered on the Monday, and Kevin named the team there and then. I was in. Not a sub this time, but in the first eleven. I would be making my first start for Manchester City.

It dawned on me that I had no routine to prepare for a first-team match. The Chelsea game was preceded by a whirlwind forty-eight hours, and this would be pretty much the same. All my experience was drawn from matches at a lower level, and now, with two days of training ahead of starting a game, I had to learn how things are done differently: set-piece work on the day before, a little more analysis than I was used to. Then the day came, and I went to college. It was a Wednesday, after all. I think it helped me avoid a long day of just waiting, over-thinking things. After finishing my classes, I drove to the stadium and made sure to go via Bradford Road, passing the old house. It only took ten minutes from Harpurhey, and I turned up to face the mighty Gunners in my silver VW Polo 1.4 with six CD changer in the back. Couldn't get better.

I'd now done enough training sessions with my teammates to know what I was about. The dynamics were very simple: I was a young player within that space. Kevin Keegan hadn't made as many changes for the game as some managers would have done, so City were at almost full strength. I was sharing a dressing room with England internationals Danny Mills, Shaun Wright-Phillips, Trevor Sinclair and Robbie Fowler. I had been picked to play in the middle of defence alongside Sylvain Distin, who at that time was a first-choice centre back. There were lots of good-luck wishes, because they knew how significant it was for me, even if the match itself wasn't the most important of the season. City weren't expected to win the League Cup, and even though Arsenal had made a lot more changes than us, they were the favourites for the match. Arsenal had won the Premier League the previous season without losing a game, an unbeaten run that had been dramatically ended by Manchester United at forty-nine games the weekend before. The match at Old Trafford became known for the 'Pizza-gate' incident, when in a post-match squabble in the tunnel area, Cesc Fàbregas had thrown a slice at Sir Alex Ferguson. This Arsenal team was prime-time, the crème de la crème, and even with the changes they'd made I was grateful that I still found those relatively new faces around me a comforting presence.

Even more fitting was that Jonathan D'Laryea also made his debut in the game. He was in the starting eleven in midfield in what was to be his only senior appearance for Manchester City. Together we had to try to keep an eye on players like Fàbregas,

Mathieu Flamini, Jermaine Pennant and a young Dutch striker who was making his first start for Arsenal, Robin van Persie. He scored the opening goal of the game, his first for the club, with twelve minutes to go. The move was sublime and had me twisting and turning trying to stop it. It wasn't the last time that happened to me against Arsenal, and it had me thinking about the moment more than a year before when Ali Benarbia had almost landed me on my backside in training. They were a younger version of the normal Arsenal team, but they still played the best football around at the time and won a lot of games doing it.

I played the whole ninety minutes and had the greatest challenge in the last half-hour, when Quincy Owusu-Abeyie came on as a sub. Now, this was the quickest man in the world, and he was determined to punish any tiredness in the City team by taking everyone on. He couldn't get past me, though. I had speed too. It was what gave me a positive feeling about my performance, despite the defeat. I know I checked my rating in the *Manchester Evening News* the next day, but I can't remember what I got. Probably a six, knowing Chris Bailey. It's hard to give a defender a really high score when a team loses, but I knew how difficult it had been to deal with the rapid Owusu-Abeyie, particularly when I was supposed to be tired. I would have given myself a seven.

We were beaten 2–1, but it still felt incredible. Just the mere fact I had been on the pitch. That pitch. With people in all four stands providing the biggest crowd I'd ever played in front of. And I'd started, against an Arsenal side that was most people's second favourite team because the way they played was so different and classy. I'd watched Robin van Persie when he was at Feyenoord, and now he was who I was up against. The whistle had gone, and suddenly I realised I was actually playing in the kind of game I'd only imagined until that point. It was special and I wasn't yet eighteen, so I allowed myself to cherish the moment, realising there were no guarantees I would ever get to taste this particular sensation again.

It was also the first time I realised I might be good enough to make it as a footballer. At no point before my first-team debut was I fully convinced it would be my career. Throughout my whole time playing at the academy or recreationally, it had been conditional. I had to invest time, effort and desire into doing well at school, because if I wasn't I wouldn't be playing. Football had always been a very enjoyable hobby, even when it got difficult. That was why I didn't do the BTEC course like the other academy players but chose instead to do A-Levels. I always thought I'd need something to fall back on, but my education wasn't just an insurance policy, it was a priority. When I started coming in full-time I knew the first team was closer, but so what? It was for everyone. I had been a good player for my age and a key player at the academy, but there was never an expectation that my future in the first team was guaranteed. You don't get to decide when your career begins because you can't select yourself. Other people have to begin it for you.

Kevin Keegan was the man to do that for me. After handing me my debut against Arsenal, he then picked me for my first Premier League appearance the following Monday night, against Norwich. The crowd at the City of Manchester Stadium was double the size of the Arsenal game, and the stakes were higher too. It was a league game and my first time coming off the bench. I'd also be replacing Richard Dunne, which would not have been the plan. When you come on as a defender, there are usually significant circumstances that lead to it. You might be winning and you're providing defensive reinforcements; you may well be required to try to quell an ongoing disaster; or it's because somebody's injured. Whatever it is, the pressure's on at least to maintain the status quo, and definitely not to make it worse. To be honest, if you're a centre back on the bench, you're almost as likely to get on as a sub goalkeeper. You serve little purpose apart from to make up the numbers, unless there's a catastrophe. So, when I saw Dunney go down, having watched the game for more than an hour either comfortably from my seat or warming up on the touchline, I was flooded with nerves. Suddenly there's a panic: I'm stretching 40 yards away from the dugout and the assistant coach Derek Fazackerley is furiously shouting at me:

'Come on. Get ready! Come on, son, come on. Quick. Are you ready?'

Whether I was ready or not, the coaching staff never appear to be when reacting to an injury, since they're bringing on a player because they have to, not because they want to. They tell you what they need and remind you about who you're marking at set-pieces. I kind of took it in before sprinting onto the pitch, watching as the heads of the players turned towards me, thinking, who is this guy? It was 1–1 at the time, and it finished 1–1. Twenty-two minutes plus injury time of doing it right.

Richard Dunne was fit again for the next game, the Manchester derby against United at Old Trafford, so I was back on the bench. It was my first senior derby and it finished goal-less, but I don't remember it at all. What I do remember is that Old Trafford provided the best food after games. Chicken sandwiches and pizzas – you know, the kind that might have been thrown at the Manchester United manager. I guess it was a pity thing: you'd normally get battered by United as an away team, but your reward for succumbing was some nice grub.

The next game against Blackburn I was again an unused substitute – two games in a row that proved Norwich was the exception to the rule – but the 1–1 draw indirectly provided me with my first Premier League start. Danny Mills was sent off, so I had the chance to come in for him at right back against Portsmouth the following week, as he'd be suspended. Typically of someone who had just turned eighteen, I spread my wings and flew at Fratton Park. I spent the whole of the first half marauding down the right flank, not giving the Portsmouth left winger Patrik Berger even an ounce of respect. I really liked the match-up and attacked him more than he attacked me. I just fully went at him, an eighteen-year-old in probably the best physical shape of his life against a 31-year-old who wasn't, even though he was a very good player. Maybe it was the joy of playing behind Shaun Wright-Phillips, or perhaps even the fact that I was only covering for Danny Mills, but I had a great time. Only for the first half, though, because I ran out of juice in the second. Luckily, Portsmouth did too, and two late goals gave us a 3–1 win.

It was the first time my performance merited a mention in the press by Kevin Keegan, who was quoted in the *Manchester Evening News* as saying, 'It must be inspirational for him to have somebody like Shaun playing in front of him.' It was. Later that season – Shaun's last of his first spell at City – I played right back with him ahead of me a little more. There was no need for any marauding whatsoever: I'd roll him the ball and just watch as he proceeded to beat sometimes as many as five or six players before putting a cross in or even scoring. It was insane, he was on fire, and he was as important a player for City at that time as I would see for any team during my entire career. He was special, and in that moment I swear he had a sort of Zen feel about his football.

That *MEN* report said something else, though. It described me as an 'impressive Nigerian teenager'. It's strange that for a player who had represented England Under-20s just the previous month, been in City's academy for several years and in the UK even longer, the most identifiable aspect for that journalist was still the fact I was born in Nigeria and how that explains my different name and different skin colour. I've come to learn that identity exists far beyond just where you're working or where you're living, but I had been in possession of a British passport for three years by then, and as a fifteen-year-old I'd thought, I'm part of a new system, I'm Mancunian, I want to fit in with this group. I'd changed, not to the detriment of my roots, but I was a teenager happy to discover a new sense of belonging. As I've got older, I've realised the importance of simply being myself and that you don't really appreciate identity until you're comfortable within your own skin. But I find it interesting that the *MEN* reporter that day had knowingly or otherwise decided that despite all the descriptions available to them, I would be most easily identified through a nationality that was likely a proxy for explaining the colour of my skin.

Kevin Keegan would only pick me to start a match on one more occasion. As it happens, it was against Arsenal again, and also because Danny Mills was suspended. The manager talked about me afterwards, resulting in another piece in the *Manchester Evening News*, which this time described me as 'Nigerian-born'. By this point Keegan had identified me as being 'highly intelligent', a 'bright boy both on and off the pitch', but also 'quick and strong'. The twin pillars on which my football career would be characterised – my ethnicity and my education – were taking root, with one offered in a little more of a considered way than the other. He also noted that he would leave me in the team for the FA Cup game at Oldham, as I'd done 'more than enough' against Arsenal. He didn't. Danny Mills came back into the side, and I dropped to the bench. City lost at Boundary Park in a big cup upset, so maybe he should have picked me! An injury in January 2005 meant I'd only play one more minute for Kevin Keegan. It was the game following the trip to Oldham, at home to Crystal Palace. I'd watched another Shaun Wright-Phillips masterclass from the bench, and with the clock ticking down Keegan turned to me.

'Do you get an appearance bonus?'

'Yeah.' I'd turned pro on my eighteenth birthday, so didn't have to wait for the money any more.

'Well, come on then. Let's get you on.'

I came on for Robbie Fowler in the ninetieth minute, playing on the right wing, and I didn't touch the ball. I tried to flick it on once, but I missed it. Ran about for a bit. For the whole minute I was on, I got an appearance bonus of £2,000. I expect I was the lowest earner in the squad by some distance, so any bonuses were incredible and way more than my salary.

The club's financial situation was not as promising. Two weeks after that Crystal Palace game, they sold their record signing Nicolas Anelka to Fenerbahçe. City had bought him for £13 million and only made just over half of that back. It happened on the final day of the first transfer window I'd experienced as a pro, and as a result I didn't have a clue what was going on or why he'd left. This still didn't feel like *my* team. I'd only recently come from an academy system in which nobody was bought or sold, and I knew nothing of transfers or how Anelka was one of a number of players who might have stayed at City if the club wasn't treading water financially. Thankfully, at that time most people, including me, didn't know that. It was business as usual, and I was just happy I'd had the chance to play with someone who was not only a very good player but who had been good to me when I'd come through.

Then, a few weeks later, another first: Kevin Keegan resigned. It was March, and City had only won once more since that home game against Palace in January. It was a wild 3–2 victory at Norwich: five goals, a last-minute winner and Delia Smith's 'Let's be 'aving you!' war cry. Following a 1–0 home defeat to Bolton, he quit, albeit on good terms with the club. His plan was to retire at the end of the season, but a poor run had seen us drift away from European contention, so he went early. As with everything I was experiencing, I had no idea what was coming next. Like transfers, academies don't do managerial resignations. Now, though, everything was a talking point: Keegan's future had been much discussed, but it still felt weird when it happened. I didn't really have anyone to talk about it with anyway. My voice within the Manchester City ecosystem was so small, and my peers at the time weren't those people directly affected by his departure. I wasn't exactly in a position to strike up a conversation with Robbie Fowler about it. We were in two completely different worlds. I was also oblivious to the fact that Gordon Strachan was the favourite to take over, with Martin O'Neill also linked with the job. I'd seen them both on TV, and that was about it. I didn't know how long it might take to go through any appointment process, or even that whole thing about how you need to im-press a new manager when they come in. Did not have a clue; I was just cracking on. In the end, the man who took over was very familiar. Stuart Pearce, who had been a first-team coach, stepped up, temporarily at first. The appointment became per-manent in the summer, by which point both he and I had had a very good nine-game run.

Stuart's first match in charge was a 2–1 defeat at Tottenham. We wouldn't lose again for the rest of the season, and he picked me for every one of those games. Kevin Keegan had given me my debut, and I was sad to see him go, but now I was being given a run in the team. The new manager selected me at right back each time, and as those nine games progressed I started to feel more and more part of the team. I was regularly in the travelling squad, starting with that trip to White Hart Lane, and on each visit to a new stadium my eyes were just a little bit wider than those of my teammates. I think I was to blame for one of the goals at Tottenham, but I remember doing well in the game apart from that. It was enough to keep my place, and then when two appearances in a row grew to five and six, I started to think differently. I allowed myself to look ahead and ask at the end of a game who we had the following week. Even though I still never rose to the level of expecting to play, and I would certainly make sure I was as coy as possible to avoid getting a bad reputation at the start of my career, there were certain moments that allowed my confidence to grow.

Often, training sessions are split into starters and non-starters, and later in your career you automatically know which side to join. But as a young pro, when you're sort of trapped in the middle, it's less clear. I'd pretend to lean towards the non-starters until someone would hopefully call me over from the other group, because I didn't want to be the one to emphatically walk over to the starters only for them to look at me and ask why I was there. You wouldn't ever live that down. I'd at least give the impression that my crew were the non-starters, as they were usually the younger players and those who'd joined from the academy, but as that run of nine games went on I was being called over to the starters' group more and more quickly. By the end, they didn't have to call me from nearly as far away, as I was hedging my bets a little less, and each time they'd start the split by saying, 'Right, same team as last week this way!' So off I'd pop.

The final two months of the 2004/05 season must have been one of the best introductions to professional football anyone has had: I was playing all the time, and we were upwardly mobile too. I was also playing behind Shaun Wright-Phillips during the best season of his career. My job was easy: literally all I had to do was get the ball and pass it to him, and then run up and support him from behind. There were plenty of other iterations of Manchester City, when it was life or death whether we won a game or not and when it would have been a bit tastier to try to begin a career, but my experience – with Shaun ahead of me and Richard Dunne, another player in the form of his life, alongside me to the left – was a very good one. After a draw at Charlton, we won four of the next six games to go into the final match of the season with a chance of qualifying for Europe, re-establishing the hope that appeared to have diminished sufficiently for Kevin Keegan to leave when he did.

The game that would decide our fate was against Middlesbrough, who sat in seventh place in the table. A win would take City above them and into the UEFA Cup. You could tell it was a big occasion in the days leading up to the match, and I felt part of it too. We'd worked hard to get to that point, and there was a sense of excitement as we walked out for the game. Middlesbrough were a good team, but their intentions were clear: needing only a point to qualify and prevent us from doing so, their goalkeeper Mark Schwarzer was time-wasting from the moment he touched the ball in minute one. Then Middlesbrough scored, Jimmy Floyd Hasselbaink slapping a free kick in off the crossbar from 30 yards out. We were losing until the first minute of the second half, and following Kiki Musampa's equaliser 'Boro were as much on the back foot as you could ever imagine a team to be. They had no interest in doing anything going forward. We were pushing and pushing but just couldn't find a winner. Then Stuart Pearce contrived to produce one of the most surreal moments ever seen within a stadium, and something I wish I could go back to just to get a real feel for exactly how ridiculous it was. With two minutes of normal time to go, the substitute board went up. Claudio Reyna, a midfielder, was coming off, for... for a goalkeeper? Despite Jon Macken, a striker, being on the bench, Stuart had decided to bring on Nicky Weaver, who'd go in goal so our original keeper David James could play up front for the rest of the game. That's a goalkeeper coming on for an outfielder while the other goalkeeper puts on an outfielder's shirt to try to win the game. It's one of the most confusing things I've ever come across, especially given the fact it was the most important game we'd played that whole season. A win would get us into the UEFA Cup. No extra qualification, like a couple of years previously. The UEFA Cup, proper. David James was no outfield player: he was there simply to cause chaos. He could barely kick the ball, although he was certainly pretty good at mis-timing tackles. There was one point when we won a corner, and I looked to the bench asking if I could go forward. They said no. This was with Nicky Weaver nearly on the halfway line and David James 40 yards further on in the penalty area. I think I'm the only player in football history to have two goalkeepers in their own team playing ahead of them – a particularly low moment considering I'd been a striker only a couple of years earlier! In the end, Stuart almost got away with making such a bizarre decision. From that corner, two minutes into the five allotted for injury time, we won a penalty. If Robbie Fowler scored, it would send us into Europe. He didn't. It was the third keeper on the pitch who in the ninety-second minute did what goalkeepers are supposed to do: Mark Schwarzer saved the penalty. The turmoil was eventually replaced by a real sadness, and I remember Robbie Fowler was desperately disappointed. He never missed penalties.

To this day I don't know why Stuart made that decision. After the game he said, 'I wanted to unsettle them, and in some ways it did. It unsettled everyone… them and us.' It certainly wasn't spontaneous: think about the time and effort that went into printing a shirt for a goalkeeper who might go and play up front in the last game of the season, one that determined whether Manchester City qualified for Europe or not. The next year, Middlesbrough reached the UEFA Cup final. There's no guarantee we'd have been like for like, but as they made their way through the competition I was just constantly thinking, 'We had a goalkeeper playing up front.' It baffles me that David James was afforded that opportunity. It also wasn't the last time I'd question the behaviour of Stuart Pearce as manager of my club and eventually my country.

Chapter 6

If my Manchester City debut was the moment I first thought I was good enough, the nine games at the end of the 2004/05 season were when I started to feel like a footballer. I was part of the group receiving information about the off-season and plans for the next pre-season. I was established enough to be kept away from reserve-team football, because I needed to be protected for the first team and would only play for the reserves to work on my match fitness. It didn't mean I was going to play all the time, but my magnet on the manager's office wall had been moved to a different side. I wasn't a transitional player any more, and I was about to be rewarded for it.

I'd been on £400 a week since turning eighteen, when my academy contract became a professional one. The appearance fee was sizeable compared to that, and the bonus for each match was £1,250 per point and thus a total of £3,750 for a win. At the end of the season I heard the club wanted to offer me a new contract, and my mum and agent started negotiating the deal. I would get constant updates but played no part in the conversations. I didn't know how it worked; when you're a kid it's parents, teachers and other people of authority telling you what to do. But I did know that I didn't want to leave, so despite getting a bit anxious when there was mention of a slight disagreement, I was happy when a three-year deal was decided. I was also excited: I was to earn just over £1,000 a week. That was the amount I'd challenged myself to save up over time once I'd turned sixteen and my salary was £80. Now I was getting it every week. Despite being probably the lowest-paid player in the team, I felt like the richest man in the whole galaxy. Absolutely stacking the cash, I was. I started saving up for a house but immediately upgraded my car. The VW Polo was replaced by an Audi A3, and this time it was bought with a 'Premier League player discount' of 18 per cent. In fact, that was the only reason I got it. It's one of the more curious things about life that the people who can afford the most get the biggest discounts. Although I didn't get the *biggest* discount, because there was also 20 per cent off if you were a 'Tier One' player – someone who played international football. Still, I got 18 per cent, bought a black A3 and drove it around like a king.

The way the money was paid also changed. When I was on £80 a week, I was literally living week to week because I got my salary every seven days. I would see it dwindling through the week, and by the time it got to Wednesday or Thursday I'd have something like £6 available. To keep myself afloat I'd have to go to the cashpoint on Corporation Street because it was one of the few that dished out £5 notes. The money started coming in monthly from the first professional contract I signed, and I didn't have to remember where all the fiver cash machines were any more. I was also able to upgrade my dates with Lucy, initially from Pizza Hut to Pizza Express, and then when I was earning upwards of £1,000 a week it was Wagamama and a movie at Ashton Moss cinema! I bought myself a couple of watches (although never anything like the APs – Audemars Piguet – I'd see other players wearing) and bags for Lucy and my mum, but apart from that I've never really been the kind of person to spend a lot of money on clothes or shoes, and still now I don't own many items that cost a significant amount of money. I spent it then as I do now: on a house, a car, a holiday.

I don't think I was consciously trying to rail against the footballer (and particularly black footballer) cliché of extravagant wealth and ill-advised spending, even though ultimately I was self-aware enough to realise that just because everybody wants something, it doesn't make it good. Perhaps it's because I inherently had different tastes, but throughout my career if I found myself thinking that something appeared desirable, I asked why. Is the thing everyone's talking about actually good, or am I just following a trend? It helped me to succumb to very little. I've not been on holiday to Ibiza, Marbella or LA. I have no issue with how footballers live their lives, but maybe in some ways I was consciously fighting the stereotype. If those were the destinations chosen by all the other players, I would try to find somewhere else to go. I lived a football life every day of every week when I was working, so when I wasn't why would I try to chase it, to be in that same environment? The world is far bigger than football, and at times it was easy to forget that, get swallowed up by it and follow the pack. There's no harm in that, as being in the pack can sometimes feel safer, but I felt like there was beauty in seeing things for what they were and making a decision based on that. You can enjoy things a little bit more when you do them as an individual. The flashiest car I ever got was in 2009, when I bought a Maserati GranTurismo. I had it for six months and had problems for four of them. It was a lesson in itself: just don't bother.

The money was increasing, as was the recognition. I was named the Manchester City young player of the year and newcomer of the year by BBC North West. I was particularly proud of the second one, as it was for all sports. I still have the trophy. In the virtual world, I was also on the new FIFA and Championship (now Football) Manager games. Yes, like everyone, I played as myself on FIFA; however, the first time I appeared on the management simulation game I was a striker. A lot of people would come up to me and say that based on the attributes Championship Manager had given me they'd signed me for their club, and within three or four years I was one of the top scorers in the Premier League. It wasn't real, but it still gave me an incredible feeling. These were two games that would get you very nerded out as a youngster, and I was buzzing that I could see myself in them.

The summer of 2005 was also when I completed my A-Levels. I'd already signed my new contract when I received my results, but the two remained separate. I wasn't playing football to secure my next deal, I was still playing to prove myself, and until that happened I wanted to keep my education going. Based on the three A-Levels I'd done, I chose an accountancy CIMA course. It felt like studying computers, maths and business funnelled me that way. I don't regret the concept, but I do regret choosing that course. It was suitable for someone who was combining studies with professional football, and Des Coffey, who was in charge of the educational side at Manchester City, was very helpful in setting it up for me, but I ended up sharing a classroom with people who were already working in the field seeking an extra qualification, another step on the ladder. It wasn't like school, where everyone was at the same stage – now I really was the exception. I didn't have the same motivations, because by that time it wasn't a career thing for me. I wanted to learn about the topic, but the other guys in those hot, stifling classrooms had much more buy-in. I didn't enjoy it at all. I didn't enjoy the environment or the time I had to commit to it, and it didn't help that it wasn't mandatory any more. I began to think it wasn't something I wanted to pursue long-term, so two thirds of the way through the year I stopped. My football schedule had started to make it difficult to attend all the lectures and lessons, and even though I was determined to keep going I was forced to ask myself why. Do I want to be an accountant? Do I want to see this through when I have the security of a three-year contract? Probably not. The wrong course at the wrong time; it just didn't fit.

That was the end of my formal education, one that had gone hand in hand with everything I'd done on a football pitch. It had defined the early part of my life and career. I was the kid at football (along with Jonathan and Nathan D'Laryea) who went to school and then to college because I actually enjoyed it. We did try to convince our academy teammates that it might have been a better path than studying a BTEC in sports science in the Platt Lane canteen, but they never wanted to swap. 'Nah, I'm good' tended to be the reply when we encouraged them to explore what they assumed was just for us 'brainy kids'. Others outside the club appeared to be more interested, as my education was a feature of my early press coverage, an obvious talking point whether the Manchester City PR department sought to encourage it or not. I certainly didn't: there was no desire on my part to wear it as a badge of honour, but I was happy to talk about it if asked. I also think the club wanted me to learn how to speak to the media by talking about something I knew. I broke through while I was still studying, and that might be more interesting than the normal conversations you'd have with a young player. My 'hopes for the future' story was based around having school the next day. It was a marked difference from how discussions went with my teammates. They didn't care, and asking how school was going was little more than an icebreaker with them. Young players didn't talk very much, either with the media or each other!

• • •

As I was committing my future to Manchester City, the club's best player was leaving. Just like in January when Nicolas Anelka was sold to bring in some vital funds, that summer Shaun Wright-Phillips joined Chelsea for £21 million. I didn't have a sense of how necessary it was that City sold Shaun, but I knew how gutted I was. Shaun was the pin-up and the pinnacle of the academy. The club would point to him and his contribution to the first team as proof of its success. I had been a ball boy when he played in the Youth Cup at Maine Road, and then in his final games for the club (in his first spell) I was behind him at right back. He had helped us young players and made sure we were being looked after, even though he was only five years older than my age group. Compared to us, though, he was handsomely paid and equally generous. I was devastated to see such a good guy leave. And a star of the team too, even amongst the likes of Nicolas Anelka and Richard Dunne. It was weird to have that guiding light extinguished: he had come from the academy, he had trained at Platt Lane and he'd left in his prime. What now for the likes of me? What was my path?

Shaun Wright-Phillips joined the Premier League champions, who had money, and lots of it. City needed money, and lots of it. I've been told since that there were those at the club secretly relieved we'd failed to qualify for Europe, because it couldn't afford to pay the bonuses players would be due for doing so. Given that was the context, perhaps it's no surprise none of the team was aware of how bad the financial situation was. The club wasn't going to reveal it was selling Shaun to stay afloat, because that would have caused panic. I just assumed it was because he'd been playing exceptionally well, and with Chelsea also being a club from the city where he grew up it was a deal that made sense for him.

People think players have insights into what goes on at boardroom level, but the separation of information keeps us away from anything that's not related to on-the-field business. The gravity of City's money problems didn't occur to me. We were playing at the City of Manchester Stadium with 40,000 people at every game, not some sort of tin-pot club down the road playing in front of 500 people in a stadium that could only hold 10,000, so I imagine I might not have understood why there were problems. Maybe I should have carried on my CIMA accountancy course!

Shaun's departure was the first of a few over the next year or so, as the foundations of my academy life slowly started to fade. In November 2005, having only played once for City's first team and having made his debut alongside me just over twelve months earlier, Jonathan D'Laryea was loaned to Mansfield. We'd been sharing football fields either on opposing teams or together at the academy since we were nine and ten. We'd taken the same subject at college, and rides in his Peugeot 207 to and from training. We'd been on the same journey all the way to the first team, and it was crazy that the Arsenal game was his only one. I thought he was good enough to play more, but there's a lot to be said about timing. He played in a position that provided fewer opportunities. We shared that moment, and being the 'hot two' just afterwards, when we'd go back to spend most of our time with the reserves. Every time a player took their first step up, they'd feel like the big boy on campus when they returned to their age group, and more often than not when I did it, Jonathan was one of those who went alongside me.

By the time Jonathan left permanently for Mansfield in January 2006, others had already gone. Danny Warrender had joined Blackpool, where Marc Laird would follow on the first of his loan spells later on. Despite an almost uninterrupted rise in an academy career, if a player reaches nineteen or twenty and they're not breaking through to the first team, it's likely they will be on their way. There's no value in just being in the reserves for two or three years, where it can be a bit bleak as you get older, so if a team is interested in you, you're unlikely to turn them down. They can get you out of purgatory. Jonathan went on to play around 150 times for Mansfield, and that's a good career.

I was sad to see my academy friends go because they were still my mates. Even though I was part of the whole rigmarole of the first team, my academy team was still the one I was closest to, and I enjoyed it when every so often I'd play with them for the reserves. I found those relationships difficult to replicate in the first team, as I always felt like a youngster and not a proper part of the collective.

As my old teammates started to move away, I was lucky enough to stay, although I was injured when I signed my new contract and that proved to be a theme for the entire length of the deal. With five minutes to go of that infamous game against Middlesbrough, I snapped my hamstring tendon. I carried on for the rest of the match, which for the first of many in my career was probably not the best idea. During the summer we went to Bermuda to play a charity game on behalf of Shaun Goater – a City legend who came from the island – and I knew I had a problem. The only reason I was even on the trip was because back in May the club medical staff had insisted I'd strained my hamstring and nothing more, but as they massaged it in Bermuda I could feel a knot in my leg. It was assumed it was scar tissue, but I was nearly in tears from the pain. I tried to remain calm like a tough guy, but it turned out the tendon had snapped, recoiled into my hamstring and formed a ball. The rehab I'd been doing up until then hadn't served any purpose because it was for the wrong injury. Three months into what was eventually a four-month layoff, I still couldn't control my leg during running sessions because there was no tendon there. I went for a scan, which revealed the severity of the problem, and I had to work my way back through the pre-season to try to be fit.

My first start of the following season brought the first red card of my career. After easing my way in after the hamstring injury, I was able to play in a League Cup game at Doncaster, a club two divisions below Manchester City. We were the better team and should have been winning comfortably, but the game went into extra time at 0–0. We eventually scored through Darius Vassell and were pushing for a second.

Racing up from right back, I was free in the penalty area and put my hands up for someone to play me in. All I could think was: 'I could score a goal here. I'm a right back, and I could score a goal.' I'd been a City first-team player for almost a year and I'd never been this far forward, let alone kicked the ball towards the goal.

Free as a bird at the back post, I was played in and took the heaviest touch the world has ever seen.

'Oh my God, what am I doing here?' I thought.

The goalkeeper was rushing out, but I could still get there first and make up for my error.

I tried to slide in and flick it over him.

And missed.

'Crap. The keeper's saved it.' I was convinced.

The referee was convinced of something else. He came flying over and thrust his hand into the air.

There was a red card in it.

'Hold on a sec, what's happened here?' I genuinely didn't have a clue.

The keeper, Andy Warrington, was on the floor, shouting and screaming. Literally five seconds earlier I'd thought I was going to score my first senior goal, and the next thing I knew I was being sent off. The home fans, packed into Doncaster's old Belle Vue stadium, hammered me as I left the pitch. Then I became even more confused. I didn't know what to do after getting sent off, as it'd never happened to me before, and certainly not at an away ground while I was getting dogs' abuse from all around. Where should I go? Where's the tunnel? I eventually found my way back to the dressing room and listened as City lost on penalties. The team had conceded an equaliser without me and then couldn't convert any of their spot kicks in the shoot-out. I was devastated. There aren't many worse feelings than being the team that gets upset by a lower league team in a cup, especially away from home, because they'll let you know all about it. There was a huge sense of embarrassment, but I was also still baffled as to why I'd been sent off. I looked at my phone in the dressing room, and all the messages were asking why it was a red card. Following the game, the referee told the City coaching staff it was a mistake and it would be rescinded. But the damage had been done, because we'd been at a disadvantage long enough for the result to go against us. I get riled about it even now, because I've looked back at the footage and I didn't even tackle Warrington. I just tried to get a toe on it as he was coming out, and as I flicked it I pulled my legs back in to reduce the severity of the impact. We collided, and he hurt his leg badly. On the pitch he was raging; he hated me for a time and may well still be angry at me.

Even though I couldn't understand the referee's decision, which was duly overturned in the days afterwards, my fury was mainly directed at myself. I'd played a part in City losing a game, but I was even more irritated about that first touch. Horrible.

One of the worst of my life. If you watch it back, you'll think I knew I was going to be sent off because my head's down as the referee comes over. 'He knows he's in trouble here!' But I was annoyed about the heavy first touch. And then I looked up and found something else to get upset about. I was very sorry that Warrington got hurt, and I tried to find him after the game to say so. I'm not sure he was interested in hearing it. His replacement won Doncaster the game, though. Jan Budtz was his name, and he saved two of our penalties. It was his first game in English football, and his best moment too. All because of my terrible first touch.

Because the red card was rescinded, I wasn't suspended and could play the next game against Newcastle. But unlike the previous season when I strung nine games together to cement my place in the first team, in 2005/06 I would only make nine appearances in total after the Doncaster match. The final one was my first senior Manchester derby. I'd experienced Old Trafford as an unused substitute, but this time, at home, I came on. The game is famous for Patrice Evra's calamitous debut. Manchester United had signed Evra (who would become hugely successful for them) just four days before, and Sir Alex Ferguson had put him straight into the team. I watched from the bench as he got completely destroyed by Trevor Sinclair in the first half. It was like man against boy, and Evra was taken off at half-time. My experience was a little better: I remember it being an early kick-off on a sunny Saturday in January, and because in the grand scheme of things Manchester City were still insignificant compared to United, there was a big buzz about the game. I was a City fan, so I also experienced it in the days before: you could feel the energy. After two goals in seven minutes from Sinclair and Darius Vassell, we found ourselves 2–0 up at half-time. Everything was going well, but we were always anxious against United: there was 'Fergie Time' to contend with, and if you're actually playing against United that means the whole game, not just the excruciating last few minutes. But, finally, when Cristiano Ronaldo was sent off for a lunge on Andy Cole, we started to think we'd cracked it. But the Alpha team in any rivalry is still the Alpha team, even when losing 2–0 and down to ten men, so when Richard Dunne got injured and assistant manager Derek Fazackerley called down the touchline to where I was warming up to say I was going on, I just thought, 'Oh my God. Don't eff it up.'

This was a serious gig. I was about to come on in a Manchester derby with twenty-one minutes to go, and Wayne Rooney and Ruud van Nistelrooy were the two strikers I'd be going up against. Once again, I had nothing to gain, everything to lose. I couldn't make the situation better; I could only make it worse. Seven minutes later, van Nistelrooy scored. I've double-checked since and it wasn't my fault, but it added to the pressure. This was full-whack Manchester United, with Sir Alex Ferguson on the sidelines and Gary Neville wearing the armband. It was surreal being on the same field as Neville; when I was younger I'd hated him with a passion because he would manifest his over-the-top love for United by provoking City fans. I really detested him. He was the personification of Manchester United in that era, the definition of the big brother who hates his little brother and takes glee in winding him up. Now, I was up against him, and his team had made it 2–1. Then, Robbie Fowler sealed it for

City, scoring on the break late on. That moment is one of my favourites; we'd been under the cosh despite having an extra man, but we'd done it. We'd won a derby – my first real derby. City rarely beat United, but we did that day, and for the next week I could leave my house safe in the knowledge Manchester was blue.

Those early days at City were riddled with injuries, and there's one in particular that still irks me to this day. It happened just after that derby win and was the one that ended my season. A trust had been established between me and Stuart Pearce after he gave me the opportunity to start those nine games. I'd played well; he'd picked me. But in January 2006 that started to erode. During a training session at Carrington, the ball came into the box I was defending from my left-hand side. As I headed it away, my fellow defender Mikkel Bischoff went for the ball too and flew into the outside of my right knee. Bang! The knee buckled, and I fell to the floor in severe pain. It was a seven or eight out of ten. Serious.

'You'll be fine. Carry on!' Stuart shouted.

I couldn't believe it. I never stayed on the floor and I'd never felt this horrible.

'You'll be fine!' He said again. 'There's nothing wrong with you.'

This was my manager, and he'd seen Mikkel crash into my knee. I was furious. He seemed to be questioning my character. If I could get up, I would have got up. I've never shirked something because of pain, and if it's hard I'll deal with it, but that night I couldn't walk up the stairs to bed and had to sleep on the sofa. It turned out I'd ruptured my medial ligament, and as well as not being 'fine' at that moment, I wasn't going to be for three months. Stuart Pearce wasn't to blame for the injury, but I felt he was to blame for his reaction to it. I did get up and try to carry on as he'd suggested, but there was no ligament holding the inside of my knee together. It had completely gone. My resentment grew over the following weeks as I realised it's an injury that's psychologically very hard to come back from. After you start to kick again and the ball catches your toe, or if you get it slightly wrong, the pain returns. It sticks with you for months afterwards. I could be fine 80 per cent of the time, and then suddenly I'd do something that gave me two or three minutes of the agony I felt when I first suffered the injury. And Stuart Pearce had tried to play it down. I wasn't happy with that at all.

One of the hardest things a player has to do is watch their team when they're not even in the mix because they're injured. It's much worse than being fit and sitting on the bench without playing. You couldn't feel any further away from it all. I was working hard to have that opportunity again, and as someone who considered themselves tough, it was weird to be so limited. I gave everything when I was injured, but the physical output was so low. It takes multiple experiences to understand how it works, because when someone says you'll be back in two weeks just as you try to kick a ball and it's like the most painful thing in the world, you don't believe them. It feels like you'll never be able to kick again, like a disaster. The injuries that followed my medial ligament rupture were to my groin and hamstring, and each time I would put in maximal effort during rehab. But my hardest only felt like 70 per cent of where I was before, and it's demoralising. The pain and the road back are the things that are hard, regardless of how tough you are. Self-doubt creeps in, particularly when one injury follows another.

Having recovered from the knee injury and while doing some low-level running around a field on the first day of the next pre-season, it felt like a zip went up my calf muscle. The rehab began again, and I wouldn't be back until November 2006. By that time I should have played more like ninety games for Manchester City, not thirty. It also meant I didn't make a first-team appearance for ten months, and it was starting to become psychologically difficult to deal with each new injury, as specific physio was required. By the time I'd recovered, I'd been a first-team player for two years but had spent a lot of that time on the treatment table.

During those ten months out someone else established themselves, not only in my position at right back but also as the new face of the academy graduates who'd made the first team. Micah Richards was also seventeen when he made his senior debut, which was also against Arsenal. In a move that might ring a few bells, Stuart Pearce sent him on in the last five minutes to play as a striker. At least David James stayed in goal for the whole game on this occasion. The match at Highbury is actually more famous for Robert Pires attempting, and failing, to pass a penalty to Thierry Henry. We lost 1–0, and it might have been very different for Micah and me. He was due to be part of the travelling party but not on the bench. That was a spot originally reserved for me, but I had a niggle and told Stuart I wasn't quite ready to play. Micah's senior career began that day, and his first season followed a remarkably similar pattern to mine the previous year, as he was a fixture in the team from the spring onwards. He announced himself to the wider world by swearing on live TV after scoring a very late equaliser in the FA Cup tie at Aston Villa. Like me, he wasn't really a natural right back. We only started forty games together in the five seasons we shared at City, and very few of them came when we were young. One of the harsh realities of football is that often two people who consider each other good guys are put in competition for one place in the team. It was often either Micah or me for the next few years. I would have loved to have played alongside him at centre back for City, but in all the games we were both in the starting eleven I only remember that happening once.

One of the few times Micah and I both played together early in our careers was in a 2–1 win over Everton on New Year's Day 2007. It was a significant match because we scored, and at home. That wouldn't happen again for the rest of the season in the Premier League, in a run that got Stuart Pearce the sack. The previous campaign hadn't been great either. We'd finished fifteenth, which after the flirtation with Europe in 2004/05 was disappointing. In May 2007 we had actually won one less point but finished a place higher, which was a miracle given that we only scored ten times in total at the City of Manchester Stadium in the whole season. It was oh so bleak. I still remember the final goal of the ten, in that game against Everton: a Georgios Samaras penalty, and a pretty good one too. I had no idea at that point that we were going to stink up the joint from then on. It took a while for the goal-less run to sink in, partly because we were both scoring and winning away from home, but after a few games people started talking about the fact we weren't doing either at the City of Manchester Stadium. That kind of narrative can weigh heavily on a team, and particularly the manager. I was never going to be the person to say someone should get sacked, but after the team failed to score for half a season at home I could understand why Stuart Pearce was. We finished the campaign only four points above the bottom three, at a time when there should have been more enthusiasm for the players like me, Micah, Stevie Ireland and Michael Johnson coming through from the academy to form a big part of the team. That excitement had completely drained away by the end of the season, and any sense of progression that the club had felt under Kevin Keegan had been lost.

On the face of it, Kevin Keegan and Stuart Pearce had a lot in common as two Englishmen noted for their passion, but their management styles were completely different. Kevin believed in the beautiful game and inspiring enthusiasm in his players, while Stuart didn't seem to have a footballing philosophy during training or when forming tactics for a game. He was very theatrical on the touchline, but usually to little effect because his message rarely had a purpose. His nickname as a player had been 'Psycho', but as a manager he was anything but. He wasn't a tough guy, which is why I was so annoyed with him for questioning the severity of my knee injury in 2006. He gave the impression that the right thing to do was grin and bear it, regardless. Tough it out. But he was fake tough. I've had managers I was scared of when they got angry, but he wasn't one of them – it was like he was nervous of upsetting people. Indeed, the biggest thing I remember about him is that he could be manipulated, and the person who manipulated him most was Joey Barton. Joey did some appalling things when he was at Manchester City, and he wouldn't have lasted nearly as long as he did without Stuart Pearce's failure to deal with it.

While any faith I had in Stuart Pearce's management dwindled significantly during his time in charge at Manchester City, it was completely extinguished two years after he left. Midway through the 2006/07 season, while he was still at City, Stuart had taken over the England Under-21s team, initially on a temporary basis. I'd been playing for them since 2005. It was strange, and I thought to myself, does this mean I'll get picked for every game? I now had the same manager for two teams, and it was hard to avoid the subject with Stuart, particularly if after a game I was in the same convoy of cars heading to join up with the Under-21s while everyone else went in a different direction. After he was sacked by City, he got the international job permanently. He carried on selecting me, and so I thought, surely no harm can come from our professional relationship being extended. Little did I know.

Everything that had happened so far between Stuart Pearce and me had soured our relationship, but at no point did I dislike him. That changed in my last game for the England Under-21s: the 2009 European Championship final against Germany. Going into the tournament in Sweden, I'd been given the impression I would be named captain as one of the most senior players in the squad, but I'd picked up an injury in the training camp which meant I'd definitely miss the first group game against Finland, if not more, so Mark Noble got the job. Mark's a solid guy, so I was cool with it. We reached the final, the biggest game you could play in Under-21s football. For those of us in that age cycle, it was our last leg. I was twenty-two so wouldn't qualify for the team after the end of the tournament. It was also the furthest we'd ever come as a group of players, following a semi-final defeat two years before, and it was a competition England hadn't ever won in this format. We'd already played Germany in the last match of the group stage, by which time we'd secured qualification for the semi-finals and so Stuart had made ten changes to the team. Germany hadn't had that luxury, so a 1–1 draw was a good result for us. I was one of those rested, having come back for the second group game, which was a win over Spain. When it came to the final, the first-choice centre back pairing had been established: it was me and Micah Richards. Unlike for our club, at international level we were getting the chance to play alongside each other in the middle of a back four. At half-time, we were losing 1–0 to a Gonzalo Castro goal. I would admit I wasn't having the best game in the history of the world, but it was certainly a million miles away from my worst. I walked into the dressing room and waited for Stuart to deliver his team talk.

'Nedum. You're coming off.' It was the first thing he said. I was stunned. Why? I wasn't injured. I wasn't at fault for the goal, which hadn't even come down my side anyway. I had no idea.

'I'm making a change. Michael, you're coming on.' Michael Mancienne, a Chelsea defender, was a good player but a back-up and part of the next cycle. He'd have another chance. We were in a final, my last game for the Under-21s, and he took me off for what I could only assume was no reason whatsoever. Nevertheless, this was the part of Stuart's character I'd become more familiar with. He had always been prone to erratic decisions in the most significant moments, but as time went on I realised the inconsistencies were starting to feed into more than just his in-game choices. If a game's going on, as a player you can get a feel for when you're going to get into trouble or when something's gone well, but Stuart would sometimes end up talking about the exact opposite. We'd have a crap game, and he'd say, 'Well done, you tried your hardest.' No, we were crap, so tell us that. Then after a win, he'd come into the dressing room and start picking us up on things we needed to work on. That wasn't the time to mention that, either. I understand the management technique of guarding against complacency or of not hammering a team when they're down, but this was a botched effort at both because the inconsistency would lead to him alienating his players.

Whether his decision to take me off at half-time against Germany was one of those attempts to perform some tactical mastery, I've never found out. You generally never change centre backs, and certainly not when things aren't going that badly. I sat in the dressing room in Malmö for at least ten minutes after the second half had started, too upset to leave. I looked at my phone to find people asking me if I was OK, because they assumed I must be injured. None of the other staff knew what to say to me, because they didn't know why I'd come off either. My family had been out with me in Sweden following the whole tournament, and they were in the stands for what was to be my last game, win or lose. After being 1–0 down at half-time, we did lose. 4–0. Since that day it's become clear how special that group of German players was: Manuel Neuer, Mesut Özil, Sami Khedira, Mats Hummels and Jérôme Boateng were all in the team. I'd been robbed of the chance to see my Under-21 career through to its conclusion. Stuart Pearce took me off, and he never told me why.

After the game I got my runner's-up medal and went over to my mum on the far side of the stadium. It didn't feel right to keep it, so I gave it to her. If I had played and lost I might have valued it more, but a tournament that I might have started as captain had ended with somebody who I thought trusted me, who knew me as a person and as a player, leaving me devastated. That night, after we returned to the hotel, the squad and staff tried to relax with a drink, but I couldn't get it out of my mind. I kept thinking, this is how it has ended. The group stayed up until the early hours, but I went to bed relatively early. I couldn't sleep, though. The next day we flew back and landed at a private terminal in the Midlands, and Stuart positioned himself by the exit door to shake everyone's hands. Not mine. I just snubbed it. Nah, I thought. Not for me. Even with all the injuries I'd had in my career to that point, this was the lowest moment. As I walked out of that door, I was never going to play for England Under-21s again, and I had no international future set out in front of me. As it turned out, it was my last game for England at any level.

For the next decade I did my best to ignore Stuart Pearce. Every time I saw him it was like he was waiting at that terminal door again, with his hand outstretched. Usually I can move on, but I still can't let that one go because I can't think of any justification for it. It was a centre back for a centre back, so it wasn't tactical. Nothing changed, and you could argue his decision made things worse. So, I can only think it must go back to David

James and Middlesbrough. To Micah making his debut up front. To telling me to get up and carry on when I'd ruptured one of my knee ligaments. You might call it quirky, but when it directly affects you it's not quite so fun any more. There is a cost. In Malmö in 2009, it wasn't just my international career that came to an end, so too did my relationship with Stuart Pearce.

Chapter 7

The reason why 2009 hurt so much was partly because of what had happened in 2007. That year, in the previous Under-21 European Championship, England reached the semi-final, and for different reasons I also didn't finish that game. The tournament was in Holland, my first international competition as a professional. Just under two years before, I'd come into the team at the end of the Euro 2006 qualifying campaign, which ended in a playoff defeat to France. After being on the margins for the younger age groups for so long, I ended up being recognised with an Under-21s cap just as I was turning nineteen. With the possibility of being in the squad for three cycles, I found myself feeling like a newbie again, not knowing anyone. I also wasn't sure if I'd ever get a game; I'd been picked as a centre back but Michael Dawson and Anton Ferdinand were the starters, and each time a match came around I was given a very high shirt number, which was a discouraging sign. These were players considered elite talent in England, and I respected my position as a rookie within the set-up by being as quiet as possible.

I roomed with Cameron Jerome, and the first time I met him

he'd travelled straight from a Sheffield Wednesday game. I'd watched it on TV from our room, and then there he was turning up just a couple of hours later, talking about it with me. I barely said a word. It was clear the other players were comfortable with how it all worked at that level, but for me it felt like having to learn everything all over again: what time was training? What did you do in the afternoon or socially? So, like my early experiences of the Manchester City first team, I just watched and tried to learn.

Peter Taylor was the manager at the time, and he eventually called on me for the second leg of the playoff against France. I was a horse for a course. The first leg had been at White Hart Lane, and as I headed out onto the pitch during the pre-match walkabout a man with huge scars across his face was heading in the other direction. Franck Ribéry was twenty-two years old at the time and already an outrageous player. He tore apart our left back Peter Whittingham in one of the best performances I've ever seen on a football pitch. I'd had no idea Ribéry had been in a car crash when he was a child and even less idea of how good he already was, but in the second leg I was picked in a position I'd never played before to try to deal with him. A man-mark job. Ribéry was quieter, but not quiet enough. He scored in a 2–1 win that provided me with an international baptism of fire but not England with a place at the finals.

Around eighteen months later, we had qualified for the 2007 tournament, and I was much closer to being first choice. Despite getting a high squad number (20) and going into the tournament with just four caps, only Anton Ferdinand and now Steven Taylor were ahead of me in the pecking order. Gary Cahill was also considered an understudy, and it was he and I who started the first game, and then me alongside Steven Taylor for the rest of the tournament. It had the feeling of a prestigious competition, and the fact I would be away from home for the longest time in my career to that point made it an experience I was keen to learn from. By the end, though, I was desperate to get home. We lost the semi-final to host nation Holland after an epic penalty shoot-out. There were twenty-five spot-kicks, and the only player in either team who couldn't step up was me: I'd injured my groin in extra time and couldn't run, let alone kick a ball. All three subs had already come on, so we'd had to play the rest of the game with ten men – though only nine fit men, as Steven Taylor also got injured. He was able to hobble on and was the last of the ten remaining on the England team to take a penalty in the shoot-out, and he scored. Anton Ferdinand missed the crucial one, though, hitting the bar with his second effort, and we lost 13–12. Anton was inconsolable; I can still remember the tears. But for me, watching from the subs bench, it felt anticlimactic. A penalty shoot-out is always dramatic, but less so when you're still taking them twenty minutes after you started. Holland went on to win the final against Serbia, and much more comprehensively.

• • •

We'd also played Serbia earlier in the tournament, a match that had a much bigger impact on me than the semi-final. It was England's final group game in Nijmegen, and after around thirty minutes I was standing near the halfway line watching an attack develop in front of me. I noticed a noise over my left shoulder. There were 10,000 people in the stadium, but it was the only thing I could hear. Certain sounds during a football game catch up with you. It might be a shout from a loved one or another voice you can instantly recognise. This noise made me turn right around.

'Oo! Oo! Oo! Oo! Oo!'

Around ten Serbian fans were doing it the first time. Moments later, the sound grew.

'Oo! Oo! Oo! Oo! Oo! Oo! Oo! Oo!'

As I snapped my head around I realised the group had become larger. The Serbian support had coalesced to the point where there were now around 200. They'd seen me looking and wanted to put on a show.

You never go out onto the field expecting to hear racist abuse. I'd been singled out by opposition supporters before. Crowds are crowds, it's going to happen. Even before becoming a professional I realised football matches aren't all people singing kumbaya. I'd been booed. I'd been called every profanity under the sun: an effing this, a C-bomb that. I'd been told to piss off and die. None of that really cut through. I'd been called fat while I was taking a throw-in, to which I'd respond by lifting my shirt, revealing my six pack as if to say, 'Yeah, OK, I guess this is fat, then?' You get used to it very quickly and realise that most of them actually react well to you engaging with them. Some do double down and get really aggressive, but you find that just like with social media these days, when they're actually recognised as individuals by the person they're abusing, the veil lifts. They don't actually hate you; they're craving attention.

The Serbian monkey chants had certainly got my attention. And not just mine.

'We will not tolerate your racist chants, please stop or leave the stadium.' This was a UEFA tournament in Holland, not Serbia, and so the authorities got involved. They made the statement through the stadium public address system. It was in English, not Serbian.

'What do I do now?' I thought. This was one of those life firsts when I didn't know how to react. I was a young man representing my country and playing in a major tournament for the first time. I had no experience on which to fall back, no world view that helped and absolutely no control of the situation. I hadn't asked them to do it, hadn't done anything to trigger it, and they certainly hadn't asked my permission. It was just happening, so I did what felt natural at the time: nothing.

Playing the game provided me with a solid distraction, especially because we were winning and that was what we needed to make the semi-finals. Afterwards I was clear-headed enough to speak to the press.

'It was horrific, a bad moment. In certain countries it seems to happen and nothing gets done about it.' And to explain why I'd stopped and stared at the Serbians racially abusing me, I said, 'I just wanted to make a stand, to be honest, and to let them know I could hear what was happening.' I would also describe the game as the 'toughest ninety minutes' of my life to that point. Even though some of my family were in Nijmegen watching, all of a sudden I felt a long way from home. I'd started to enjoy the new environment and being away with England was becoming familiar, but that's when something bad happening can really knock you. It completely changed my perspective on being in Holland and the whole trip. I remember talking with the coaching staff about the monkey chants, and the English FA made a formal complaint to UEFA. The Serbian team was eventually fined around £16,000. 'Who's going to pay that?' I thought at the time. 'The local millionaire might as well.' What purpose did that fine serve? I know it would have been in response to rules that are agreed to, but £16,000 makes no difference to anything. Even putting a monetary value on racist abuse suggests the focus is not on ethics or beliefs but on a governing body essentially saying, 'We'd rather you didn't do that, so here's a slap on the wrist.' There's no real consequence when you can just pay money to get rid of a problem, especially if those being fined don't deem it to have been a problem in the first place.

If I had been older when this stuff happened, I probably would have made a bigger deal of it, but this was 2007 and I was twenty. Three years previously, Shaun Wright-Phillips had been one of the senior England players racially abused during a friendly in Spain, and when he returned to Manchester City I'd noticed that he didn't want to talk about it. Not because he was too shaken, but because he never sought out controversy. He just left it to those in power and concentrated on playing. Shaun's upbringing in south London had hardened him to a point where nothing that happened around football appeared too dramatic. When something went wrong, it was literally the least of his issues. He was tough physically and mentally, and the game was a release for him, not a burden. When later asked to reflect on the abuse he'd received in Spain, Shaun did say that were it the convention, or even allowed, he would have walked off the pitch in response to the monkey chants. Things had not changed at all by the time I heard them directed at me in Nijmegen, so it wasn't an option for me either. Had it been, I wouldn't have said no, let's not walk off. But I wouldn't have been the one to make that decision, because choosing to do something like that at a time when it would have been almost unprecedented comes from a position of comfort, safety and strength. I felt none of those things. The experience was foreign, both literally and metaphorically, and so it would have needed someone to say, the consensus is we should make a stand and walk off.

Making it about me alone was, like for Shaun, not something I was prepared to do. But in this day and age, with the things I've seen, I now know that making a bigger deal of it wouldn't have been making it about me. I understand the bigger picture that speaking out is about everyone of colour on the field or in the stadium. I'd be representing those people, making a statement for those who aren't under the spotlight. A person might be aiming their racial abuse at a particular player, but they're actually saying every black person on the pitch or alongside them in the stands shouldn't be there, and that means football isn't fair for everyone. My response is to say the racists aren't welcome, their chants shouldn't be tolerated and they shouldn't just stop but should leave the stadium themselves.

It's about leverage. People speak out more when they have some or if they will gain more by doing so. Too many people have no power whatsoever and accept things they shouldn't have to. They need someone to speak on their behalf. That's what age and experience give you, and it's taken me a long time to get to that point. And it works both ways; when Bukayo Saka, Marcus Rashford and Jadon Sancho were racially abused online after failing to score in the penalty shoot-out at the end of England's defeat to Italy in the final of Euro 2020, it was because they were black footballers. Well, until recently I was a black footballer, so when those racists call Bukayo, Marcus and Jadon that, they call me that. It doesn't matter to them who they're sending their messages to, because that's what they think about all of us. Now I can't just leave it like I did in Nijmegen and how I would in Podgorica the following September.

After what had happened against Serbia, I was a little nervous flying into Montenegro. It was the first of our qualifying games for the next European Championship, and my initial impression of the country was that it was very pleasant. We were staying in a rural area, and driving around it appeared to be a really nice place. The stadium, however, was extremely hostile. Montenegro had just gained independence, and this was their first competitive match. The crowd were loud. Joe Hart was in goal and told us of things being thrown at him. I scored the first goal in a 3–0 win from a yard out. I had jumped as if there were five people around me challenging for the ball. There were none. Not even the goalkeeper. Despite the noise, I didn't clock any obvious abuse towards me or any of the other England players. It was after the game, away from the glare of the cameras, that I had monkey chants directed at me for the second time in three international games and within the space of three months.

With another game against Bulgaria to come just a few days later, we went out onto the pitch for a post-match warm down. Afterwards, Joe and I walked back down the tunnel, which was in the corner of the stadium and lined with Montenegrin police officers. We were halfway to our dressing room when I heard it again.

'Oo oo oo oo oo.'

It was quieter this time, from just one mouth, but I could instantly tell where it had originated. As I turned around, the space darkened as the stadium floodlights appeared to be extinguished. A guard with a rifle slung across his chest had moved to block the tunnel entrance. I thought about going up to him and addressing it, but as I did others started to join him. Just like the Serbia fans in Nijmegen, racism emboldened the guards. Two became four, standing next to each other with their stares fixed on me. Deadpan. They gathered together in a show of force to make sure I had no way of escaping past them. Now I was scared.

'Let's keep walking,' I said to Joe. There was no confronting a situation when those abusing me were a group of uniformed men holding guns in an enclosed space. For the second time in my life I chose flight not fight, but this time it was the right decision. I wanted to question them, ask them what they were doing, but when they came together and I saw the rifles, I realised we had to get out of there. I was frustrated, but I'm not stupid. I feared the worst, which is why I chose to do nothing. A police officer had called me a monkey, and when I turned round it was clear he wasn't the only one who thought so. So, we carried on down the tunnel and found sanctuary in the dressing room.

It was another occasion when I was made to feel a long way from home, and again it had come after a real high: scoring a goal and winning in a hostile atmosphere. Perhaps that was why the guard did it in the first place. But this was still the era of not making a fuss, so after a couple of conversations with my teammates in the immediate aftermath, the incident was never spoken about again. In some ways I think they were just glad it didn't happen to them. There were other black players in that England Under-21 team, but I don't know if they were having the same experiences as me because it was almost like it wasn't worth talking about. My young life with my family in Manchester had taught me about isolation within a larger community;

we were Nigerians who spent most of our time with other Nigerians in an environment filled with people who didn't look like us, and even though that was an experience some of my teammates may have shared in different parts of the country, there was no concept of strength in numbers. We didn't have our own community within that team, so we weren't going to go en masse to seek change or consequences for the abuse we'd received. At worst we'd have to share those events only with each other, and at best we could share them with the whole team. You wouldn't come together and demand the FA made sure it never happened again, because as young players we still felt subservient to those people we considered to be our bosses. My voice was not one of a man who was able to dictate anything in an environment which at that time didn't deal well with racism. It certainly didn't feel like a solution was something the game's governing bodies – including the FA – or any club were really pushing for, and racism didn't register as something of significance because otherwise incidents would have been dealt with far more quickly.

I don't think I had to take that attitude in Montenegro, but I felt like I needed to. I was one person in a 23-man squad, with coaches and support staff in addition to that. This happened only to me. I could lodge a complaint concerning an incident which the Montenegrin police would likely say never happened. Were the FA going to press UEFA to do a full, thorough investigation when that's the starting point? Then, as time went by fewer people would care about it even though it might still affect the very person involved. It was a shame it didn't come more naturally to me to escalate it, but by my recollection it wasn't until five years later, when Danny Rose was also subjected to monkey chants by Serbia fans while playing for the England Under-21s (although this time in the Serbian city of Kruševac), that it was a big enough story to feel like something might be done. In 2007, I didn't think about the wider implications of choosing to do nothing. I didn't understand how it takes bravery for someone to say something and that drawing attention to abuse is not making trouble, is not kicking up a fuss. It's to highlight an example of what has been going on, systematically, for years and years and to try to stop it. All I thought about in Podgorica was getting out of there and playing the next game.

•   •   •

It was even more problematic trying to convince people of all the racially charged episodes away from football. My life has been split into two around the point when people started to listen to me about being subjected to racist abuse. Before that, if something happened I might tell my black friends and turn it into a joke. Outside of that context, some would claim I was making it up. If, because they're white, they aren't followed – remarkably indiscreetly – around shops by security guards or called Donkey Kong because they're a big guy driving a smaller car, then they might deny to this day that it ever happens to me because I'm black. The only solace to be found in having my experiences dismissed was to share with those who'd experienced it themselves. Even though those things still happen, now most people have a better perspective and actually want to hear the stories.

I would like to think this is reflected in football, but I can't help but be sceptical. I try to be realistic and at least admit that the reaction to racist abuse is now more than nothing. And that's something, but it's not enough. I'm glad that racism in this context is being taken more seriously and reported more often, because you never really know who might be picking it up. People say the message of players taking the knee before matches has become diluted, but I've had someone tell me how their child asked why their favourite team was kneeling, and the father was able to explain. So, a young person gained an understanding of something important that they might not otherwise have known. Change can come from people who are still forming their worldviews now, from people who are still taking things in and learning about these topics through conversations with others. We are products of what we were told when we were younger, so if somebody is listening to a point of view that says monkey chants are wrong, that the punishments for racist abuse are insufficient, that it's just talking and nothing's changing, as that young person gets older they'll know what's wrong and will understand why.

Here's the problem, though. Something is only wrong if the majority of people in society declare it to be wrong. If you're in the minority, nothing will happen. In 2021, Hungary were punished for a series of incidents involving its fans, some of which were during games against England. UEFA or FIFA can, in theory, force them to play behind closed doors, but to what effect? Hungary as a country won't accept it, will maybe even deny that anything happened in the first place because they'll feel like their identity is being questioned. It might be that for them racism is a matter of perspective. A Hungarian football fan could call me the N-word and declare it isn't racist and therefore not offensive. But if I'm offended, why is it not racist? It blows my mind that discrimination can be contested. When the Rangers midfielder Glen Kamara was allegedly called a 'f***ing monkey' by Slavia Prague's Ondrej Kudela, the defender received a ten-game ban. The following season Rangers played against another Prague team, Sparta, during which 10,000 children booed Kamara for his role in Kudela's suspension. The reason the crowd was almost entirely made up of fourteen-year-olds or under? UEFA had punished Sparta for repeated instances of racial abuse against black players and banned their fans from attending the game. The boos came because those kids knew no different to what they were being told. Kudela had denied making the comment, and so the table was set.

The statements from the Czech government, football federation and clubs all spoke in terms of persecution, and even the office of the country's President sent a letter to UEFA accusing them of 'discriminating against non-black people'. The defence of racist behaviour plays out in the same way each time: first, it's not many fans doing it; second, the accusations are 'unfair'; third, they attempt to discredit those making the complaint; and finally, they accept what will likely be a meagre punishment. The racists know the playbook too. Those Serbian fans could have said and done whatever they wanted to me in 2007, knowing there were going to be no consequences for them or their team. What is £16,000 to a football federation or to a country?

This is the divided international community within which FIFA and UEFA are operating, but I don't sympathise with them. The path most often chosen is that of least resistance, and not just because of all the pushback they might get from the football authorities in countries like Hungary or the Czech Republic. It's not because of the excuses or the suggestion they shouldn't punish everyone for the sins of a minority. It's because of money. It appears to me that they're driven solely by cash, and racism doesn't cost them anything. As a consequence, I don't think they're motivated to deal with discrimination in the same way they rally to reject an idea like the European Super League (ESL), when twelve clubs attempted to form a breakaway league in 2021. Look how much of a big deal that was, how energised the football community was to snuff it out within seconds as it threatened to divert billions of pounds away from those clubs and governing bodies that benefit from the existing structure. I've never seen such a swift call to action involving so many stakeholders in the game. Where is that conviction on matters of discrimination? Instead, we hear, 'We'll do an investigation,' 'We'll see how this goes,' 'We'll fine Serbia £16,000.' And so often the punishments are suspended or reduced on appeal with weak pleas for those responsible to please not do it again. This is the system in which FIFA and UEFA function. It is one they've built for themselves and which they've settled in to. Racism doesn't matter if they can still host their competitions in countries or cities that pay for the privilege but some of whose inhabitants may have discriminatory views.

The only way to deal with this problem is to remove some football teams from the system. Incidents that speak for themselves – clear, obvious racism – should lead to teams being banned. This is the only consequence that will prove to be a deterrent. I've seen it away from football. Even if some people believe I'm an N-word, they'll be discouraged from using the term if they foresee significant punishment. Take an experience they want away from them. If there's no real threat, people won't change. If football, and society for that matter, wants to create an environment that is 'fair', there must be consequences for racism. The

ESL was deemed to be a force for unfairness, so the system reacted to protect itself. Governing bodies should apply the same
principles to discrimination. If you're responsible for it, you're
out. Close stadia, take away points and ban teams. Then we'll see
if 60,000 people in Budapest start a monkey chant. Or even one
person; they need to understand that doing so would amount to
letting down their own country and result in their football team
being expelled from international competition.

I understand how unlikely this is to happen. Would every federation agree to a new set of rules which dictate that if you cross
the line you will be severely punished? I expect not, particularly
if that country denies the very existence of racism within its bor-
ders. This is why I fear that trying to end discrimination in football is an unwinnable fight. Tribalism has become so toxic that
fans will defend their players, clubs and institutions to the bitter
end. If someone plays for your team and racially abuses a rival,
all logic completely vanishes from the argument. Why defend
a stranger when you can defend a friend? And this extends to
England too. Outrage here doesn't carry far internationally.
The coverage and awareness of racist abuse is admittedly much
better, but our desire for action elsewhere in Europe is mostly
met with deaf, and sometimes disbelieving, ears. We are naïve
if we think another country is going to hear our complaints and
say, 'You know what, you're right, we're going to change.'

•   •   •

If somebody threw racial slurs at me as a professional in England, my initial reaction would be to take a swing. I can say that

as a matter of fact based on my other experiences of racism. I accept that you'd get into massive trouble for fighting on the pitch, but I always thought it would be an interesting case if you explained why. I feel like you might not lose your job because of it. Not that there's any reasoned thought at that point, because the red mist just kicks in. Even though violence isn't necessarily justified, I think there would be some leeway. Racism tends to take you out of professional mode and into the real-life situation, and I am black whether I'm on a football pitch or the street, now and for the rest of my life. This is who I am, and even though I think I'm quite calculated I know that by the end of my career I would have lost my mind if a player had racially abused me during a game. No flight here, only fight. I wouldn't be taking off but taking a step forward. I'm not the nine-year-old I was when our house was being robbed in Miles Platting.

My instinct now, like in the tunnel in Podgorica, is to ad-dress abuse. I wasn't going to try to fight a guard with a gun, but until the situation became potentially dangerous I wanted to do something. If someone writes something or there's a debate, I'll dismantle the theory behind the racism. On the street, though? There would be no argument. If I'm called the N-word by a stranger, something that's incredibly insulting to me and millions of other people, am I going to say, 'Well, I think you're wrong there' and talk it out? The racist is not presenting an argument for debate; they're telling me what they think I am. How do I educate somebody in that moment? I'm happy to talk to people about certain topics in which I can put forward a point of view knowing they might not change their mind, but how convinced do you have to be to think it's a good idea to come up to somebody and say, 'N****r'? If they're looking for a fight, they're going to get one. It's a shame that in Manchester, Nijmegen and Podgorica I needed the older me to be there. But maybe those younger experiences are what caused me to become the older me.

Chapter 8

I was standing directly behind it.

The ball was just to the right of centre for a free kick more than 30 yards out. Newcastle goalkeeper Shay Given had set his wall up to protect the goal to his left-hand side.

That was the way most would go. Try to whip it over the wall. No point going to the keeper's side from this distance because Shay had it covered.

Four unhurried steps later, Elano let his strike go.

'H-h-h-h-hold on a second…' He'd gone keeper's side.

The ball never rose above the crossbar as it flew into the top corner. I watched it all the way. Then I ran over to the corner where Elano had slid to his knees in celebration and turned to Martin Petrov, who had arrived just before me.

'Oh. My. God.' I mouthed, giving him a conspiratorial side-eyed glance. The keeper had been set, the wall had been set, but the ball… uh-uh.

Absolutely outrageous. Without doubt one of the best goals I've ever seen.

This was the end of September 2007, and everything at

Manchester City reflected that sunny autumn afternoon. The previous season we'd gone out with a whimper and Stuart Pearce had been sacked. Over the summer, more than just the manager had changed. The club had been sold to former Thai Prime Minister Thaksin Shinawatra, and I'd signed a new contract, although the fact that the former happened just after the latter made me wonder how much more money I might have got if it was the other way around. The wage ceiling certainly went up, and therefore perhaps it was no surprise that the club wanted me to agree the deal as quickly as possible before the investment arrived. I was a City fan and very happy to sign, but I knew I was on the back foot. City had appointed Sven-Göran Eriksson as the new manager, and part of the £50 million transfer kitty he'd been promised had been spent on Vedran 'Charlie' Ćorluka, a Croatian who could play both right back and centre back. Now there were three young players fighting for a place in the team: Charlie, Micah Richards and me.

City ended up spending most of the kitty on Rolando Bianchi, Gelson Fernandes, Javier Garrido, Valeri Bojinov, Martin Petrov and two Brazilians: Geovanni and another who represented all that was exciting at that time. Elano cost around £8 million and made an immediate impression. He was a bouncy Brazilian, a really friendly guy who clearly loved to come to training. He wanted to have fun, and in five-a-side matches or rondo exercises he would really express himself which would entertain us greatly – unless you were playing against him, in which case you'd have no idea what was going on. He'd play toe-poked 40-yard diagonal balls that would fade over a player's shoulder to put them through on goal. That is absolutely not a thing. It was, however, pure genius. In shooting practice, when the coaches would always shout, 'Match tempo! Match tempo!' to try to keep up the intensity, Elano would lay the ball off to a player, who'd then set it for him to casually jog on to before he caressed it into whichever corner he fancied. Made it look like a passing drill. Meanwhile, Rolando Bianchi and another striker, Bernardo Corradi, would be trying to kick everything so hard, with a much lower conversion rate. Elano became our penalty-taker, and the first five or six of his City career were so precise they hit exactly the same bit of netting. I assumed a goalkeeper would figure this out soon enough, and when one did Elano rolled it at 1mph into the other corner. He was different, and when things were going well he provided exactly the energy we needed.

The new signings' impact was instant. In the opening match of the season at West Ham, Elano produced a glorious pass to set up Rolando Bianchi, while Geovanni scored thanks to what I'd say was an even better assist. Charlie Ćorluka started the game but had only been with the club just over a week, so on a hot day at Upton Park he was tiring with about half an hour to go. I came on to replace him at right back. With three minutes left, Michael Johnson played me the ball. I was already inside the West Ham half and took it on the turn. I'd been on runs before, but you never remember the ones that don't produce anything. This one is clear as day in my mind. I left one player for dead as he attempted a sliding tackle, then I powered away from two more. I always felt comfortable if someone was on my back shoulder or even slightly behind, as I was quite good at holding them off. I kept going but was running out of space on two sides: the byline was in front of me, as was a third West Ham defender to the left. Then in a flash I stopped to let one past me, nutmegged the second and in typical fashion for me passed to Geovanni with a toe-poke slide tackle just before the third arrived. He took a touch and drilled it into the far corner. Nedum Onuoha: quick, strong *and* skilful. It was 2–0, and I was knackered. Dribbling the ball is so tiring. You don't realise that when you're actually doing it, just afterwards, and that was a long enough dribble to leave me absolutely shattered. And I wasn't the only one. Following the celebrations, I got back to my position and Craig Bellamy wandered over. He was playing on the left wing for West Ham and had watched me go on my excursion.

'Right. If you don't run at me for the rest of the game, I won't run at you.'

I laughed nervously. Bellamy was a very fast player. There was merit to his suggestion, even with just a couple of minutes remaining.

'You and me. We don't run at each other. Deal?'

I never replied, but he never ran at me. Every time he got the ball, he'd just immediately pass it inside. So I figured that meant I couldn't run at him. Little did he know, despite only playing half an hour I had no intention of doing anything particularly energetic. I was spent and wanted to stay back. If he had taken me on, I would have been diving in for fun because I had nothing left. He could have run rings around me. This is weird, I thought. But I'm going to run with it. Or not, as it happened. We shook hands at the end of the game as if there had been no pact.

'Thanks, man. All the best.' And that was it.

• • •

I only started one Premier League game in the first four months of the season, finding myself behind Charlie and Micah in the pecking order. I didn't resent either player or the manager, and despite being disappointed, previous seasons had showed me I could always force my way in before a campaign had finished. It was one of the reasons I didn't leave Manchester City in those early years, even though I might have got more games, more often, elsewhere. I was the next in, and the next in always plays. It's not like I was the substitute goalkeeper. There are so many injuries and suspensions, and the fact I could play in two positions meant the options were there for me. I wasn't starting, but I tried to use it as a positive, as that's when I would be motivated to train the best I could. My week would look different because I wouldn't have the satisfaction of working towards a match on Saturday, so I'd find enjoyment elsewhere. I'd try to win every game on the training field Monday through Friday. If I couldn't get ready for Saturday, I'd get ready for the next day. If a teammate said I should be in the team based on my training performances, I'd often consider that a bigger vindication than being selected in the first place, because the people who are most able to see the effect you're having think you deserve to be playing.

I was frustrated I wasn't first choice, but that's the nature of who was fighting for my position at that point. I believed in myself, and every time I played I felt like I was doing all right. It was a rare moment in my career that I was dropped for not playing well enough, but it's not always the case in football that you're left out for those reasons alone. A player's relationship with a coach and how that affects their place in the team is not always founded on merit, and that then has an impact on their training. If a player knows he's going to be selected regardless of how he performs in matches, he's much less likely to give everything in the days between. It's one of the game's big injustices, because it has a demoralising effect on those who *aren't* playing but *are* trying in training. Nothing they do makes a difference, yet if they consider not bothering, the same coach will hold that against them. I had about four or five training sessions in my entire career when I was in such a foul mood I thought about trying to toss it off, but I've never been able to. It was never long before I snapped out of it. I've got high standards and I'm competitive, and the shame in not trying was too overwhelming. I insisted to myself that giving my all was the bare minimum, particularly because of the position I played. I felt like I was an important person in my team, and if I stopped trying the whole thing would collapse. There were lots of training sessions where someone sacked it off, but that made me double my efforts in response. It disappointed me, and I'd never follow their lead. My attitude was in part inspired by my parents, who made all those sacrifices when I was younger. Throughout my life I've never been in a position where I could just down tools and do what I wanted, and I'd learned from them that you have to try to do what is right. There were tons of times I could have been lazy in training and got away with it, but I found the sense of guilt horrendous.

So why do managers have favourites? It's another, albeit smaller, part of 'the system'. When you consider that a manager will, whether it be for a small academy or a Premier League first team, encounter hundreds of players over the years, you might understand that they'd prefer to have just eleven in their mind who all play well all the time. But there's always more to it than that. Managers are judged for the decisions they make, so they can be very protective of the results of that process. For example, if a player is bought by a manager, how much time will they be given to prove the manager was right to buy them? More than others? Sometimes a player won't play well because they're not as good as the manager thought, but they'll be given countless more opportunities than a person in the squad who's playing better but whose performances reflect less directly on the manager. And that's the problem: players further down the pecking order suffer because of the manager's fear of being proved wrong.

To be at the whim of a manager's ego is a tough position for a player, and I had that a few times in my career. Sometimes the slights are a little less direct, like when a signing is made in your position the summer after a season in which you've performed really well and been given a new contract. They haven't come to you and said anything wild, but they're recruiting for a slot where you think there isn't a vacancy, so you get the message. Sven-Göran Eriksson was the perfect manager for this. For some, there's a starting eleven and then everyone else. Sven never made it feel like that. Most Premier League squads are big enough to have players left over when there's an eleven-a-side match in training, but Sven made sure those three or four were never the same, mixing it up so everyone felt like they'd had some game time as they walked off the training field and like they'd therefore gained something from the session. He never wanted anybody sitting it out. As a result, nobody felt alienated, and we grew to respect and even like him. When you have a manager like that, you will do everything you can for them. It's a rare thing, and it came from Sven believing in every single player. Whether he said something about your performance in training, how good he thought you'd been or could be, he meant it.

The Manchester City job was Sven's first since being England manager, and getting a pat on the back from somebody of such significance, rightly or wrongly, felt different to getting one from a manager with less experience. He had an even higher profile than Kevin Keegan, who was also a former England boss, because overall Sven had been a more successful coach, and you could tell immediately that he had an air about him. He was so charming. Regardless of your position in the hierarchy of the squad, you never dreaded coming into the training ground for work. If Sven was disappointed with you, he'd not be too down on you, and he certainly wouldn't bear a grudge. He'd keep things positive, which in turn would motivate players.

Sessions were competitive, but they were fun too. Sven had Tord Grip and Hans Backe alongside him on the coaching staff, and together they created a good atmosphere. They also instituted something that was full of subtle genius: a five- and six-a-side tournament. Small-sided games in training are nothing new, but Sven and his assistants would keep score, give points and put the teams into a league. Each day the line-ups would change, and the players would hold on to the tally they'd personally accrued over the course of a season. At the end of every month, those with the most points would be given a prize, usually a token amount (for a footballer) of £200 or so, and those at the bottom of the table would face a minor punishment. It was really exciting as we headed towards the end of each section of the tournament, as you didn't want to be near the bottom, and it was a massive motivation as you went into training. The money wouldn't make any difference, but the status did. And this was the purpose for Sven: through this ongoing competition he was able to see who the best trainers were. They were the ones who, regardless of whom they played alongside on any given day, affected the performance of that team in a positive way.

As well as a new atmosphere in training, there was also a new style of football in matches. Sven wanted us to play, all the time. That was a big transition from what we'd been doing under Stuart Pearce, although, unlike Stuart, he did have money to spend. The previous season had ended so disappointingly that the change in ownership created a lot of excitement. Thaksin Shinawatra came into the club promising the world, and one of the first things he did was to get Sven involved, so we felt very optimistic. There appeared to be an injection of ambition, and the new manager was the right person to handle the cultural shift that was happening at Manchester City. He could deal with those who had grown up in the traditions of English football but also brought the experience, and the languages, of other countries. The new players who had to adjust to playing in England would find Sven easing that process with words they could understand. He wanted his team to enjoy playing football, and it was centred around the genius of Elano as his No. 10.

Despite having an influx of foreign talent, two academy products were also able to shine in support of Elano. Michael Johnson had broken through to the first team and was playing in midfield alongside Stevie Ireland. They were nineteen and twenty-one respectively, the same ages as Micah Richards and me, so even though there'd been investment, the team maintained its links to the club's youth system. Stevie in particular flourished, and it was perhaps no coincidence that he was always at the top of that training league table too.

• • •

The 2007/08 season started with three straight league wins, the third of which was in the derby against Manchester United at Eastlands. Geovanni scored the only goal in a game in which Michael Johnson, a teenager from Urmston, was the standout player. I was really excited about the result despite being an unused substitute – at least until I left the stadium. The victory had compounded the positive feeling at City; there was a new style, new players, a change in philosophy, and now beating United had given us a new high. But it dawned on me that I hadn't been part of it. As a fan I was happy, but as a player I asked myself: where do I go from here? It was one of the first times I was really down on myself. Something great had happened, and I had celebrated, but it had nothing whatsoever to do with me. Was I just a passenger on this journey? City felt like a whole new club, which made it tougher, walking away from the ground that day, to feel like I was on the outside. There hadn't been a ton of great moments for Manchester City during my time as a player, and suddenly when the hope had arrived and we'd won the biggest game of the season so far, I wasn't part of the conversation.

The reverse fixture told a different story. By February 2008 I was in the team, but we hadn't been playing well. Heading into the derby at Old Trafford we'd won just one of our previous eight league games, and the expectation was that United would get revenge for their defeat at Eastlands and roll us over. In contrast to our strong start in August, the first derby was the third of three games United had failed to win from the beginning of the season, but since then they had won all but four of their Premier League matches. Four days prior to the second meeting they'd also marked fifty years since the Munich Air Disaster, so this particular Manchester derby was more significant than most. The two teams had agreed to wear old-fashioned kits reminiscent of those worn in 1958, with no sponsors or players' names, and United's jerseys were numbered 1 to 11. The occasion was commemorated with a pre-match wreath-laying by the two managers, Sir Alex Ferguson and Sven-Göran Eriksson, and a minute's silence. Even as someone who's never liked Manchester United that much, I appreciated what felt a poignant moment. All this only increased the anticipation that it would be a procession for the home team, who would fittingly honour those who died in Munich in the process. Whether it was the weight of history or the strange atmosphere, it didn't go that way at all.

By half-time we were 2–0 up. We went into the break on a high, because Benjani Mwaruwari, a new signing in the previous month's transfer window, had just got our second goal. But it was the first that was dominating our thoughts in the dressing room. Darius Vassell had given City the lead in the twenty-fifth minute. Stevie Ireland and I were both close to him at the time – enough to know the statistic that had followed the striker since before he'd joined the club from Aston Villa in 2005: his team had won every Premier League game in which he'd scored. What came next was a wordless conversation between the three of us, all communicated through furtive looks and raised eyebrows:

Stevie: Is this happening?

Me: Is this really a thing?

Darius: Don't ruin it!

I'd never been leading in a game at Old Trafford, and the script for this one was getting torn up. But even with Darius's goal appearing to seal the deal, we couldn't believe that this derby, with everything surrounding it, would be one we'd win. The City fans weren't quite so apprehensive. They spent half-time enjoying themselves, and it was into this positive atmosphere that we returned for the second forty-five minutes. The clock ticked, but for some reason no more slowly than it should have. United pushed, but not like in times gone by. It should have felt like the longest half of football ever played, but somehow, even after Michael Carrick pulled one back in the ninetieth minute, it never did. That was City's first win at the home of their big rivals since 1974. It was understandably not how United wanted this particular derby to go, but they weren't used to losing to City at Old Trafford in any context. It made for a weird atmosphere on the final whistle. City's fans occupied a corner between the south and east stands, and for security reasons they weren't allowed to leave until the United supporters had vacated the area. Not that they wanted to or that they'd be waiting long. As we walked off the pitch alongside the scores of empty seats towards the tunnel, a man came sprinting alongside us, jumping up or down a row to avoid those few stragglers supporting United who were still in the stadium. He eventually caught up with us and unleashed a sweary tirade, jabbing his finger violently. It was the most enjoyable abuse I've received in my career. He was truly rattled, the angriest man I'd seen at a football match, all because we'd beaten his team. Not many have the luxury of leaving the field at Old Trafford with big smiles on their faces having won three points against Manchester United. As we returned to the dressing room for the second time, there was no longer anything to curse by speaking about Darius's statistic.

'Of course we were going to win!'

'It was obvious. Darius scored!'

'Never in doubt.'

It was a run that would never be broken. Darius Vassell retired having scored in forty-six Premier League games, and the team for which he was playing won every single one of them. Very few will have meant as much as the goal after twenty-five minutes against Manchester United on 10 February 2008. It was probably the last time Manchester City went to Old Trafford as significant underdogs. We weren't supposed to win, but we did, and instead of watching from the bench I'd played all ninety minutes.

Just over a month later, I scored my first City goal. It's terrible it took so long, and it's a measure of our overall form at the time that it came in our first win since that derby. I've always loved out-swinging corners, and Elano picked me out with one against Spurs. If it's an in-swinger I often struggle to get my head on it, but this curved perfectly towards me. Jumping over Pascal Chimbonda, I met the ball firmly and it cannoned into the top part of the net to the keeper's left. I caught it so flush I probably headed the ball as hard as I could kick it. Some of my worst headers have been after I've had time to think about them, and I was always better at playing football when it was instinctive, so it helped that the moment came and went in a flash. The celebration I took a little longer over. I wheeled off towards the box where my family was, overlooking the north-west corner of the pitch. To my mum, who had been there for every single game I'd played since the age of eight and was now jumping up and down and watching her son blow her kisses, it's hard to overstate how incredible it was. She'd lived every moment of my career, both bad and good; she was there when there were just twenty people standing on the sidelines at a Sunday League match; and now 40,000 people were all celebrating her son's goal. It's understandable that someone might go nuts at a time like that. My teammates were clambering all over me, but my gaze never left that box. I knew immediately where it was, because, like every game, I'd identified it during the pre-match warm-up, just to make sure my mum knew I knew she was there.

It's weird scoring a goal in a full stadium. I milked the celebration, but moments later I had to be back in position and playing again. I'd scored what I thought was a good goal, and I couldn't believe it. I honestly couldn't, and there's no time to allow it to sink in. I'd given us a 2–1 lead, and we had eighteen minutes to see it out. We did, and my own little statistic was born. I got eighteen goals in my career for club and country, and right up until the eighteenth I never lost a game in which I scored.

• • •

The weekend Manchester City beat Spurs, we were in our lowest league position of the season so far. The next game we drew at Bolton and dropped even further. The promise of the early matches had ebbed away, and we only managed four Premier League wins after 2 January. The signs had been there as early as the previous October, when City had been thrashed 6–0 at Chelsea. Sven-Göran Eriksson had apologised to the fans immediately after the game, and I think he did it partly because their expectations had been raised through the previous weeks. The team had gone into the game in third place and surrounded by conversations about City 'arriving' and asking if we were the 'real deal'. There was no questioning Chelsea; they were the standard at the time, having won two of the previous three Premier League titles. Legit, certified heavyweights. It was then that we realised our team, with new signings in the mix and attempting to play nice football, was not yet the kind to win at Stamford Bridge. They ate us alive. I was on the bench and started to think that everyone, including us, had jumped the gun with the optimistic narrative. That match showed the difference between looking up towards the top of the table and aspiring to be there, and a team that was firmly part of that picture.

The return game against Chelsea was in April, during our second-half slide down the table. I started but didn't finish the match, which ended up being my final one of the season and last under Sven. In the second half I was tussling with Michael Essien when I fell forward, landing awkwardly on my left arm. I'd never felt anything like it. I was almost blacking out, the pain from my shoulder was so intense. I started shouting, yelling in agony. Medical staff ran onto the field, both the club's physio and the paramedics. They tried to get me to calm down and offered me some air through an oxygen mask. I'd never used one before and had no idea what the technique was. Instead of puffing slowly I took loads of quick deep breaths. So now on top of all the pain, I started having a panic attack. Confusion reigned; I realised my mum was watching from the stands, that my girlfriend Lucy would be wondering what was going on. They know I don't stay down, but I was rolling about on the pitch, in bits, screaming, hyperventilating and, as it turned out, not telling the medics what was wrong with me. When they found me incapable of speaking, they started putting a splint on my wrist. I have a joint that has always stuck out, and when they saw it they assumed it was broken. Anybody who's had a splint put on knows that you have to rotate your arm, at the shoulder. Each time they moved it to wrap my wrist, the pain got worse, making me less able to tell them to stop. I was put on a stretcher and taken down the tunnel. Five minutes later I'd figured out how to take on the gas and air, and I was calm enough to say that my wrist was fine. My shoulder was not. They cut open my shirt and it was out of its socket, hanging in a funny position. It was dislocated. At the third attempt they managed to put it back in, and the pain went from a 10.5 out of ten down to a four.

It's the worst pain I've felt in my life, and I was reminded of it just afterwards during the MRI scan. I had dye injected into the joint, and when it passed through that was the second worst pain I've ever felt. I had to have a full shoulder reconstruction, and just before the operation they did a test to see how loose it was. It was easy to tell: each time they lifted my arm above my shoulder it just popped out. The third worst pain was during the first two weeks of recovery. It was awful. The tiniest things became incredibly hard to do. To work on improving the range of motion, I had to dangle my arm and spin it around in a little circle. Then I had to try to claw at things like a tube of toothpaste. It was impossible. Lucy and I went on holiday to America that summer, and she bought me a dumbbell to exercise my left arm because it had shrunk to the size of a small child's.

Dislocating my shoulder meant I missed the final five games of the season, which not for the first time was to end with a match against Middlesbrough and one that for most would be unforgettable. I wasn't there and was glad, as it would have scarred me for the rest of my life. Despite the derby double over Manchester United and the initial impact made by the new signings, it was an open secret that Sven-Göran Eriksson would be sacked following the last game at the Riverside. It was almost because of how upwardly mobile he'd made the club feel in those early weeks that the downward trend since the turn of the year appeared so stark by comparison. By the end of April it felt inevitable, to the extent that Sven knew he'd be leaving and so did the fans. They launched a 'Save our Sven' campaign, which included a petition signed by thousands of supporters and banners that were on display at the away end in Middlesbrough. But the season, and the support for Sven, fell flat. City lost 8–1. Richard Dunne, despite having been sent off after just fifteen minutes, gathered everyone together in the dressing room after the game and thanked the manager on behalf of all the players. After losing 8–1. Sven was about to lose his job, but he hadn't lost the team. Injuries, including mine and one to Micah Richards, had decimated the side to the extent that Elano was sometimes called upon to fill in at right back. In a metaphor for the whole season, the exuberant No. 10 from Brazil was now trudging up and down the flank as an auxiliary defender. Despite the players' disappointment, losing so heavily at the Riverside brought a natural end to Sven's time and to any thoughts of fighting it. Dunney also said in his speech that we would miss him, and I agreed. He'd been very good to me and would speak to me all the time, particularly about using stretching to limit my injuries. I was pretty half-hearted about it at the end of each training session, but he'd continually remind me. At the time I didn't understand, but he was right. Even though I was still young at the time, I'd missed a lot of football and might have played much more for City if I had listened to Sven. He was trying to teach me that the most important ability of a professional is availability, and I regret that it was only later in my career that I could see that.

Sven Göran-Eriksson brought hope, but that had eventually killed him. Manchester City felt different that year, and for those of us who'd been there when there was very little optimism, we enjoyed working surrounded by the positivity conveyed by Sven, Tord Grip and Hans Backe. They gave us a taste of what it might be like to play for a successful City team, and I'd waited most of my life for that. I was a ball boy when City lost to Bury on the way to being relegated from the old Division One in 1998, and ten years on I was there still. You don't forget where you come from, and like for many of the fans who'd signed petitions or painted banners, Sven had given me a taste of something new. What neither he nor I realised when he left in June 2008 was that he parted ways with Manchester City in the most seismic summer in the club's history.

Chapter 9

Transfer deadline day, 1 September 2008. It's a cliché, but I was watching it unfold on Sky Sports News. The clip still does the rounds; a slightly baffled-looking Mark Hughes holding up a No. 10 shirt, standing next to Robinho. He'd apparently only found out about the deal while playing golf earlier in the day. We'd had no idea about any of it during training. The reporter said the football world was 'gobsmacked'. I was too. In the space of a few hours, Manchester City had been bought by something called the Abu Dhabi United Group and spent more than £32 million on one of the finest players around. I used to watch highlight reels of Robinho on YouTube and had seen him play for Real Madrid in the Bernabéu on television just two weeks prior. A superstar at the pinnacle of European football was about to be wearing City's baggy Le Coq Sportif training kit alongside the rest of us at Carrington.

When the club was sold in 2007, it had been to alleviate a dire financial situation. Thirteen months later, it was again in deep trouble because of the personal peril faced by Thaksin Shinawatra. Hundreds of millions of pounds of the former Prime

Minister of Thailand's assets had been frozen in his home country, and when he was sentenced to three years in prison he fled to the UK. It was clear he wasn't going to get his money back, so he agreed to sell the club. I was aware enough of what was happening, but at no point were we kept informed by City. It's understandable they wouldn't sit the players down before a match and say, well, today's crisis is that we're going to cease trading because we're struggling financially. The problem was that every time we turned on the TV somebody else would be telling us, so it was unavoidable. We knew that for some reason we had money, then we didn't.

We also had Sven, and then we didn't. The club's first foreign manager lasted just one season and was replaced by Mark Hughes. He would be my fourth manager at City and another journey into the unknown. Mark had done well at Blackburn, and those I knew at the club told me he was a solid guy and that I'd like him because he's funny, chilled out, relaxed. Well, we didn't get that at all. He came in and tried to be very stern, to set a new tone. Managers know that clubs hire them because they need something different, and it can lead to them playing up to that, even if it's not their natural personality. Like almost every new manager, he wanted to make us fitter. The number of times I've heard someone say on day one that the players aren't fit enough. It's nonsense. But on our pre-season tour in Germany, Mark made a point of it. We'd get our boots and kit together in the hotel, put them on the bus for the journey to the training ground nearby. With a mile to go, he'd make us get off the bus and jog the rest of the way, while the kit was driven there. Nobody was allowed to sit on the bus for that final mile, so the whole squad ran to training. This was before any of us had got a hold of Mark as a person, so it felt like a weird psychological test from a man attempting to be authoritative. Mind you, it did work initially, because we had no option but to take it very seriously.

Perhaps Mark was drilling us so intensely in pre-season because our competitive matches started in mid-July. The irony of the 8–1 defeat to Middlesbrough compared to the 1–1 draw with the same team three years prior, was that despite being thrashed City qualified for Europe in 2008. We didn't qualify through our league position; losing five of the last seven games meant we'd finished ninth. It was, like in 2002, through the fair play rankings, which rewarded a team not already in Europe and that had the best disciplinary record with a place in the UEFA Cup, and it was sealed on the final day in spite of Richard Dunne doing his best to ruin it by being sent off at the Riverside! That's how nice we were as human beings. Our opening tie in the competition was in the first of two qualifying rounds we'd need to get through before reaching the group stage, and it was against a team from the Faroe Islands called EB/Streymur. It made my first European match for Manchester City a curious experience. We flew into an airport where the runway was shorter than I would have liked, and on a cliff edge. Having survived the precarious landing, we drove through some mountains to a hotel with a grass roof. All this in a country where in July the sun barely set. Not all European football is glamorous. It's a peculiar situation when you're used to playing teams you know all about; all we had on EB/Streymur were a couple of videos, because it's fair to say nobody had spent any of their spare time tracking the Faroese league.

It was a good introduction to the sometimes peculiar nature of playing in Europe, where you had to adapt to the location, the teams and the perilous travel.

The Manchester City fans embraced the trip, however. It was typical of City's supporters, whose emotions had been on a rollercoaster ride for decades and particularly in the previous year, that they approached the opportunity to travel to a group of islands in the North Atlantic Ocean with such enthusiasm. Qualifying for the UEFA Cup twice in six years through the fair play league was the most City thing going, and the wackier the destination the more time they'd invest in being part of that story. Even if it took them three days to get there and they had to row the final 800 metres. It's the perfect example of City fans' adoration for the insanity of their football club. It hadn't been stable for so long, neither on nor off the field, and so many of the identifiable things about the club were frankly bizarre. I mean, remember when Stuart Pearce brought his daughter's toy horse into the dugout with him? But the fans bought into that and embraced the underdog mantle. It defined their experience for so long: we might win a game, but we won't win a trophy. You support your team for different reasons when that's the case, and it makes you stick with them through thick and a lot of thin.

Despite the unravelling financial situation, Mark Hughes was able to spend some money before the Abu Dhabi Group take-over, which suggests someone might have known it was coming. Jô had arrived for around £18 million, while Tal Ben Haim was also signed. There have been many incredible signings during the Abu Dhabi regime, but the three in the ten days prior were some of the most important the club could have made: Pablo Zabaleta, Vincent Kompany and the return of Shaun

Wright-Phillips. Shaun coming back was big. He'd done well at Chelsea, although you could argue he wasn't able to achieve his potential based on how much they spent on him, but his return was a huge deal – for him, and for me. He came back to a place he hadn't really wanted to leave and with which he was familiar, allowing me and other academy graduates to reconnect with the player who'd inspired us all those years ago. It might have also been a bit strange for Shaun, as the club had changed a great deal in just three years. It had also been transformed just before he arrived as one of the things Mark Hughes did, as with all the clubs he managed, was to revamp the training ground. His intention was to make Carrington feel like a place of work. It was the foundation of his philosophy to provide players with an environment that allowed us to be the best we could be. People might complain about his tactics or his personality, but Mark would squeeze out every last bit to make sure that when everyone came to work, we felt good. This was what Shaun returned to and what Pablo and Vincent joined.

I had already met Vinny Kompany, twice. I knew his best friend, Floribert N'Galula, through my agent. Flo had moved over to Manchester to join United's academy having been at Anderlecht with Vinny, and we'd played against each other. One weekend in March 2008 we'd all gone to Germany to spend a couple of days together and watch Vinny's team, Hamburg, play. They beat Eintracht Frankfurt 4–1, and Vinny came on wearing the No. 10 to spend around half an hour alongside Rafael van der Vaart as an attacking midfielder. He was a really solid guy, a nice dude. I liked him enough to recommend that he get in touch with a girl I'd known since I was around seventeen or eighteen, someone who I thought he would get on well with. Her name was Carla, and that was the first Vinny Kompany heard of the woman he would marry. I had no idea at the time that he would soon be moving to Manchester. Our second meeting was during that rigorous pre-season in Germany, when we played Hamburg in a friendly. Less than a month later he joined City and as far as I'm aware called Carla for the first time. Now, I'm not saying City signed one of the most important players in their history because five months previously I gave him the number of a Mancunian girl I was friendly with, but OK, maybe I am.

Vinny joined City ten days before the Abu Dhabi takeover, but Pablo Zabaleta was one of two to arrive just one day before. Pablo became one of the most loved City players of recent years, but City fans also ended up being very fond of the other player who signed on 31 August 2008 – only for different reasons. Gláuber Berti was a Brazilian centre back who became a cult hero for being named as a substitute nineteen times and never coming on. The twentieth time he was on the bench was the final game of the season, and his last chance to play in his one-year deal. In the eighty-fourth minute against Bolton, Mark Hughes brought him on to make his debut, nine months after he'd joined the club. The reception he got was incredible, and he was cheered every time he touched the ball. He was proof of the fact substitute defenders are rarely called upon out of choice, but also of something about football clubs that's missed by those on the outside: teams are more than just the eleven players who start each game. There are those who will expect to play and maybe a handful of others on the fringes of the first team who more often than not get on from the bench, but the rest will be disappointed when each game comes around. Find a group that works well together in this context, and you'll be successful.

Managers say the hardest thing they have to do every week is not to pick the team but to tell the people they're missing out and why. Sven-Göran Eriksson had a way of keeping spirits high, but it's not always down to the boss. Sometimes the players have to be relied upon to do it themselves, and Berti was the perfect example. He was a great guy and a brilliant trainer. He worked as hard as he could every day to get a chance. One which, until the final six minutes of the season, didn't come. But he didn't go around kicking anyone or cursing the coaching staff. Disappointment can easily spill over into negativity, but he was really professional, even as each week passed and Mark Hughes still didn't bring him on. He never quite gained the manager's trust enough to play, but the fact he always gave 100 per cent in training gained ours, and the ovation he got against Bolton was the very least he deserved. He knew that nine months previously he'd signed for Manchester City the club, not the first eleven, and that there's a much stronger chance of a club succeeding if everyone's pulling in the right direction.

Seeing the way Berti behaved was an affirmation for me. At the beginning of the 2008/09 season I also wasn't playing, but seeing that someone lower on the pecking order than me wasn't sacking it off made me even more determined to win back my place. We even developed a partnership in training, as we'd often be on the same team. We could see the value in helping each other to play well and worked together to stop those people who were in the team ahead of us. Not in a sinister way, but we enjoyed doing our jobs in training, as that was the only platform for us if we weren't being picked. That's the way I was when I wasn't in the team. I would never say to a manager that I should be starting; all I was seeking was closure, and if I ever spoke to the manager I asked what I needed to do to get into the team. It's the same concept but the wording is less hostile. If they told me, I could go and work on that. Closure. That's all I ever wanted.

Three of the six players who arrived at Manchester City before the transfer window closed that summer could play in my positions. Perhaps it's a good thing the takeover happened so late and they weren't able to buy anyone else! Charlie Ćorluka had left for Spurs on deadline day, so at least there was one less player competing for those spots in the team. Throughout the early years of my career the right side of the defence was constantly being strengthened. I was aware of people coming in to replace me, but I was still only twenty-one and had no desire to leave. I was from Manchester and playing for Manchester City, and that aligned with me more than thoughts of moving elsewhere. If I had been bought by the club I would have felt differently, as the ties wouldn't have been so strong, but I didn't know anything other than City. I didn't know what it would be like to leave, and being a young player who was considered next in at right back or centre back, I wasn't looking for it either. What more could I want? It might have put me on the back foot, but I understood that they wanted to reinforce the defence and thought I could maybe learn from the players they brought in anyway. It was my club, and I was still invested in them doing well, even if my own role in the team was less certain. I also had a habit of working my way back into the team for the latter part of seasons and knew time was on my side; nothing could change until the next transfer window in January.

For the next four months, Manchester City were linked with everyone. Agents were putting their players' names into the fold, saying they were all considering a move to City. But while the club was prevented from buying anyone new, the big signing it had already made had a chance to flourish. Despite now being the richest club in the world, very little had changed overnight. Robinho was the exception. He scored on his debut in a home game against Chelsea and another eleven times before the end of 2008. This alone challenges the narrative of Robinho being a failure at City. He scored fifteen goals that season, all from wide left, and that's not too bad. We hadn't been blessed with true goal-scorers for a while, so when all of a sudden somebody came in and made it look easy, it was exciting. Off the pitch, things were a little more difficult. Robinho was a player who was off-the-cuff, based on feel; Mark Hughes was an organised, scientific manager, and that didn't add up. Each morning the players' readiness to train was assessed using saliva and urine tests, and Robinho hated them.

'Aaaargh! Pish test!' He would get so angry, and he had a sympathetic ear from his fellow Brazilian Elano too.

'Every day a pish test!'

All I can think now is how good it was that Robinho wasn't around for that pre-season trip to Germany. He wasn't comfortable operating within the structure Mark Hughes wanted in place. If he felt good, he played well, and it made no difference what his preparation was like. You just had to watch his less-than-vigorous pre-match warm-up to know that. But in trying to create a team that was tough to play against and which rigidly moved together as one, Mark Hughes would get frustrated when his most expensive player indulged his maverick streak. It also didn't help that Robinho's English wasn't great. Mark would call him over and tell him something ten times, but at no point would Robinho understand. Perhaps he would have prospered more in the previous City team under Sven. He certainly didn't under the next manager, because Roberto Mancini hated him with a passion. Overall, though, Robinho served the purpose City wanted him to. He made an impact, both in terms of his signing and his first season. We only finished tenth, but he made us better. Take his goals away and where would we have ended up? Some might say we'd have been more of a collective on the pitch, but with people like him in the team, anything could happen. He also increased the standard of those around him, with young players like Stevie Ireland and Daniel Sturridge upping their game simply because Robinho existed, and defenders needing to be better against him in training. He wasn't physically strong, but he could read your body shape and move where you couldn't follow. I remember a couple of years previously Micah just laughing when Bernardo Corradi tried to dribble at him, because he knew Bernardo wasn't getting past. Robinho, on the other hand, would nutmeg you.

If Robinho was the first indicator of the calibre of player Manchester City were now interested in, the January transfer window provided more evidence. Four players signed, all of them internationals. These were serious players: Nigel de Jong, Wayne Bridge, Shay Given and Craig Bellamy. They were technically very good, but they also meant business. All the time. More examples of the kind of player the rest of us could learn from. Manchester City might not have meant everything to them, but success did, and it was clear this was the first crop of players who were being brought in to achieve something. I could feel a change, and I liked it. Training was more competitive, and the fact the new players were difference-makers made us feel better going into games too. The problem for me was that by the time January came around I'd only started two matches in the Premier League. I'd also come off the bench twice, including at half-time in the Boxing Day game at home to Hull City, which I admit was not the most memorable thing to happen during the fifteen-minute break.

As I was warming up to come on for Micah, Hull manager Phil Brown was delivering his team talk, on the pitch, with the players sat around him. They were losing 4–0, and he was trying to make the point that they'd let down the fans who were now watching him berate them. I understand they were getting battered, but to have the manager think they can do that in front of other players? I was embarrassed for them. No player would go into half-time 4–0 down and not have a reaction. Their manager reacted by humiliating them in front of everyone. That kind of thing turns a team against their boss, because at that point he's not doing it for their benefit but for his. He's trying to show the world it means something to *him* and that the attention should be focused on *his* attempts to put it right. The stunt might have appeared inventive at the time, but these things don't age well. I doubt you'd find any players who look back on it as a masterstroke. They've essentially been publicly accused of not caring, while their manager has put on a show to suggest he does. This is the kind of quirkiness that can alienate a team. Like, just for example, playing with two goalkeepers on the pitch.

• • •

2008/09 ended up being my best season at Manchester City. From mid-January, I started all twenty-four games. I was in the team and playing well, in a match rhythm of Thursday–Sunday as we played UEFA Cup knock-out games in midweek. The heavy schedule meant we never really did full training sessions, just prepared for games instead. I became more robust because the load on my body was different, and it helped me get into a groove. It took a month or so before I started thinking of myself as a true starter in the team. By now, instead of the first team moving to one side before each training session, they'd get bibs handed to them. Four years on from hovering between the two groups, never quite having enough confidence to even inch towards the starters, this was the first time I instinctively took a couple of steps in the direction of the bibs. It had taken me that long, and that many games, to think of myself as a fixture in the Manchester City first team. There had been times when I'd played a run of games, enough to give me a rough idea of my status, but because of the competition for my place I'd never allowed it to develop into an expectation. But now Mark Hughes was picking almost the same team every time. Enough to take just those couple of steps.

The routine provided a nice feeling. I could base my week around the relative certainty of playing games, which was a significantly better mentality than waiting to see if I'd been picked. You don't worry about negative outcomes when you play regularly and well. Whereas if you only get a chance either from the start or as a sub after a number of weeks out of the team, you're preoccupied with making sure you don't do badly. The distinction is very subtle, but it can define your performance. It's the difference between stepping up to take a penalty and seeing a big goal to aim at versus just seeing the goalkeeper. The difference between worrying about what could go wrong and making sure everything goes right. Being confident in my position, I was excited about going out and showing what I could do and what impact I could have in every game, rather than being concerned about whether I was going to play in the next one or looking over my shoulder to see if I was going to be replaced. It's no surprise that I played my best football and was voted the club's player of the month on two occasions during the second half of that season. I felt incredible, and probably the most confident of all my time at Manchester City. It's a great position to be in to have as much faith in yourself as others appear to have in you; no opposition was too tough, and I felt like I was always going to be competitive, both individually and as part of a team. I'd hit the sweet spot. During one game, the opposition played a high ball over the top towards me. It was uncontested, so I had time to run back, jump up and pull it out of the sky with the cushioned control of someone at the peak of their power. I remember feeling great as the fans clapped me – just as I was asking myself what on earth I was doing.

Then, by way of contrast, there was my goal against FC Copenhagen, which was not going to win any awards at all. After the qualifier against EB/Streymur in the Faroe Islands, City had made it past another qualifying round and a mini group stage to the third round of the UEFA Cup. I hadn't played since the first leg of the Streymur tie but had enjoyed travelling to places like Spain's Santander before we arrived in Denmark in February. By then I was unequivocally a starter and would therefore be playing a European game-proper for the first time. The journey the club was on was also exciting; after all, we were only in the competition because we'd qualified through the fair play rankings. We were not a top-six English side on yet another European campaign. We travelled to each away game the day before and usually had a training session in the stadium, and this was the case in Copenhagen. Stevie Ireland and I were walking onto the pitch at the Parken and looked to the right. There was no stand. There should have been a giant two-tier structure to match the other three sides of the ground, but it was being redeveloped so instead there was a huge canvas sheet with a picture of a stand on it, complete with cheering fans.

'If I score, I'm celebrating over there,' I promised Stevie. I must have said 'If I score...' on a hundred occasions before games, and the vast majority of times it hadn't worked out. Stevie had been there for most of them and rolled his eyes. The next night, with half an hour gone against FC Copenhagen, Stevie rolled me the ball. We were kicking towards the building site, and even though I was playing centre back for some reason I found myself in on goal. Running through, one-on-one with the goalkeeper, I looked to my right. Craig Bellamy was there, asking for the ball to be squared to him. Alarm bells should have been going off in my head: I must play it to him; he would have a simple tap in. But something else was in my mind. I thought I was Thierry Henry. (It wasn't the first time I'd invoked one of my heroes. I'd once scored a goal for AFC Clayton just like George Weah's famous pitch-length dribble for AC Milan. I'd watched it on TV and then delivered a less dramatic version for the Under-10s. I was overwhelmed when George joined City for a few ultimately unsuccessful months in 2000, partly because he was a guy from West Africa. I don't think he would have been impressed with my version of his goal.) Henry's signature move was his finish. Approaching the goal from his starting position on the left-hand side, he would open up his body and place the ball across the goalkeeper into the far corner. I'd tried to replicate that before too, but it was the chance I'd missed in what proved to be my final academy game as a striker. Now, Craig Bellamy was literally right there, imploring me to pass it. That would have been the sensible move, partly because if I made the incorrect decision, Craig would let me know about it. But I was in Thierry territory, just left of centre, inside the box. The finish was on, low to the keeper's left.

Let me do this, I thought to myself. Very ballsy. I shaped my body to open up the angle and took aim. Sweeping my right leg forward, I imagined all the balletic grace of my French idol and completely mis-hit it off my heel. I panicked; Bella was going to kill me. It was a horrible strike. So horrible that it completely fooled the goalkeeper. I looked up to see it trickle under him and go in, nowhere near the corner. Relief washed over me, mainly because I wasn't going to perish at Bellamy's hand – and then I kept my promise. I celebrated in front of the stand that didn't exist with the fake fans drawn onto a big sheet.

'Wow. Called it. Did it.' I thought.

'If that hadn't gone in...' Craig had arrived at my shoulder. He didn't need to say anything else. I had no business being in that part of the pitch, and I had no business scoring, but I was very lucky I did because with the finish I produced it could have gone a whole lot worse. Maybe if I'd clunked it off my heel when I'd had the chance at the academy, I'd have still been a striker.

The game finished 2–2, and we went through after winning the home leg. Bellamy scored both goals in a 2–1 victory. I wasn't anywhere near either, which is probably just as well. We eventually lost to Hamburg in the quarter-finals, coming one goal short in the second leg at Eastlands. The UEFA Cup run was really cool. As good as Premier League football was, there was something different about playing in Europe, and we enjoyed getting a taste for it. Part of the fun was the people I shared it with. Between the Copenhagen and Hamburg ties was one against another Danish side, Aalborg. We beat them on penalties, and the dancing in the dressing room afterwards, music blaring, was extra special. I appreciated it's not an experience every team gets to have, and I'm glad I did, because not only was it my first, it also turned out to be my last.

Chapter 10

Gareth Barry, Roque Santa Cruz, Carlos Tevez, Emmanuel Adebayor, Kolo Touré and Joleon Lescott. The first summer transfer window since becoming the richest club in the world. Close to £140 million spent, and in the cases of Kolo and Joleon, on two new centre backs. I'd just ended a season with my place in the team more secure than ever, but I immediately knew I wouldn't be playing at the start of the next one even though I'd signed a new five-year contract. This was the first time there was true conflict within me; City had rewarded my best season with a deal that increased my salary to more than £1 million a year but had simultaneously relegated me back to a young, albeit trustworthy, squad player. I tried to figure out what it meant.

I knew I didn't care about the money. I had my own progression, and a lot of contracts for players my age were triggered by the amount of games we'd played anyway, so I wasn't banging on the door having been in the team for two solid years, asking to be paid the same as the other starters. I'd been a regular for six months and the contract was a fair reflection of that. It was enough for me. Looking back it makes sense, as City were trying to reach the next stage, one where success had to arrive, and they felt they needed to invest in players like Joleon and Kolo for that particular moment. They were two of the best centre backs from two of the bigger teams in the Premier League. I was a 22-year-old defender who had come through the academy, and it was unlikely they would choose to build the side around me. I also wasn't bothered about what the players who had been signed since the takeover were getting paid. In fact, I'd never been concerned about comparing salaries, even though everyone was distinctly aware from the news reports that the latest signings were in a different tier to most of those already at the club. There was a lot of attention given in the press to how much money was being spent, so it was hard to ignore. But I was paid very well to play for my club, and I felt great. What more could I ask for? So, I thought, right, leave it there. Trust the process. I'd worked my way into the team in almost every season I'd been a professional. There had been players bought to replace me before, like Tal Ben Haim just a year previously, and I'd fought my way past them. The new signings were good players, so I resolved to learn from them and compete with them, and I would get my chance.

Up until the summer of 2009, Manchester City had retained the feel of a club that was familiar to me, even with everything that had happened. I was late to pre-season after playing in the Under-21 European Championship and took my own flight out to South Africa where the team, including most of the new players, was on tour. This was the first time I sensed things changing just a little. The squad was much larger, and more than half of it was new. By the end of the transfer window there would be eighteen players who had joined City in just twelve months. Of these, only Shaun Wright-Phillips could claim to have a connection with the club but all were being paid handsomely. They were called mercenaries, but that's not accurate. I wouldn't expect new signings to understand a club's history if they're going to be successful in creating its future. It's hard for a new player to engage immediately with a club anyway; it takes time to get a feel for it. These were more players I'd describe as serious; really good professionals who took personal pride in their own performance and that of their team. They didn't like losing. That got them to where they were, and it's why they cost the money they did.

As for each player's motivation in signing for a team to which they might not have a personal link or long-held ambition to join, the money mattered, but it's not necessarily the only thing that persuades footballers. Imagine being told that you can be the foundation for a club's push into the Premier League's top six, that a team will be built around you and a host of players you're excited to play alongside, let alone who could be signed in the future with the funds available. What's the negative? It seems like a no-brainer to me. It's enticing to be part of a project that intends to achieve so much.

It certainly appealed to Carlos Tevez, although he might have had even further motivation to join City. He'd won five major trophies in two years at Manchester United, where he'd been on a complicated loan deal involving a third-party company. Despite his success, towards the end of the previous season he'd become frustrated with what he saw as United stalling on signing him permanently. In swept City, who made him the first player since 1999 to move across from the red to the blue side of Manchester. Seizing on the opportunity to make a point, City's chief executive Garry Cook came up with something spicy: a massive poster of Tevez with the words 'Welcome to Manchester' was erected on Deansgate where the city of Manchester officially ends. Old Trafford is, strictly speaking, in the Metropolitan Borough of Trafford, not Manchester, and City fans enjoy that fact greatly. Cook's plan was to challenge United's dominance aggressively, and if he could do that by undermining them, so be it. The poster made a huge splash and did exactly what he wanted; he annoyed United fans and delighted City fans in equal measure.

As a supporter I kind of liked it. As a player, though, I wasn't so sure it was the right thing to do. I like to go about my business subtly, and this brought a lot more heat on us. We weren't ready to go about saying we're great at this or we're going to do that, and I would have rather just done it and then bragged about it afterwards. Manchester City were a team that wanted to win something; United had been winning and had to carry on doing it too. The next season United finished second in the league to Chelsea: for them, a failure. If City had done exactly the same, it would have been our biggest success in Premier League history. There was still a separation between the two clubs, and the poster put more pressure on us to immediately bridge the gap. That's not to say bringing Carlos Tevez across wasn't a coup. But if we thought eyes were on us before, they really were now. It was another thing that was changing about City. That was the first year it felt like there had to be success, because the players being brought in was one thing, but now one of them had come from Manchester United and he was in his prime. The chant at Old Trafford had been 'Fergie, Fergie, sign him up!' He didn't; we did, knowing (and I imagine in Garry Cook's office revelling in) how much it would have annoyed the United manager. It might have cost £47 million, but we'd stolen an asset, and that was significant.

Just under a year after City's first statement signing in the hours after the Abu Dhabi takeover, it had another. Both Tevez and Robinho were forwards from South America, but they were very different players. Carlos just felt tougher. He was obsessed with winning and worked really hard in games. We could rely on him to set the tone and energise the rest of the team as much as the crowd, and he provided a lot more than just scoring goals. Robinho liked winning too, but to him it seemed more about enjoying the game. He loved having the ball at his feet, moving it around (usually between him and Elano) and delivering the odd nutmeg. Carlos was about the end result. If that required sticking his head or his boot in, he was happy if that helped the team be successful. He also had the technique to add to his incredibly driven, passionate character, all of which made it easy to buy into him as the person who defined the City project at that time. He was the cherry on top of everything, and the way he played and behaved suggested he took that mantle very well.

Sir Alex Ferguson took the bait provided by the poster. Having ignored City for most of his time as United manager, he now said we'd become their 'noisy neighbours'. He chose his moment to use the phrase well, waiting until United had a chance to prove their dominance on the field. The September 2009 Manchester derby at Old Trafford was one of the most dramatic in history. Whoever won had the chance of going top of the table, and we went into the game in third with a 100 per cent record, just behind United on goal difference. It felt like the first derby

I'd seen that was genuinely competitive, which was why it was so crushing when Michael Owen scored an injury time goal for a 4–3 United win. I was devastated. Craig Bellamy, who was the first player in my experience to really expose Rio Ferdinand, had got his second of the game in the ninetieth minute to make it 3–3. But then the familiar feeling. We had taken our first few steps on a different path, but Manchester United were still winning against us. We'd taken one of their players, but until we achieved more than the odd derby win we were still the little brother. United fans had the recent success, and with it came leverage. That win allowed them to carry on treating us as they had done for years, and even though it was close, to them the result proved we were the same old City, nothing more than the neighbours who'd turned up the volume a bit.

Carlos Tevez played that day but didn't score in his first game against his old club. He did in his second. Twice. Then in his third he got another, and it nearly helped us reach the League Cup final. The disappointment of the September derby had been so great because it reminded me, in this new era, of how the relationship between City and United had always been; the outcome of the semi-final the following January hurt just as much but left me encouraged about the future. We won the first leg 2–1 at home, with Carlos celebrating his first goal by running to the United bench and provocatively cupping his ears.

'Fergie, Fergie, sign him up! Fergie, Fergie, sign him up!' City fans co-opted the chant and made sure the Manchester United manager was left in no doubt as to how noisily they could sing it. You could tell their confidence in City to compete on an equal footing was growing with every encounter, and it was being channelled through Carlos Tevez. The away leg was just eight days later, and this was when I got a real sense of how United fans were reacting to the status quo being challenged. We were travelling to Old Trafford from the hotel, fittingly on Deansgate, and at almost every turn on the journey there were United supporters raging at us. Some threw things at the bus. That type of behaviour hadn't existed in my experience before; it had been limited to the odd fan like the one who'd been furious enough to run alongside us shouting after we'd won at Old Trafford in 2008. It was happening now because suddenly we were relevant. A threat. In the past the United fans hadn't cared enough about us to get that angry, as to them we'd been insignificant. But now, things had changed. They were so mad it was like they wanted to burn the bus and throw it off a cliff. I looked at them, thinking, 'They're rattled. This is brilliant.' The League Cup semi-final second leg was to them, as much as to us, a meaningful game. It was big because they were playing against a team they could no longer afford to lose to, and they were worried they might not win.

The game finished 4–3 to United again, this time on aggregate. Another late winner, this time from Wayne Rooney. As jaded as I was from losing, particularly with a final at Wembley on the line, there was something else that happened in that semi-final that hurt me more personally. While the tie had given a glimpse of the future for Manchester City, it had also made me think, for the first time, that that future might not include me. The two legs against United came just a few weeks after Mark Hughes had been sacked. I'd only just got back into the team for the trip to Spurs in December, a match we lost 3–0 and after which the club decided they wanted a change of manager. It was just our second league defeat of the season, but too many draws had left us in eighth place. Not good enough for the new City.

Plans were made to recruit a replacement for Mark before he was told of his fate, which led to a really weird situation in the next game. We arrived at the City of Manchester Stadium to play Sunderland with the press reporting Mark would be sacked that day. But until he had been, he was still the manager. He knew of the rumours, and despite his attempts to get the team ready to win a game in the normal way, it felt different. Mark didn't directly address his situation, but his team talk didn't really reference the game we were about to play either, as if he wanted to say good-bye without using the word itself. We went out the same way we always did, trying to win a match, but it felt like it didn't matter because the consequences had already happened. In an eerie atmosphere, the result was 4–3 again, this time in our favour. Mark waved to the crowd as he left the pitch and was officially gone ninety minutes later, with the delay apparently because the chairman Khaldoon Al Mubarak wanted to deliver the news in person. I was disappointed for him but also preoccupied with my own problems. I'd played the last few minutes with a calf injury, which hadn't prevented me from running (albeit in a slightly weird way) but had affected my ability to walk properly. I knew I was in trouble because I limped my way off the field as soon as the adrenaline of the game had worn off and all I could feel was a sharp pain. I wouldn't be fit when the new manager arrived.

• • •

Roberto Mancini was introduced to the Manchester City squad upstairs at the Carrington training ground. You still attend meetings like that when you're injured, so I was in the room. My first interaction with him just afterwards set the tone for what was to come and took place while I was outside doing some rehab.

'How long until you are back?' Mancini asked me.

I wanted to be personable, as first impressions matter.

'Dunno,' I said with a smile and pointed at the physio who'd been working with me that day. 'You'll have to ask this guy.'

Mancini's face didn't move. I thought he'd match my smile, understanding that I'd made a joke. But he was dead serious. Then he started shaking his head. This was not a man with a sense of humour. Even if I hadn't taken the chance of trying to engage with him on a personal level, I still hadn't been lying. The recovery schedule of a calf injury is dictated to you, you can't change it through working harder. I genuinely didn't know how long I would be out for, and the physio would have been able to give a much more informed answer. I'd tried to show that I had a personality, and it had been a disaster. Mancini took against me immediately, and the situation was made worse by the fact I wasn't training, which was how I'd won over any managers who had doubted me previously. In those first few sessions the new coaching staff invested a lot of time into working on tactics and team shape, bringing in floodlights to allow the team to train in the late afternoon. There was a complete culture change going on, and I wasn't involved.

It was in this context that I fell down the pecking order. I was out of Roberto Mancini's sight and mind, and soon enough I wasn't the young defender who was trusted to be the next in, as I had been for more than five years. I was replaced by Dedryck Boyata. Dedryck is a Belgian centre back who joined the academy in 2006. He'd been brought in from the reserves that season, had just turned nineteen when Mancini arrived and hadn't yet made his first-team debut. I liked Dedryck, and I'm still friends with him now. At that time he was on a path with which I was very familiar, and one I greatly valued. But I was ahead of him by any measure: status, experience and recent form – I'd started in the two games before Mancini arrived. After missing the new manager's first four matches due to my calf injury, I was back in the squad and on the bench, alongside Dedryck, for a trip to Everton. Dedryck had made his debut by then, and two appearances in total in the preceding two games. Pablo Zabaleta was playing right back and went down injured. I was the only substitute who could play in the position, so I looked over to the coaching staff expectantly. They sent Dedryck to go and get warm. Even though he was a centre back and Pablo didn't need to come off in the end, Mancini had made it clear: Dedryck was next in. I was rocked. I understood the significance of what appeared to be a minor decision. If I wasn't starting, I'd always had the insurance of being the one called on to step up. Now I wasn't. Three days later was the first leg of the League Cup semi-final against Manchester United. Both Joleon Lescott and Kolo Touré were unavailable, and Dedryck started. The second leg was the same story, and I only got some game time coming on for him in the second half. I should say he played well in both, and I remember Carlos Tevez praising his performance after the game at Old Trafford, but it probably sticks in my mind because while I didn't resent Dedryck, I resented the manager's decision to play him. For the first time I was adrift and nowhere near the team.

I might have felt like an outcast, but others were simply cast out. After the semi-final I made two rare starts for Mancini. The first was in an FA Cup tie with Scunthorpe, a game which allowed the manager to make several changes. I played right back and scored, although the other full back Sylvinho also got one, and it was much, much better. Robinho scored the final goal in a 4–2 win, and it was to be his last match for City. It had just about worked for him under Mark Hughes but was never going to under Mancini. He'd missed part of the season through injury and wasn't nearly the influence he had been in the first half of the previous campaign. His significance to the club had also waned because of how the talent pool had grown around him, and he was exactly the opposite of the kind of player Mancini wanted in his team. It was clear Mancini was going to be the death of a lot of people, and Robinho was the first – he left for Santos on loan for the rest of the season.

Another player marginalised by the new manager was Stevie Ireland. He had prospered under Sven-Göran Eriksson, and even amongst all the new signings after the takeover he had been City's player of the year in 2008/09. He was the perfect example of how someone can improve just by having better talent around them, and winning the award was a huge statement of his own ability. He was also a very dedicated player in training, as his performance in Sven's league table consistently proved; his body of work showed how capable he was, but for Stevie it was a higher point from which to fall. I didn't take Mancini's attitude towards me particularly well, mostly because it was only six months removed from the end of my best season, but Stevie had had an even better campaign, and being overlooked was definitely more detrimental to his mental health. Mark Hughes had trusted and understood us, but now it felt like we were on the scrap heap, victims of the next step the club had made and the manager it had appointed. We couldn't have been further away from where we had been, and it was a shock how quickly everything had changed. All of a sudden, being a youngster from the academy became a weakness, and at a time when we were playing as well as we ever had. If we had been afforded the opportunity to take that next step, we could have become even better players.

After beating Scunthorpe, the next round of the FA Cup was against Stoke. That fifth-round replay in February was the last time Stevie Ireland and I started a match together. It had been close to ten years of shared football experience. Two players from the same academy year who had made more than 100 appearances for the first team. We spent the majority of the rest of the season together but in what was essentially the training 'B' team, working hard but finding only frustration and disappointment. None of it was directed at those playing ahead of us, and we certainly didn't want them to pity us, but it was getting to a point where training well was making no difference. If Mancini liked you, you were fine; if he didn't, there was nothing you could do about it. My value was being dictated not by anything I could do, but by one person who said, 'yes' or 'no'.

After the Stoke replay, Mancini only said 'yes' to me starting three more times that season. It was on consecutive weekends in March, and the first was a match at Burnley. We were coasting by half-time, 4–0 up. Just before the break Burnley had been awarded a free kick, which they crossed into our penalty area. A half-chance arrived, but it went harmlessly wide. As we came back into the dressing room, a very angry Mancini came straight up to me.

'What were you doing?' he asked.

He was referring to my position at the free kick. Mancini was very particular about defending set-pieces and how everybody had to be in their exact spots. I had been in mine.

'The chance at the end. You were supposed to be *there*.'

I wasn't, and I told him so. It was Craig Bellamy who hadn't been in his spot, not me.

'Craig wasn't there. I was in the right place.'

It was another occasion when the manager's face didn't change and no words came from his mouth. He fell silent for a bit, and just as I started to walk out for the second half he pulled me to the side.

'Don't ever speak back to me again.' He hissed.

I had defended myself against a false accusation. I had been in the exact position his coaching staff had told me to be. We were 4–0 up. And yet he was furious with me because of a half-chance from a set-piece when I'd done nothing wrong, and from which they didn't score. I thought, something's off here. What's going on?

It wasn't the first time Mancini had singled me out and blamed me for something I hadn't done, and on those previous occasions I took it without speaking up. He would get angry if things didn't go perfectly in training or if he could detect any semblance of fun during a session. He had a vision for how he wanted the team to play and was married to it, so if it didn't happen completely as planned every time, he would get very frustrated.

'You stand here, you do this. The ball goes here, you all go here. If the ball goes there, you all go there. If it's gone over the top, you run there and do this. Then when you get the ball, you play it here, or here, or here.' That was how we had to play on every single day, and it was always uncontested. Even on Sundays after a Saturday game, when he'd conduct a replica session for those who hadn't played and a few call-ups from the academy and the reserves. On one occasion I was playing right back and the centre back alongside me was actually a reserve-team striker, and he was determined for it to be no fun whatsoever. One passing drill had me at right back again with Shaun Wright-Phillips ahead of me. All of us were under strict instructions not to play a diagonal ball to the other side of the field, so we'd pass it short inside to a midfielder. After I passed it to Nigel de Jong, he proceeded to switch play with a long diagonal. That was against the rules. Mancini immediately stopped the session.

'What were you doing?'

It would become a familiar question. Although he wasn't asking Nigel: he had directed it to Shaun and me. He then delivered a line that will follow me to the grave.

'It's like you've never played football before.'

I had, like my entire career, done what I was told. Shaun had too. And yet we were the ones being accused of having never played the game. Was I going to give him the benefit of the doubt and say that perhaps it was lost in translation? Or was I going to get angry about it? It occurred to me that either way I still had no real say. There was no comeback. Nothing I could do. Despite us doing the right thing, he said it was like we hadn't played football before. Imagine hearing that as a professional. I had no idea why he'd even blamed us for Nigel's pass, and the way he reacted later in the season when I pointed out Craig Bellamy's mistake at Burnley suggested I was right not to ask him to direct his irritation elsewhere.

Mancini compounded a humourless attitude to training with an inability to accept his players speaking up in their own defence.

Some of his criticisms appeared completely random: he once told a physio I was too slow. Me? My pace was so obvious to everyone it was often what descriptions of my game boiled down to. He said Joleon Lescott's calves and Roque Santa Cruz's quads were too small. He said Stevie Ireland needed to 'change his head' to have a chance of getting back into the team. The reason Stevie was in that frame of mind was because of his treatment by Roberto Mancini. The manager would get things into his head that were impossible to counter, as set in stone as his team-shape training sessions. Whether it was to justify his decisions to himself I'm not sure, but he was acting on them in one way or another because none of me, Joleon, Roque or Stevie were playing.

By the time I had the chance to come back into the team for the Burnley game, I was struggling badly with my mental health. Talking back to Mancini at half-time at Turf Moor was partly a consequence of that, as was the way I celebrated scoring a goal in the following game. Well, a goal I thought I'd scored. We were playing Birmingham at Eastlands and were 1–0 up through a Carlos Tevez penalty. Two minutes later, I connected with a corner with an impressive diving header. I saw it bounce up into the top corner, without realising that Carlos had got a slight touch. Nobody else had either, because they followed me as I got up off the floor and wheeled away in celebration. This time my destination was not the box where my family were but the City dugout. All my frustration was being let out, and instead of blowing kisses at my mum, I gave Roberto Mancini some different hand gestures. I doubt he saw it, and I know he wouldn't have cared. But there was a whole load of spice to it.

Then in the second half I got another one, which was just as well as Carlos was eventually awarded the first. With the frustration already released, this time the emotion was much more like ecstasy – although that may have been an attempt to cover more than a little embarrassment at how the goal had come about. I received the ball in a more attacking, more central position than I would have expected. There was space for me to run into, but I saw Emmanuel Adebayor in a good position ahead and slightly to the left of me, so I decided on this occasion it would be the right thing to give the ball to him. I proceeded to play one of the worst passes of my whole career. It went nowhere near Manu. Having learned from all those times I'd completely messed up a touch, pass or shot when in a position of potential excitement, this time I reacted. I immediately realised it was a terrible pass and just carried on running. As I went past Manu, his head turned slowly, tracking my movement with total disbelief. He had just been preparing to take the ball from me, and now he's just watching as the ball and then I go past. I eventually caught up with my own pass on the edge of the penalty area and in an instant slammed it into the bottom corner with my left foot. Not a lot of defenders score with their wrong foot from 18 yards out. Even fewer after a one-two with themselves.

The final game of the three in a row ended up being my last Manchester derby. City lost, again. To a late winner, again. This time it was Paul Scholes who got it. It was also my final Premier League start for City, and perhaps fitting that it was in the latest episode of my city's great rivalry. If there was any suggestion that my performance against Birmingham was the reason I kept my place for this match, even when Pablo Zabaleta had returned to the squad, the rest of the season would put that out of my mind. I didn't play another minute of City's attempts to qualify for the Champions League for the first time. They all boiled down to the penultimate match of the season, a winner-takes-all game against Spurs. Whoever got the three points would get the Champions League place too. A Peter Crouch goal was enough for them to win 1–0: a reminder that Spurs were another club just a little further ahead of us, one of the big four or five teams in the Premier League we wanted to be part of. I wasn't anywhere near being a part of it, but I still felt the disappointment of losing a huge game.

Even at that point, with my chances of playing dwindling by the match, I couldn't think too far ahead. Certainly not to the next season. Four days later, that changed. In each campaign I'd faced adversity, I'd ended it in the team. So, what happened on the final day of the season at West Ham really brought home how different things were this time. I'd started to lose faith in my ability to change Mancini's mind about me very early on, but things deteriorated to such an extent that if he named a squad of twenty players to stay at the hotel the night before a game, I'd pack a hat, coat and gloves. I had a feeling I'd be one of the two left out, sitting in the stands. The first time it had happened to me, back at Newcastle with Jonathan D'Laryea, was a surprise to an enthusiastic teenager. Now I was struggling so much for confidence that I'd become convinced I would be 'that' guy. One who fell outside of the eleven in the team and the seven on the bench. The way I found out at Upton Park was horrid. Each game, the starters would be told just before leaving the hotel, and then there'd be a ban on all players using their phones. I wouldn't know if I was a substitute until we got to the stadium, and I wanted to text my mum to tell her if I was involved. Just one message. But that was the rule, and Mancini would get very annoyed if he saw anyone breaking it. He tried to fine me once for being on my phone in the dressing room, even though I was just listening to music. He hated that too, but I wasn't breaking any rules.

The West Ham game wouldn't decide anything for City; we'd definitely be in the Europa League even if we lost. So, Mancini made a few changes which increased my chances of being part of the match-day squad. Once we'd made our way into the dressing room, the coaching staff started pinning sheets of paper on the wall. I knew the bench would be the last thing, even after all the set-piece instructions. I really didn't like that, as it showed how little the substitutes mattered to them. Sometimes the coaches would be all blasé about it and deliberately extend the process, moping around and keeping those players outside of the first eleven waiting. Up went all the free kicks, all the throw-ins, and then the final piece of paper was attached to the wall. It was blank. There were no names on it. We had to remind Mancini to fill in the names, and moments later they put the new sheet up on the wall. I went to check it, and my name wasn't there.

'What am I doing?' I thought to myself, completely exasperated. 'What is this? I've gone from playing to being the next in, to being the first out.' It was truly horrendous, because it had been pretty much the same squad throughout the season. Not that much had changed, except my place within it. And worse still, this was how Mancini told me I was out, in a way that showed he didn't care about me as a human being at all. It was toxic, and symptomatic of how the lines of communication between the players and Mancini had been severed. I knew I didn't have control over my own career, as I couldn't pick myself, but at no point did this manager give me the closure I needed. There would be a whole host of reasons for not playing under previous coaches, but at least there was trust in those relationships. If the players ahead of me were injured or suspended and I had been training well, I would get my chance. Now, without any explanation, that wasn't true any more. Why did he call on Dedryck Boyata for the League Cup derby? He wouldn't tell me. Why did he suddenly order me to play for the reserves? He wouldn't tell me. Why was I not getting an opportunity after training well with the first team? He wouldn't tell me. My whole set of circumstances had changed, but the group of players around me hadn't. It seemed personal, but I still would have accepted it if he had told me why. Say you don't like me as a player, that's closure. Tell me I need to work on something. Closure. Cast me out and promise I'm never going to play for him again. Even that's closure. The only certainty I had was that my status in the team was dropping lower and lower and lower. It took me back to my days being obsessed with the ratings in the *Manchester Evening News*.

For six months I just existed, with little purpose. I wasn't a starter, I wasn't there to fill in. I wasn't injured or in rehab. I wasn't there just because I was a good guy. Mancini didn't even tell me to leave, so I wasn't contributing and I wasn't getting ready to move either. I was stuck, asking, 'Why am I here?'

I wasn't the only one who felt this way about Roberto Mancini. I didn't like him at all, and I don't remember anyone in the dressing room enjoying how hostile he was, particularly at the beginning. He lacked personality, and if you didn't do things his way you were deemed not good enough. What infuriated me further was that in front of the media he was so different. In that environment he was happy to laugh and joke, and yet we had the opposite, every single day. He's been able to successfully maintain a good reputation because of how he presents himself in public. To this day I'd say he's well thought of in the media, and particularly recently because of Italy's success at Euro 2020. International football is perfect for him because he can have total control. He can work in a culture he's familiar with, and part of the Euro 2020 narrative was about how he'd restored the country's connection with its football team. As an international manager he gets to hand-pick each and every one of the people he wants to work with. And if someone plays the wrong pass, uses their phone in the dressing room or talks back to him, he can drop them and never see them again. If he could have done that at Manchester City, I'm convinced he would have: a squad of around twenty-five players, all of whom he'd signed. But instead, the playing staff were already there, and he was hired to work with them. In that environment he couldn't place his trust in the whole squad, because he wasn't responsible for them all being there. At various times he would fall out with City's head physio, the therapists, the fitness coaches and other members of staff, let alone the players he didn't like.

Those people were associated with Manchester City, whereas he wanted people associated with *him*. If they shared his culture and his coaching methods were familiar, it would be much easier for Mancini to build a sense of pride in what they're doing. It would also lead to an environment he would find it much easier to control. Therefore, seeing him be successful with Italy was no surprise at all, although to watch him do it against England at Wembley and all the love he subsequently received, that was the stars aligning to create my worst nightmare.

Some might feel differently to me, that there's a trade-off to be made if you want to win. Maybe it's a privilege to enjoy playing for a manager and it's a rarity to find an instant respect that

At 391 Bradford Road, Miles Platting. Our first house after moving to Manchester from Nigeria was small and had a lot of mould and very little security.
Author's collection

Alongside my three sisters while on holiday. Diuto's the eldest, and she's at the back holding Lynda, the youngest of the four. I'm standing next to Chidi, who is three years younger than me. Author's collection

Lynda with the person she was named after, Linda Wyon, who's sat with her husband Andrew. Spending time with the Wyons in Bath gave us our first experiences of traditional English culture, a garden to play in and rhubarb.
Author's collection

LEFT My first year at Hulme Grammar in Oldham. I was ten, because I passed the entrance exam a year early. It was the beginning of the education my parents had hoped to provide me with when we moved to England. Author's collection

BELOW LEFT Before football took over, it had to share my affections with track and field. I loved sprinting and only stopped when I couldn't afford the time for both sports. It also played a small part in introducing me to my future wife! Author's collection

BELOW RIGHT At home on Rochdale Road, Harpurhey. A slightly bigger house for a slightly bigger family, and on a main road close to the bus stop, which meant I could get to school, friends and football a little easier. Author's collection

BOTTOM My class at Hulme, with me third from the left in the back row. In the front row, also third from the left, is Okey, the only other black boy in my year. Author's collection

At Platt Lane with my other classmates, from the Manchester City Academy. I'm on the back row of this one too! Next to me is the coach, John Ferguson. To my left are Ian Bennett, Jonathan D'Laryea, Paul Collins and Nathan D'Laryea. Carlos Logan is below me, and Danny Warrender is two to his left. These were the kids I'd played Sunday League against, and now I was alongside them for City. Author's collection

FAR LEFT I'm pretty sure not all those medals are mine... Author's collection

LEFT ...but these are. I was invited onto the Maine Road pitch during the 2000/01 season to show the athletics medals I'd won while representing Manchester. I'm standing alongside the legendary City academy scout Barry Poynton, and I was chuffed to be there. Author's collection

Signing my first professional contract on my eighteenth birthday with Mum alongside me, as she had been, and would be, until she passed away. Author's collection

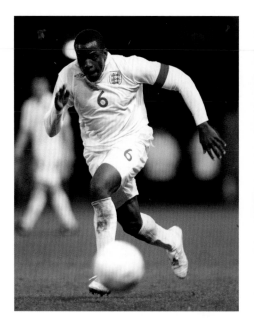

Captaining England Under-21s.
© Laurence Griffiths/Getty Images

With Richard Dunne and Sun Jihai after City had done the double over Manchester United, winning at Old Trafford for the first time in thirty-five years in February 2008. © PA Images/Alamy Stock Photo

My first senior Manchester City goal, against Spurs in March 2008.
© AMA/Corbis via Getty Images

After blowing kisses to my mum in the stands, I was joined in my celebrations by Benjani, who had what looks like an expression of some surprise on his face!
© Ed Garvey/Manchester City FC via Getty Images

Celebrating scoring in the Euro 2009 semi-final win over hosts Sweden, with Micah Richards the first to catch up with me this time. © Phil Cole/Getty Images

Martin Onuoha and
Dr Anthonia Onuoha.
Author's collection

The beginning of a long
sprint after scoring against
Birmingham. The City
dugout was the destination
for a celebration that released
a lot of pent-up emotion.
© Alex Livesey/Getty Images

A bear hug from Joe Hart.
© Andrew Yates/AFP via Getty Images

Perhaps this time it's me who's surprised, after a mazy dribble that brought Sunderland's goal of the season at Stamford Bridge in November 2010.
© AMA/Corbis via Getty Images

RIGHT Loftus Road can be an intimidating place, but when it's behind you there's very little like it. © Nathan Stirk/Getty Images

BELOW My celebration after scoring in my first game following Amaia's birth. © Ben Queenborough/BPI/Shutterstock

Ruben, Lucy, Teia and Amaia. Author's collection

Being able to share my experience at Real Salt Lake with my family is something I'm incredibly proud of. Author's collection

With Lucy at a University of Utah football game.
Author's collection

My final game as a professional in November 2020, with accompanying blizzard.

ABOVE A tribute from the RSL ground staff before my last match.

LEFT Once a Blue, always a Blue.

© Laurence Griffiths/Getty Images

means you look forward to going into work. Playing football is a job, but we're so lucky to do it that it shouldn't feel like work. Roberto Mancini made it feel like work, and work that was very, very tough. He hated giving players time off, so we would see him every day. I'd walk by him and wish I didn't completely dislike him, but his disregard for those he'd decided weren't for him made it unavoidable. He will ride or die with his rules, his mentality, his ideas, until the bitter end. You were either with him or against him.

The results eventually came for Manchester City, but after winning the FA Cup in 2011 and the Premier League title in 2012 – the club's first trophies in more than three decades – it was only a year later he was sacked. I certainly got the impression there wasn't much sadness at the decision, either amongst the players or the staff, and I'm convinced his inability to develop personal relationships with all those around him was eventually why it was a relatively easy choice for the club to let him go. It takes a lot for a group of players to turn against a manager who's brought that kind of success. Losing a dressing room because of results is easy enough, but at City that wasn't the reason. It was the other stuff. The team was still winning, but they'd got to the point with Mancini when winning wasn't enough. What does that say about the person in charge?

Chapter 11

I had no desire to leave Manchester City. It's my club. But with three strikes it was clear I was out. The first had come when Dedryck Boyata was picked ahead of me for the League Cup semi-final. The second was on the final day of the 2009/10 season, when I wasn't included against West Ham. The third was a very specific moment in the following pre-season.

The club was on a tour of the USA, and the opening match was in Oregon against the Portland Timbers, a team with whom I'd end up having a few significant meetings. It is a pre-season standard that to set players on the right path to fitness, each gets forty-five minutes in the opening game. I was at a low ebb, having suffered more mentally over the previous six months than at any time in my career, but I understood why I wasn't in the first-half team. Cool, I thought. No stress. Everybody's going to play forty-five minutes. But the second-half team went out and I was still sitting on the bench. Goodness gracious me. Why is this happening?

It was a new season, but nothing had changed. I came on for the last ten minutes. That's what you do if you're a sixteen-year-old who's part of pre-season to make up the numbers. I should know, I've been that player. Next there were two games on consecutive days, and because there were eleven changes for the second one, I played the full ninety minutes against the New York Red Bulls – and then that was it. That was my whole pre-season. There were two more matches in the US, followed by a trip to Germany to play Borussia Dortmund and a home friendly against Valencia. I didn't get one minute. It was completely pointless. If Roberto Mancini had had any intention of having me as a member of the squad, he would have given me time on the pitch just to improve my fitness. But he wasn't interested. He gave me nothing apart from a strong feeling that I was no longer a part of the club. He could have told me in the first week of pre-season that my future was elsewhere, but he wasn't for giving closure. He made me travel around the USA, to Germany and back, forcing me into making the decision I'd never wanted to. Mancini had diluted then broken the emotional relationship I had with my club. The people who'd been at Manchester City the longest were no longer forming the culture there; we'd become peripheral at best, to the extent that new players wouldn't even think we mattered. I don't believe the club had forgotten or didn't care about its history in this new era of wealth and winning, because what happened to me and others – Stevie Ireland also left that summer as part of a deal that brought James Milner from Aston Villa – was very specific to the manager. The players who had arrived in recent years, either pre-takeover like Vincent Kompany or like David Silva that very summer, bought into where Manchester City had come from and where it was trying to go. Roberto Mancini appeared to strongly dislike some players: me,

Stevie, Wayne Bridge are three who particularly come to mind. (I'm also convinced he hated Carlos Tevez, but if he did he realised he couldn't do without him.) We weren't cast aside because of the club's ambition but on Mancini's whim.

Being ignored that pre-season meant I had no option but to look elsewhere. After the Under-21s European Championship in 2009 I'd gone on holiday to Barbados, and while Lucy and I were waiting for our flight at the airport one of my England teammates arrived in the departure lounge. Fraizer Campbell had just agreed to leave Manchester United and join Sunderland, and he and his then girlfriend were on the same flight. We ended up spending the whole week together, with Fraizer insistent that Sunderland manager Steve Bruce wanted to sign me. I politely told him it wasn't going to happen. A year later, a loan offer arrived. By that time it was clear there was no future for me at City, so for the first time I had to get my head around playing for someone else. The day the move was confirmed, I went to my parents' house next door and cried my eyes out. I didn't want to leave City. I'd never wanted to leave anywhere, and since the age of five in Nigeria I'd not had to. The tears weren't just about football; I had just agreed to move away from my family, my friends, my city, and to enter the unknown. It wasn't anything to do with where I was going but the fact I had to put distance between myself and all I'd ever known and wanted. I was bawling in my sister Chidi's arms. I wasn't excited; I was devastated. And frustrated too. Some of those tears were about not being able to break back into a team that was once my own. Frustration more than failure: I still didn't understand how I'd got to this point. The way I perceived football was that people would leave because they weren't playing well enough. That wasn't my problem. I just wasn't playing. I wasn't falling down the pecking order because of my performances, because there weren't any I could be judged on.

It was only to be for a year, so I had in the back of my mind that it might not be the end for me and Manchester City. But still, everything changed. I was going somewhere else, and no longer would I have the routine of finishing training at Carrington and then going to Didsbury or Stretford to see friends. They were always within half an hour, but now they'd be more than five times that. Lucy and I had got engaged in the spring of 2010, so she decided to quit her job working for Bury Council and follow me to the north-east. Sunderland paid for us to live at the Malmaison in Newcastle for the first month, and then we found a house in a place called Seaham. It was right on the beach and used to be owned by Paul Gascoigne. It was also just five minutes from where Fraizer Campbell lived. Some of my worries were being alleviated.

I was also encouraged by the football situation. Steve Bruce was the first manager in my career who'd actually chosen me to be at their club. The others had inherited me. Now I had a boss who wanted me, and considering the situation I'd come from I really appreciated being welcomed with open arms. Steve was a man-manager, which, ironically, means someone who doesn't spend every moment managing his men. He wasn't the main point of contact for the players, but what he wanted was clear: work hard and do your best. It was tough; I was the lightest I'd ever been while playing for Sunderland, and both training and gym sessions were hard. But I enjoyed it, as everyone bought into the standards that were being set, and we were pushed and pushed to make sure we met them.

Sunderland is a one-club city, which was another thing that was alien to me. You can feel it around the place: football sets the mood of the whole city, not just the more than 45,000 who would fill the Stadium of Light. If you're doing well, you're royalty, but in return for their passion the fans demand commitment. I was happy to provide mine – although this wavered as early as the second Premier League home game of the season, because it was against Manchester City. The league's rules state that a player on loan cannot appear against his parent club, so I watched from Fraizer Campbell's box as Sunderland beat City 1–0. Darren Bent was fouled by Micah Richards in injury time and scored the penalty himself. It was a really weird feeling. I was split, to say the very least. I was surrounded by people cheering against the team I'd supported and played for, and it's hard not to be swept along by that. I found the failure of my old peers a tough thing to truly celebrate (although I did allow myself to think, 'This is interesting, isn't it, Roberto?') It was also a shame to miss out on a big win for my new team. The mixed emotions of the day were intensified by Fraizer suffering a serious knee injury, which meant I wouldn't be able to play alongside him for the whole season.

Fraizer wasn't the only player I already knew at Sunderland. I'd played with Darren Bent and Lee Cattermole before, as well as Anton Ferdinand, all for the England Under-21s. It was a high-quality squad with the likes of Asamoah Gyan, Steed Malbranque, Bolo Zenden and a young Jordan Henderson. Kieran Richardson was there too: my Manchester United nemesis during the academy days, who I had enough genuine distaste for to almost fight with him on more than one occasion. But now I realised he'd become a completely different person, far more humble, subtle, calm and driven by success. I came into the club worried that our previous relationship might lead to some hostility and ended up thinking he's one of the nicest guys I've ever met. Bizarre.

All those in the squad who provided a connection to my career to that point helped me overcome another part of the move I'd been concerned about. My plan had always been to make it through the Manchester City Academy, play for the first team and stay there for the duration of my career. That simply doesn't happen any more. Playing for the same club for more than five years is something only around 5 per cent of professionals can claim. I had entered into a more realistic world and was now like almost everyone else on this journey. The ideal scenario might be an ambition, but the more realistic one is to have a successful career, and that doesn't have to be at the club where you first started.

· · ·

Steve Bruce had a lot of options in central defence, so he'd brought me in to play right back. Neither he nor I thought I'd score Sunderland's goal of the season. I still have the award displayed in my house.

On the way down to London to play Chelsea, who had won the Premier League and FA Cup double the previous season, Steve had made an unprompted speech to the whole team.

'This is a big game, and I wanted to remind you all that if you ever want to get noticed for doing something, then do it in London. This is where all the eyes are.'

'What are you talking about?' I thought. 'How is geography

relevant?' I didn't give it any further thought. I was more concerned about keeping Chelsea out; they were top of the league and had Didier Drogba and my old teammate Nicolas Anelka up front. Along with the other Sunderland defenders, I managed to do that until just before half-time, when a Branislav Ivanović clearing header fell to me, dead centre, about 35 yards from the Chelsea goal. Now, throughout my career I scored plenty of goals. In training. Every kind of goal: overhead kicks, volleys, tap-ins. In games, it's obviously different. You're focused on your role, and very rarely do defenders get in scoring positions.

When I controlled the ball, the Chelsea players clearly only considered the body of evidence provided by my games, because nobody came towards me. If I've got the ball at my feet and no player comes to engage me, I'll keep going forward. Enough people had looked at me and seen only pace and strength over the years, so the Chelsea defenders should have known better. I continued running towards goal, and still no respect was being given. The principle was initially to hold on to it until I could find the right pass. But then I saw a gap. It sounds nonchalant, but with a bit of movement I just went through it between John Mikel Obi and José Bosingwa, and now I was clean through on goal. Ivanović realised too late and didn't reach me until I'd hit a shot with my left foot. Well, slightly scuffed a shot with my left foot. But once again the imperfection of the strike helped me, as it went between Ivanović and Petr Čech's dive. Another Premier League goal after a mazy dribble (though this one was intentional) with my left foot into the same corner. I admit not quite the same as either George Weah or Thierry Henry, but clearly I'm clinical from that sort of range.

It was also obvious that I was knackered. Again. I didn't have enough energy for a full celebration. If your whole game is about dribbling, you can do it all day long. I'd never get tired from wrestling with a striker, for example, but ask me to run at high speed while controlling a ball and it's clear my game isn't built for it. Thankfully, I had half-time to catch my breath and receive my teammates' congratulations. It's true what they say about the importance of a goal just before the break, and as we were coming into the dressing room 1–0 up on the champions, everyone was tapping me on the head to say well done. If players do that away from the cameras, it shows they genuinely like you. It was just under a year since my whole footballing world had changed, and it felt so good to be celebrated and appreciated in that moment.

That goal is the only one from my whole career that I've consistently looked back at, not because of where it took place but because of what it meant. It wasn't just about the victory at Stamford Bridge. It was the other stuff. After the game, which finished 3–0 to Sunderland, I looked at my phone to find more messages than I'd ever received before. Steve Bruce had been right about people noticing things that happen in London.

The win at Chelsea took Sunderland to sixth in the Premier League, which is where we'd stay until the following February and the reverse fixture. This time Chelsea won, and it started a slide. The momentum of the first half of the season died, and all the focus we had in training made way for a group of players going through the motions. The desire had gone, and there was no drive coming from Steve Bruce. He appeared to have become distracted and looked and felt different to earlier in the campaign. We dropped as low as fifteenth and sat only a place higher than that before the last game of the season, which would determine our final position. The bonus scheme at Sunderland dictated that we'd be rewarded with a lump sum if we finished in the Top 10, so there was a financial incentive heading into the match at West Ham. For the second year in a row, my season would end at Upton Park, but this time I was playing, and we won 3–0. Elsewhere, Bolton and Stoke lost (it wouldn't be the last time those two clubs played a part in my final-day dramas), while Newcastle and West Brom drew. We leapfrogged over all four of them and finished tenth. The bonus was nice, as was ending up higher in the table than Newcastle, which somewhat made up for the fact that earlier in the season they had provided me with one of the lowest points in my career by beating us 5–1 in the Tyne–Wear derby at St James' Park.

It felt like I'd completed my tasks of the season: we finished where we needed to finish, and above Newcastle. I'd played most of the games, making thirty-two appearances in total. Tick, tick, tick. I had restored some confidence, but there wasn't a lot of clarity about what came next. I hadn't had any conversations with Steve Bruce about a permanent deal, and I didn't push for one even though my time with Sunderland had been enjoyable. That was partly because a week before the final Premier League game of the season, I'd watched Manchester City win the FA Cup, their first trophy in thirty-five years, from my house in Seaham. To reach the final, City had beaten Manchester United in the semi-final at Wembley, overcoming the hurdle at which we'd fallen in the other cup competition the previous year. There was euphoria for those in blue; it didn't matter if City beat United at the national stadium, on Mars or at the kitchen table, the joy of a derby victory, and one of such significance, was huge, even for me all those miles away.

The final was different. It was against Stoke, and all I could think about was not being there. I wasn't at Wembley. I wasn't in the squad. I was at another club, watching it all on TV. I was conflicted: on one hand I was happy for City; on the other I was desperate to return. I wanted to be part of a team that could win trophies, rather than just existing at Sunderland. I'd not been sold, and I still belonged to Manchester City, but the FA Cup final was the first time I truly realised that, as things stood, they weren't my team. I was determined to figure out what I needed to do to change that.

• • •

When players are loaned out, it can be for any number of reasons. It might be to give a player on the fringes some game time, or to get them out of the club. I thought the nature of the Manchester City squad dictated that I'd followed the first option. Little did I know, it was the second: they hoped I'd never come back. Perhaps I was naïve in thinking my future was at City, but towards the end of the loan my agent advised me to speak to Roberto Mancini about the following season and what I had to do to become part of his plans. I thought I was good enough to play for his team, and I wanted to stay. Whatever had happened in the past was over, and I wanted to get back and show him that. So, I went to see the manager at the training ground, where I appeared to catch him off-guard, because the conversation, while short, was more cordial than I was used to.

'Roberto. Can I have a word?'

'OK, no problem.'

'I'd like to get back into the City team and really want to know what I have to do to be part of it next season.'

Mancini paused.

'I'll get back to you.'

OK, fine. Cool. He hadn't dismissed me completely, and I was happy with that at least, as I'd become increasingly sure I wanted my future to be at my club. There was no other thought in my mind as I went back to complete the season at Sunderland.

That summer Lucy and I got married, and our honeymoon was to be in the US. On the first day in San Francisco, we booked a helicopter tour ride around the Golden Gate Bridge, and I turned my phone off for the duration of the flight. When we landed, I had a missed call and voicemail from Mike Rigg. Mike had been at City since Mark Hughes's time and had been my point of contact during the Sunderland loan spell. He'd phoned on day one of my honeymoon to tell me I had to find a new club for the next season. Mancini had got Mike to tell me his decision: I had to leave Manchester City.

My first reaction, as was always the case with Mancini, was why? I hadn't demanded that I play fifty games, I'd just said I wanted to be part of the team. Instead, I'd been told I had to leave, even before I'd had any chance to prove my worth in pre-season. I'd decided Sunderland wasn't an option, even if they wanted me, so I had no idea what to do next. Mancini did, though. Having returned from our honeymoon, Lucy and I were spending a weekend with friends at Center Parcs ahead of what was supposed to be the first day of pre-season on Monday. It was Saturday afternoon, and this time it was a text from first-team support manager Clare Marsden.

'Hi Nedum. You don't need to come in on Monday for pre-season. Come in next Saturday instead.'

OK, fine. Cool. They've pushed pre-season back a few days, I thought. Plans change all the time, and Mancini had been fluid with them before. I was happy at the idea of having a few more days' holiday and texted Micah Richards to that effect.

'Are you off as well?' I asked.

'No. We start training on Monday and fly out to America on Friday.'

My heart sank for the second time in just a few weeks. Not only had I been told to get a new team, my current one was going off on their pre-season tour without me. I wouldn't get my chance to prove my worth. I wouldn't even be training with them. The following Saturday I was with Craig Bellamy, Wayne Bridge, Emmanuel Adebayor, Roque Santa Cruz and a group of players who were essentially the Under-16s. The senior pros on that pitch were outcasts too, but I was the only one of those left behind who had been part of the club over the long term, and that's why it hurt more. If the message hadn't got through the first time, now it was being hammered home: you're not part of it and you need to leave. Still the question was, why? I wasn't an expensive signing the club was trying to cut its losses on. I certainly didn't have a salary that meant they needed to get me off the wage bill. The others were on long-term, high-salary deals, and that's why I felt I was different. I don't imagine they had the club in their hearts like I still did. They weren't at home.

Suddenly everything that was so familiar appeared alien. My daily trip to work was a horrible one, driving into a completely different world, never further away from the team I'd called my own since the age of ten and those I'd called teammates. While they were playing the likes of Inter Milan, I was in my track-suit driving to turn out against Stalybridge Celtic and Curzon Ashton with the youth players. It got worse when the USA tour was over. The team came back, and we were kept separated from them, training at the same time on two separate pitches, 50 yards apart. And yet, before and after the session, we'd be sharing the same dressing room.

'See you guys later!' I'd say with false enthusiasm. 'Enjoy it!'

It was meant to be a joke, but it was heartbreaking. I'd still not been told why I was being put through this. I'd never felt anything like it, even through all the injuries in the early part of my career. And worst of all was the fact I had no control over any aspect of the situation. Was the treatment I was receiving an indictment of my ability? Of my attitude? I thought I was a pretty good player, and nobody had ever had reason to question my commitment. Emmanuel Adebayor was less anxious about the predicament we found ourselves in, at least at the start. He reckoned that if City were trying to force him out, he'd dig his heels in, sit there and take it until he found a place to move to. He was determined not to let the club dictate when that happened. For the first two weeks he was happy to shrug his shoulders, relax and enjoy himself. But it wasn't long before he cracked. One day he came in and just started giving the Under-16s a kicking during training. He was just fed up, and even though he was getting his full salary, it's proof that some emotions in football can't be solved through money. Even the control Manu thought he had of his own situation wasn't enough to get him through more than a few weeks of the punishment.

A little later on our group was relegated further. To prevent us having any contact at all with the first team, our training sessions were moved to a 3 p.m. start. It's a very specific time, to make sure everyone else would have left the building, so now we weren't just 50 yards away from our teammates but having no interactions whatsoever with anybody. I felt sorry for the young players who were being dragged into it. Mancini seemed to be creating an environment in which the older players felt we had no option other than to give up and walk out. But what was his end goal? Surely I'm more of an asset if I'm training and playing well and can be put out in the open for someone to buy. I never kicked up a stink, and I never would, because it's my club. I also have a sense of personal pride, and even though I was now firmly footballing deadwood – those outside of the starting eleven and regular subs – if I had been given the chance to train, I would have given my best. That improves the quality of training and the standards of the team.

Instead, they made a decision without thinking about the true consequences for the players it affected, and they did that because it didn't matter to them. It may well have been so inconsequential to Mancini that it never crossed his desk, but if he didn't make the call about me directly, he certainly decided it was acceptable. Perhaps he just didn't have the emotional maturity to deal with us one on one. I don't think he enjoyed having real heart-to-heart conversations, and clearly he was good at avoiding them.

That pre-season was horrible. But I was conflicted: I didn't want to go through it any more, but I also couldn't bear the thought of leaving. A chance to join QPR came and went, partly because they never made an official bid after talking with my agent and partly because I didn't feel right about playing for then manager Neil Warnock, given his reputation as an old-fashioned English manager and the style of play that went with that. When the last day of the transfer window arrived, I assumed I was going to be a deadline-day signing for someone. So, at the end of what I thought would be my final training session for Manchester City I emptied my locker and packed all my things into a black bin bag. I said goodbye to everyone I met on the way out. It was clear I had no future with the club, so I took my stuff home and sat by the TV waiting for a phone call. The hours passed by, and it never came. The sinking feeling of not being wanted was as bad as it comes. I was literally sick, throwing up as the stress overwhelmed me. I had been convinced something was going to happen, that one club would make an offer for me. Everybody knew City wanted to get rid of me, but the clock ticked past the deadline. The next day I drove to work with the bin bag in the back of my car and slung it over my shoulder as I walked into the training ground. It is one of the most humiliating things I have ever had to do.

I continued to train away from the first team for the days that followed, and then to my complete surprise I was in the squad for the club's first ever Champions League match. I'd not been rewarded for anything, not been spoken to by the manager, and he'd not even seen me train, but suddenly Roberto Mancini wanted me for the game against Napoli. Except he didn't. Just like the last occasion he'd picked me as one of the twenty players for a match-day squad more than a year previously against West Ham, I travelled to the hotel and was one of the two left out of the first eleven and seven subs. At least I'd got one training session with the rest of the team. A week later I got another one, and this time a match too. It was in the League Cup against Birmingham, and I started in a 2–0 win. The following round I was on the bench but didn't get on, although my involvement in the main sessions was increasing. By the November international break, I was with the first team most days and at least felt less like an Under-16s player.

Ahead of a QPR game in the Premier League, Mancini told the squad that if any players weren't playing for their countries in the ten days that followed, they could have the week off. We had a lot of international players at the time, but there were plenty involved in the first team who weren't, and for quite a few of us there was cause for celebration, as it was very rare to get so much time off in the middle of the season. I said to Lucy that we should go away, and we booked a relatively expensive trip to Dubai. But then, on the Saturday night after the QPR match, I got another text from Clare Marsden that sent me back to rock bottom:

'Please come in for training on Monday, Tuesday, Thursday, Friday and Saturday next week.'

'What's going on? I thought we had the week off?' I replied.

'The manager says you don't.'

I phoned Mancini. It rang out and went to voicemail. I tried again. It rang twice and then diverted to voicemail. I sent him a text. No response. I ended up pleading with him, asking to have the week off reinstated. Nothing came back. I went in on the Monday and discovered that me and Wayne Bridge were the only senior players who had been told to train. The rest were youth-team players. Then, on the Friday, it got even worse. Every single player was off, except Wayne and me. Just the two of us, having been told to do a gym session. The academy teams, the reserves, the first team, everyone in the complex was out, but we were in. Figure that one out.

Roberto Mancini could be very unsympathetic to his players and didn't seem to care about upsetting people. Once after a match Yaya Touré missed, he gathered the team together and told them they were nothing without Yaya. This was a side that included Vincent Kompany, David Silva, Joleon Lescott and Edin Džeko. His treatment of Wayne and me felt spiteful, and there was no benefit to him doing it. It wasn't an attempt to keep us fit to play because we weren't playing; he wasn't providing a carrot, just hitting us constantly with a stick. And at no point was there an explanation, even after multiple attempts to get one on the phone. Or in person: twice after playing in the League Cup midweek and then being left out for the weekend's Premier League game, I was told to play for the reserves the following week. Nobody else was, so I was confused and went to Mancini to ask why it was just me.

'What's wrong?' he said. 'Don't you want to play football?'

It was one of the few times in my life I was left speechless. I did want to play football, but he framed it in such a way that after everything he'd put me through, if I turned down the chance I would have been the bad guy. He could be manipulative and it struck me that our relationship had become completely dysfunctional. I was twenty-five but he was treating me like a teenager, as if I was brand new and should be grateful for any scrap he gave me. Then, if someone didn't do what he wanted in exactly the way he wanted, he'd on occasion punish them and then shape his alternative view when speaking to the media. Take the case of Carlos

Tevez refusing to warm up when he was on the bench for a Champions League match against Bayern Munich. Most, if not all, of the players in that team would say Carlos did nothing wrong, but he was disciplined so heavily because of Mancini's own perception of the situation and how he had decided to frame it – as someone so out of line that Mancini insisted Tevez would never play for the club again. It seemed to me that the goalposts would move as and when it suited him and even though, like with Carlos Tevez, the consensus amongst my teammates was that I had done nothing wrong, Mancini was casting me as the bad guy. Meanwhile there were plenty of imperfect players at the club, and they were training just fine. I had been separated from the rest and was being treated differently, despite not being a negative person or a bad influence. I basically spent the best part of two years wondering what was going on, having no answer, and then when I tried to address it, he'd send me to voicemail, literally and figuratively.

I was broken. A lost soul. I was also really, really angry. I didn't think I deserved it, and amongst all those in the Manchester City squad I was probably the only one who truly loved the club. Yet I was being treated like the villain of the football club. I thought I was good enough to be training, and I thought I was a good enough person to be around the team; my best season for City was the year before Roberto Mancini came in, with 75 per cent of the same players. I'd been there from the age of ten, a ball boy at Maine Road. I'd got hold of all those old programmes, signed up to be a Junior Blue and proudly showed everyone my membership card. I had been all-in, but now Mancini had not only dismantled my self-esteem but eroded my relationship with City to such an extent I realised I might have to get out. I didn't receive any support from my teammates, because the atmosphere had become sufficiently cut-throat for them to have their own issues to deal with. You sometimes need to be a leader with a strong foundation or have a devil-may-care attitude to do the right thing in that environment, and even though they understood what was happening with me, I don't think any players had the ability to provide the help I truly needed.

At home it was very different, and my family did the best they could to support me. Having a proper conversation about football with someone on the outside isn't easy, as while they appreciate the highs and lows they see on the pitch, the bits in the middle are harder to understand. Family and friends would listen and offer advice, but it was hard to convey the nuances of my situation. Why can't you just talk to him, they'd ask. I couldn't expect them to fully get it and tried not to affect other people's moods when I was trudging to and from 3 p.m. training sessions with no prospect of playing. I might only be in the building for three hours or so, but I'd spend the rest of the day respecting the need for rest or preparation. I'd come home and try to be normal, but the bad vibes at City were hanging over my head. The evenings would sneak up on me, and suddenly it'd be time to get ready for the next shambles of a day. I used to enjoy everything about football, but the man in charge was making me fall out of love with both the game and the club I held so dearly.

• • •

My mum, as she had been for my whole career, was there for me when I was at my lowest ebb. She and Dad were living next door in Middleton, in the first house I'd bought for the family. I'd check in with them on a daily basis, but not just because of what I was facing at City. Mum had her own problems. In the days before I had moved to Sunderland on loan, a deal she had helped to organise alongside my agent, she had been very ill. She was constantly vomiting and went to have it investigated. My mum was diagnosed with stomach cancer in late July 2010 and was given nine months to live. The first part she revealed to her shocked children, but the second she did not. We were convinced she would have chemotherapy and radiotherapy and she'd be all right, and nobody told us otherwise. It was reassurance enough to go through with the move to Sunderland, and we promised to speak over the phone every day. I also planned to travel back as much as possible to help out and take her to appointments at Manchester's cancer hospital, The Christie.

However, soon after that, the treatment led to her losing her hair, and a woman who had never showed weakness started to appear more and more frail. She required assistance for physical things, chores that needed doing. Lucy, my sisters and I would tidy up for her, help with the cooking or just simply take her out for a walk for some fresh air. All her energy needed to be spent on getting better, and not knowing about the terminal prognosis we were sure she would. At times she was even able to travel up to Sunderland and was still trying to come to every game she possibly could, but it was incredibly sad to see her changing. The sense of mortality hits hardest when it arises with someone so strong struggling so much. I was grateful she was attempting to be herself, and I knew that being myself would help her do that because she was desperate not to make it about her, even with all her suffering. My dad, on the other hand, faced the burden of the true diagnosis. He would offer up all kinds of holistic remedies, whereas Mum was happy to trust the conventional medicine and also her faith, which comforted her greatly. The good days were shared by all, but the bad ones they had to suffer alone and in their own way.

Then, on 3 November 2010, part-way through my season in Sunderland, my mum received an email.

Chapter 12

While receiving treatment for stomach cancer, my mother had been attempting to rectify an ongoing contractual dispute with Manchester City. The source of my appearance fee while at Sunderland was being contested by Brian Marwood, who at the time was the chief football operations officer at my parent club. He claimed they were paying me correctly but Sunderland were not fully reimbursing City for the share of my salary they'd agreed to take on; Mum had already confirmed with Marwood that City would agree to 'preserve Nedum's contractual terms and conditions' during my loan at the Stadium of Light. This guarantee was made on a phone call between the two on 10 August 2010 and signalled that an initial £14,000-a-week shortfall had been rectified.

However, my next pay slip from Sunderland suggested otherwise. Another person at City claimed my Sunderland deal included a clause which acknowledged that an appearance for my loan club didn't constitute one for City, and therefore I wouldn't be paid an appearance fee – but it was included in a part of the document that had remained confidential. A series of emails were exchanged to this effect, and Marwood continued to insist that an appearance fee was something I should negotiate with Sunderland, even though that was part of the 'terms and conditions' he had said would be protected. My mum wrote back:

Dear Brian,

Thank you for getting back to me.

My body might be ravaged by cancer and ongoing chemotherapy but, thankfully, my intellectual and mental capacities remain fully functional. I fail to see where any of the explanations you have offered justify the exclusion of any aspect of Nedum's Manchester City contracted terms and conditions.

The last conversation we had was about a shortfall of £14,000. You called me back after consulting Garry [Cook, Manchester City CEO] and Graham [Wallace, COO] and stated that it had been sorted out. I asked you to confirm that what was agreed was the protection of Nedum's contracted terms and conditions during the period of his loan. You replied in the affirmative, informing me that you had done me a big favour which you hoped I would return in the future.

Nedum is being paid £8,000 per game for each Premier League start whilst on loan, contrary to the guarantee you gave during our conversation.

I intend to seek formal advice as soon as I feel less fatigued but would prefer an informal resolution of the matter. I will be happy to attend a short meeting at your office, if it helps resolve the matter satisfactorily.

My health problems remain entirely confidential.

Regards,

Anthonia

Cook and Wallace had been included on the emails, and the former replied. But he sent his message to the wrong person:

Brian,

 Ravaged with it!! I don't know how you sleep at night.

 You used to be such a nice man when I worked with you at Nike … You handled this very well.

 G

Sent from my iPad

It was supposed to be for Brian Marwood, but it came to my mum. She called me that day to reveal that Garry Cook had sent an email mocking her illness. I'd known that there was a conversation going on about a sticking point in my contract, but as on all previous occasions I'd been happy to let others deal with it. I was literally 130 miles away. So, the severity of the escalation shocked me; I was disgusted, outraged and upset for my mum. But then I made the wrong decision. Like the nine-year-old in Miles Platting and the twenty-year-old in Nijmegen and Podgorica, I didn't do enough. I certainly didn't do what I would now. Then, I was very different and lacked leverage because of my situation with City. I didn't want to ruffle too many feathers. I wasn't able to catch the full gravity of the situation, even though my mum, dad and agent were all furious. I considered it a classless act by an idiot; ridiculous and unprofessional. You simply can't joke about things like cancer, particularly behind someone's back. But I still thought it was best not to cause a fuss and to stay in line.

Part of my reaction was based on not knowing that her diagnosis was terminal and an assumption she would get better. But that same fact is what makes me angry to this day. If I were to put present-day me in that situation, knowing what I now know, I'd be going to war, all by myself if necessary, and I would not relent. Fight, not flight. I know speaking up isn't an easy thing to do because people fear what could happen to them. Even if they know they're in the right, it's difficult to attack a system that protects those in power. But speaking up can nip in the bud patterns of terrible behaviour, preventing the suffering of a lot of people. It does take courage, though, and while I have that now, I didn't when I learned about the email. I didn't have a platform or influence enough to make a big issue of it.

Less than a year later, it became a big issue when the email was leaked to the press. Neither I nor my mum was responsible for the newspapers getting hold of the story, so I'm assuming it came from within Manchester City. My agent did confirm some of the details to a journalist, who he describes as someone who 'didn't like Brian Marwood'. They'd apparently had the piece ready for a while but needed certain information before running it, which my agent was happy to provide.

But Marwood didn't bear the brunt of the contempt that both men received, Garry Cook did. He initially denied that he had sent the offending email but resigned after an internal investigation concluded he had. He was caught out by the 'Sent from my iPad'. As the story of the email, investigation and resignation played out in the press, I felt like an extra in a film. I didn't have any more information than what my mum had told me at the time and certainly wasn't in direct communication with Cook. I was there in the story, but it's not like I was lifting Thor's hammer. I was just in the background, even though a lot of the attention was being put on me. By then I was back at City and being forced to train with the youth teams, so I was in a very difficult place mentally. Then all this happened on top of it, piling on to what was the worst period of my career. There was even an accusation levelled at me that I had leaked the email because I was a disgruntled employee who was seeking retribution for being left out of the team, that the timing couldn't have been a coincidence. It wasn't that at all. How would trying to take someone down get me back in the team? I also, perhaps stupidly, wanted to think the best of the club, even though it was being run by those two and managed by *him*.

I wasn't pleased that the email became public, and Cook losing his job didn't please me either. It was the right thing that it came out and it's understandable that he resigned, but I didn't celebrate in any way. I would never defend him, because what he did was wrong, but I wasn't planning to go on strike if he didn't get sacked or anything like that. My mum felt differently. She recognised the egregious nature of his error because she knew the seriousness of her condition, so she was satisfied with the outcome. This was not 'banter', forgivable if one of those involved is considered to be a charismatic figure, as Cook was. I don't receive emails like that, and I guess very few others do. There's a reason for that: most people know it's wrong. Look a little deeper into an environment in which this sort of email exchange takes place and you risk opening up a can of worms. If staff are happy to send this kind of stuff from a company account, what else might be going on in private?

That's why there was not a great deal of difference between Garry Cook and Brian Marwood in my mind. They were a pair, and not just because they'd known each other during their time working together at Nike. Marwood was the intended recipient of that email, and even though it was not him who composed the message it was written in a way that would suggest he was a willing participant in the joke. The difference is that I've barely spotted Cook anywhere for the past ten years, but Marwood still works at Manchester City's parent company as their managing director of global football, and that's why I've ended up being angrier with him than with Cook. If I'd known when I first read that email that my mum's cancer was terminal, I would have hated him. And I stress the word hate. In the moment I thought I'd – we'd – be able to move on. No way on Planet Earth would I let that fly now in the way I did back then. But although I can't go back and change how I reacted then, I can guarantee I'll never forgive him.

Since becoming a father I've realised why my parents didn't reveal that my mum wasn't expected to recover, and for all the reasons apart from how I was able to deal with the email, I think they got it right. I can imagine wanting to protect my children from something like that, and my youngest sister Lynda was only fifteen when Mum got her diagnosis. None of us were old, none of us were mature adults. Perhaps we weren't ready to have that type of information.

Now there's another kind of conflict. I do some work for Manchester City and Brian Marwood is still there. I've seen him twice, and both times he's come up and said hello, all cordial, although he's never apologised. Maybe he cares, maybe he doesn't. Maybe his regret is that he didn't get the chance to work with his friend Garry Cook for longer, and he thinks I'm to blame, so the cordiality he shows is a sacrifice he thinks *he's* making. He might also think there's nothing to apologise for, and if that's the case I guess he'll never understand where I'm coming from.

I'm business-like when I'm in his company, and I can always be polite with anyone if I'm in a professional setting, but I can't look at him and not think about that time.

• • •

Just over a year after the email became public, my mum phoned me. It was our daily chat, and I picked up the call on my way to a game. I had moved to QPR by this point, and I was heading to Loftus Road for a home match against Reading. We talked about what was coming up, as we normally would, and then hung up. Later, the phone went again. It was Mum. She'd called to ask me about the game as if we'd never had the first conversation.

'Mum, what are you talking about? We've just spoken about this!'

'No, we haven't.'

I thought it was really weird that she couldn't remember. A few days later my dad told me that the cancer had accelerated, reached her brain, and she wasn't well at all. Her memory had been affected, and this was likely to be the final stage of her life.

There had been times before when she was sick and really struggling, but I'd always been comforted by the conviction that she'd get better. After all the highs and lows of the more than two years she'd been living with cancer, now I found out she'd taken a big leap to what was being described as the inevitable. Then, at the beginning of November, another call from Dad. QPR had a game against Stoke, and afterwards I should carry on heading north, he said. It was time. I had to go back home.

When she was able, my mum would be at every game I played. Every game. For the entire first half of my career, I put down two tickets under the name of Dr Anthonia Onuoha. Never Mrs, always Dr. Too many times when she was younger, being black and foreign, she fought in vain to gain the respect she deserved, so now she insisted I put her proper title. She wanted people to know who and what she was. Mum was a supporter of me and everything I was involved in. She would get to know my team-mates, my friends and wanted to be part of my world. She was beloved by everybody who was in my orbit because of her posi-tivity and joy in any success we shared. After each match, we had two different routines: at home games, we'd meet in the players' lounge; at away matches, by the team bus before it departed and she left in her car. She had a huge smile, and she'd swamp me when I arrived. Regardless of how the game had gone for me personally, I got a buzz off her happiness. When you know that you have people who care about you and really root for you, it gets you through the tough times and the good times feel so much better.

I used to rush to get ready to make sure I saw her, because whether it was in Manchester or Molde in Norway, she would be there, literally every step of my journey. From the grotty parks of AFC Clayton to the glamour of the executive box at Manchester City, where she received the kisses I blew to her after scoring my first senior goal. When we had away trips with the City academy teams, she'd always bring food with her to hand out to the team. It tended to be puff-puff, a Nigerian doughnut, or some dried meat. Sometimes, if she had to rush off, she'd leave it with the bus driver. As we clambered on after the game, he'd produce a bag full of food, and nobody was in any doubt as to who had provided it. That's who she was and why everyone loved her. She didn't just look after me but all those around me too.

The obsession with keeping me fed didn't begin or end there. There were the boxes of bananas, and I still jump headfirst into them when I buy a bunch now. The amount of food I ate compared to others suggested I was from a completely different world. She would feed me constantly, even when I moved into the house next door. Initially, we lived in Middleton in a home I could afford to buy after becoming a professional. It was the first house anyone in my family had ever owned. Then, when the house I'm now in became available, my mum liked the idea of me being close, so she encouraged me to buy it. Soon after I did, we decided to replace the fences between the two houses. Mum asked for a hatch to be inserted within one of the panels, one that was just big enough to fit a plate through. It's almost the size of a letter box, and food was passed from her to me on countless occasions. Her nickname for me was Mr Universe, and she did everything to make sure I stayed that way.

If I went next door to see my parents, I was greeted by my mum's beaming smile and would kiss her on her right cheek as I walked through the door. She'd immediately sit me down and try to give me food, and then we'd just talk and talk. These were the conversations we replaced with our daily phone calls when I moved away from Manchester. She'd been there for the duration so understood the nuances of my career more than almost anybody else and could appreciate the grey areas that others couldn't. It wasn't the cliché of a parent being a second coach, as she knew that wasn't her area of expertise, but she could read the mood very well. If I was unhappy, she wouldn't demand that I perk up but could spot when I needed to talk. Even though she knew that opinions offered by those outside the game don't make any difference to how successful a footballer is, she would still tell me about things made her particularly happy, including if someone had got in touch from Nigeria to talk about my progress. Both my mum and my dad would gain such a sense of pride from speaking to people back home who'd seen their son play on TV! Her enthusiasm was matched by her selflessness, and she was so loving she'd give you the shirt off her back in a snowstorm if it meant you'd be warmer for just a split second.

Still, when she needed to be stern, she was. She took no nonsense from anyone, the kind of person who if she's unhappy with the food at a restaurant, would complain so effectively she might as well have shut the whole place down. She was a fighter, and even though I might have been a little embarrassed when I was a child, I've come to appreciate the many reasons why you need a harsher edge when you're older. Now I get why she didn't take any nonsense, and I think there are similarities with who I've become.

This was the woman I found on a ventilator on Saturday 10 November 2012, the evening after the game against Stoke. She was at home and struggling. I could hear with each breath the pain she was in, as if her lungs were flooded with liquid. She was on morphine and could still muster a few words on that first day, but soon enough her suffering prevented her from managing even that. We spent a powerless few days just waiting for her to die. Then, on the Thursday evening, she was gone. Lorna D'Laryea, Nathan and Jonathan's mother, who is a nurse and one of my mum's best friends, came into the living room where we were sitting.

'You guys need to go to her. She's passed away.'

I walked into the room next door and saw my mum. My instinct was to kiss her. It always had been, whether it was each time I arrived at her house or when celebrating a goal. I went to kiss her on her head, but stopped. It didn't feel like her. I'm not spiritual, but it was as if something wasn't there any more. I was reluctant to do what I'd done impulsively a million times, so instead I just looked at her. She was lying there, dead, and I didn't know what to say or what to do. For days I'd thought she was dying, but until you see death happen in front of you, you have no idea what dying is like. All of a sudden, the story is finished. The first person of any significance I'd lost in my life happened to be the one closest to me on Planet Earth. It's over, it's done.

My sister Lynda's birthday is 9 November. Mine is the 12th. Dr Anthonia Onuoha passed away on the 15th, at the age of fifty-three. Immediately after she died, we were told for the first time that her original cancer diagnosis had been terminal. It became clear that the four children were the only ones in the family who hadn't known all along. The adults' reaction to my mum's passing was different; they were sad she had gone, but they'd been preparing for it, and for longer than expected because she had significantly outlived the original prognosis of nine months. My older sister Diuto was very angry at not being told. I was too, but I accepted why my parents had decided to keep it from us. I reasoned that there was little value in being angry at a time when I was so overwhelmed with sadness.

It was a moment that came almost exactly halfway through my career, and it affected everything I experienced in football afterwards. She'd been there from Sunday League at Clayton, for my Manchester City trial at the Armitage Centre, then at Maine Road when I was a ball boy. Nobody else had been to as many games. Lucy, my dad and sisters all went to a lot of my matches, but now there was a void. One that felt bigger with every attempt to fill it. Football started to feel like business now that she wasn't there. I started to go to games by myself, saying goodbye to my family on the way out of the door, saying I'd see them later but I had work to do. I'd discourage them from coming to watch me, because even though I loved playing at QPR, Loftus Road could be hostile at times, and if I thought it might be a bit toxic because the team wasn't doing so well, I decided I didn't want them to go through that. Football had become work, devoid of the emotional context of the first half of my career, and if I couldn't appreciate any upside to my family coming, why subject them to a possible downside? There were no more trips to the players' lounge, no more waiting around by the bus. There were no more daily calls, which I quickly realised had become a crutch for me. They had been intertwined for so long, but now football and life went in two different directions.

Another bond had been broken too. The past few years have been very tough for my father. He's better today than he was, but he'd lost his companion. I can't imagine what it must have been like for him to cope without her. I think of how it would be for me to lose Lucy, with whom I've been for twenty years, and whether my eldest daughter Amaia would understand. She couldn't possibly, and nor could I with my dad. I know who I am with Lucy in my life, but if she wasn't here, I don't know who I'd be. My dad tried his best to be who he thought he needed to be for himself and his children, and he always sends the family WhatsApp group a little message on the anniversary of Mum's death. He hasn't attempted to replace the role she played in my career, because that was unique to her, but don't think for one moment that her dominance meant he didn't make a significant contribution. They both supported me, albeit in different ways.

It was my dad, after all, who spurned the advances of the Manchester United scout and encouraged the one from City. While my parents would have made so many decisions that concerned me together, that was one where Dad went out on a limb. I genuinely think if it had been down to my mum, she would have chosen United for me. She would have analysed it from a practical point of view, and this was at a time when United were the best team in the country and had just won the double, while City had been relegated. She would have also known that I owned a cassette of United's 1996 FA Cup final song. I had only been in Manchester for five years, so while I liked football, I hadn't yet nailed my colours to the mast. But my dad saw or heard something. Something that meant he didn't make the decision in a vacuum, something that made him think Manchester City was the team for me. Where he also differed from my mum is that once he made the decision, that was it. Mum might have consulted me or given me a series of options; Dad wouldn't choose to involve me in a question to which he thought he knew the answer.

Nigerian fathers can typically be quite tough on their kids. They expect discipline and dedication to education, and at times my dad came down quite hard on me. He's softened a little over time, and when he and my mum provided a united front it was a very caring one. But in the early years in Manchester he was strict, a proud Nigerian man with traditions, and the upbringing that Diuto, Chidi and I had was different to Lynda's. When us three older siblings were young, there was no way we would ever speak back to our parents at all. By the time Lynda was born, Dad was adopting more of the philosophies of his new home and what was more normal in British culture. He didn't let me go on that double-date to the cinema on a school night, but when Lynda was the same age she was going on sleepovers! I'd never had one in my life, because Dad felt it was important for the family to maintain the standards he'd grown up with himself, ones that would have been expected in Nigeria. I can understand why, because let me put it this way, there were people in the Nigerian community in the UK who were sent back home if they'd been messing about. They'd get straightened out and then come back to England to behave how they were supposed to. If it was felt they were being too socially liberal, doing whatever they wanted, they were told that was not the way to operate. They were reminded that the younger generation are not peers of their parents, as they might be in British society. In Nigerian culture, respect for your elders is an undefeatable requirement.

The focus on education is almost as important. The day of my GCSE results, I was a bit nervous but felt particularly positive about maths. I thought I was going to get an A*, and my teacher loved me, so maths was going to be solid. I also thought geography would go well, but I wasn't quite so confident about English. My dad drove me to school to pick up the results, and he'd barely ever done that before. Clearly this was a big moment. I was handed an envelope, opened it and showed it to him. Eight As, two Bs. No A* in maths and only a B in geography. We drove home, and there was silence in the car. I was panicking that I hadn't received any approval from my dad, let alone any congratulations. I was objectively disappointed about the A in maths, but I'd like to think I performed to the best of my abilities in the moment and met the expectations people had of me. I wasn't one of the best students at a school that regularly produced brilliant results, but I was nowhere near the bottom of the pile. But still, silence in the car. My sense of anxiety was growing at what Dad was going to say. We got home, and he was apoplectic. Whether it was because he didn't think the results were sufficient reward for his and Mum's sacrifices or he thought I didn't put in as much effort as I should have, he made it clear I should have done better. I felt like I had let him down, and it motivated me to outperform expectations in my A-Levels. I had learned from that silence in the car, and I didn't want to repeat it.

Even when I'm with my dad now, I'm the same person I was then. If I went to his house next door and he told me to sweep the floor, I'd sweep the floor. The respect remains. I don't talk back to him. He might say something I disagree with 1,000 per cent, but I will still dutifully sit there and listen to it. I won't tell him he's wrong, even if it's about football and I feel I'm qualified enough to contradict him. 'Fine, Dad. Yeah,' I'll say, appreciating that he has his own opinions. My sisters are totally different. They call him out all the time, which I imagine provides a little hit to his pride. But my relationship with him still shows an understanding for Nigerian hierarchy. I am not my dad's peer. He is my father, and I must act as such.

For my part, I like to be chilled with my kids. I want them to do well, but more than that I want them to be happy, healthy, good people. That doesn't revolve around them being incredibly successful in school. It'd be nice if they were, but I'm not going to fall out with them over a bad test result like I did with my dad. I won't be angry with them, but it's because I'm lucky enough to be able to afford to send them to a good school. I'm not making the same sacrifices my parents did to give me that opportunity. My efforts go into ensuring they are loving people whose creativity is not limited. If they were being destructive in any way I'd discipline them, but am I a Nigerian father? No. I'm still a Nigerian son, and there's a subtle difference between the two.

My wife Lucy gets it. She understands my culture, my background, my heritage and why I do and say certain things. She respects it and doesn't question it, because she knows I'm not in a position to question it either. The first time I saw her, she was running 800 metres round a track in a pair of horrible gym knickers. It was a big joke at the time that all the girls at Hulme had to wear them when they did athletics, and it was pretty funny. Despite this I immediately thought she was very attractive, but I had no confidence she'd like me back. I wasn't one of the coolest kids around or anything, and I had a litany of brief unsuccessful relationships behind me. I was always getting dumped, sometimes after just a day or two. It was an achievement if a girl stuck with me for a week. One of them broke up with me, only to demand a couple of days later that we get back together after a rumour emerged I'd moved on to someone else. OK, fair enough, I said. I was so soft. But my failures, fleeting as they were, led me to Lucy, with whom I have clearly overcompensated.

After that first time, we both did enough sport that I saw her again on a few occasions before I properly started talking to her. Around a month later, on 22 May 2002, we were boyfriend and girlfriend, making it official with an exchange on MSN Messenger. And then I went big. Within another month, I'd told her I loved her. Then, just two months after getting together, I left Hulme and she stayed. That would have been enough reason for it not to work, because now we were in the teenage version of a long-distance relationship. I was full-time at Manchester City and attending college nearby, while she lived in Failsworth – at least a couple of buses away. While she was in the sixth form, experiencing the comparative freedom you get from that, I was doing the exact opposite. I couldn't join her on Tuesday nights out in Oldham because I was either training or playing. It also shouldn't have worked when she left for Leeds University, which took her even further away at a time when my stock was rising within Manchester and I was getting a lot of attention. But then, and now, I couldn't imagine being with anybody else. I'm just incredibly happy, and she's clearly the right one for me, because we've been together twenty years and I've loved it all.

Prior to the March international break in 2010, I asked Lucy's mum and dad if I could have her hand in marriage. With their consent, I then took her to Paris, having had a ring made based on a famous Tiffany design that, somehow, I had managed to find out she liked without making it too obvious. Before getting on the flight I realised I didn't have a plan to store the ring, so I did what you're never supposed to: I put it in the hold luggage. I panicked for the whole flight, thinking it was going to go missing for ever. But I got away with it, and after arriving at the Hôtel Barrière Le Fouquet's just off the Champs-Élysées we ordered room service and I uttered a much-practised piece of French my sister Diuto had taught me:

'*Veux-tu m'épouser?*'

'What are you talking about?' was the less than romantic reply.

'*Veux-tu m'épouser?*'

Her face was blank. I produced the ring.

'What I'm trying to say is, will you marry me?'

There was a tear in her eye as she took the ring. A few moments later I realised she hadn't made it official. Perhaps we needed MSN Messenger.

'Can I have an answer?' I asked.

'Yes,' she said.

We spent a year looking for places to get married and settled on Sotogrande in southern Spain. The two of us and close family stayed out there for a week, with guests joining us from Friday to Sunday. We were legally married on 2 June 2011 in Gibraltar, before the ceremony two days later on the 4th. It was an incredible day, one of the happiest of my life. There were 100 guests, and as they arrived on the Friday night it occurred to me how surreal it was to have all those I cared about most in the world in the same place when that place wasn't home. I'd become accustomed to people looking at me, and while I was made a big deal of on my wedding day, it wasn't about me. Any man who's ever got married will tell you it's about the bride, and even though she doesn't enjoy being in the limelight and everyone knew not to make a massive fuss of her, it was definitely Lucy who was the centre of attention.

About twenty of the guests might not have been to a conventional British wedding before. Some of those I hadn't seen for maybe twenty years. But within Nigerian culture, those guests were the kind that simply must be invited to your wedding. They came from Nigeria itself, America and elsewhere. We are a mixed-race couple, bringing together two very different traditions. I was nervous the first time I told my mum and dad that I had a girlfriend who was white. But that was me messing up, because neither of them cared, and they were happy that I was happy. Lucy's grandmother had barely ever seen a black person before I met her, but soon she got to know me and liked me. I'm lucky because I've lived in the only culture Lucy's known, so I understand it, but she's been absolutely brilliant listening to me explain how mine is a bit different. She recognises it's part of who I am. She takes that on board and doesn't expect me to be anything else.

At some point I'd like to take Lucy to Nigeria for the first time. Our three kids, Amaia, Teia and Ruben too. Amaia is now well aware that although she was born in England, she's half-Nigerian. She likes it because she's inquisitive, and she wants to go and see where it is and what being half-Nigerian actually means. All three are lucky they're growing up in a different environment than those of previous generations. I'm sure at some point they'll face difficulties, because when it comes to race there will always be those who consider people who aren't 100 per cent white to be non-pure in some way. I'm hoping they'll be more readily accepted by others who might also be part of minorities, as well as by that other group to which they belong as British kids with a white mother. So far it's not been an issue, and that is down to Lucy. My life has been blessed by two women who have been the most amazing mothers. My biggest regret is that one wasn't around to witness the other. My mum was everything to me. She looked after me so well from literally minute one, but she never got the chance to see me with children. Amaia arrived two years after my mum passed, and that fills me with sadness to this day because I know how much she, Teia and Ruben would have loved their grandmother, and she them in return.

Chapter 13th of May

Nearly nine years after my first experience of the Manchester City first team, I had my final one. It lasted nine minutes. Edin Džeko had given us a 1–0 lead against Wigan at the DW Stadium, and Roberto Mancini wanted to hold on to it, so he replaced David Silva with a central defender to make it three at the back. This was a tactic he regularly used, although this was the only time he used me as part of it. For some reason, in a decision as unclear as most he made involving me, I had been picked for a Premier League game. He hadn't done that once before in the 2011/12 season, but I was in the squad for Wigan in January, named as one of the substitutes.

Midway through the second half, he looked over and asked me to get ready to come on. After two years of waiting for him to need me, now, all of a sudden, he did. I was confounded by the fact he now depended on me to affect a match on his behalf, given he'd apparently not even trusted me to train with the first team for so much of the season. But what meant more to me was the reception I got from my teammates. Joe Hart and Joleon

Lescott high-fived me as I came on, both happy for me personally and reassured that I would help them see out the game. At
least they still had faith in me. I had little to do – I remember
shielding a ball out of play to stem a Wigan attack – but I was
so gratified to see the comfort I provided to my defensive col-
leagues and the respect they gave me for it, that after all those
months of Mancini's manipulation and my own mental disinte-
gration it ended up being my nicest moment during the manager's time at the club.

I didn't know for sure that it would be my last City game, but
the rarity of my selection suggested it would be. Nor did I know
that the team I was part of that day would eventually become a
Premier League-winning side. I contributed nine minutes to that
achievement, and I can live just fine with the fact that it came
way short of the threshold for getting a medal! After all, ten days
after that Wigan game I left Manchester City, for good this time.
I'd been at the club since the age of ten, and now, having turned
twenty-five two months prior, my association with my team in
my home city was over.

I had come to terms with the fact things wouldn't improve
under Mancini, and the advice I'd been given was that I couldn't
waste a whole season at that stage of my career. So having never
courted a transfer before, I knew the January 2012 transfer
window provided an opportunity I should now take. I had to
move on, and that was tough to realise. Emotionally it felt weird
to be leaving permanently, but also practically. I simply didn't
know how transfers worked. Newspaper speculation is invaria-
bly based on what might happen, not what is actually happening,
and I would see stories about Middlesbrough being interested in

me or Aston Villa bidding £6 million, but neither amounted to anything concrete. Even if a bid is lodged, the line will be that there's a negotiation and perhaps a counter-offer, but if you're the player at the centre of it all, you're one of the last to know. I had been told that QPR had resurrected their previous interest in me, and then before I knew it City were asking me to go down to London because I had to speak to them about it. My inclination was to say, no I don't, but I was naïve: QPR had had a bid accepted, so I did indeed have to talk to them. Meanwhile I also learned that Everton were interested in a loan deal until the end of the season, which would then become permanent. I liked that idea more as it would allow me to stay in the north-west, so I was encouraged to go and speak to Brian Marwood to find out if it was true and if I could pursue it. Going straight to the man in charge wasn't something I would normally do, but this appeared a significant enough reason to do so. Given what had happened over the previous eighteen months between Marwood and my mother, I made sure to be polite.

'Brian, I know this QPR thing is happening and I need to go and speak to them about it, but I've heard there's something at Everton for me.' I wasn't in a rage or even impatient. Perhaps I should have been. 'If there is, I'd rather do that.'

He looked me dead in the eye.

'Nope. There's nothing at Everton. Nothing. We've accepted a bid from QPR and it's the only option that's there. You have to go.'

A denial, point-blank. So, I had two conflicting pieces of information. One from my friend Peter Morrison, who, while he wasn't directly representing me at the time, had been my agent since I was a teenager; the other from a man who did not have my interests at heart. I had reluctantly to accept Marwood's version, because what else could I do? He had the power to push me in the direction he preferred but in doing so he dismissed out of hand what Peter, one of my best friends, had said. By insisting that I didn't have more than one option, Marwood got what he wanted: me out of Manchester City.

•   •   •

I didn't know much about QPR when I signed for them. They were sixteenth in the table at the time and had been in the top ten earlier in the season, but a slump in form leading up to Christmas had cost manager Neil Warnock his job. If he had still been there, I imagine I would have tried to hunt out more options. I ended up playing under him when he returned to the club as the caretaker manager and it was fine, but at that time playing for him didn't appeal to me at all. His replacement removed that significant hurdle: Mark Hughes. Shaun Wright-Phillips and Joey Barton were familiar names too. Apart from that, though, I was entering a level of the unknown I'd not experienced before. When I moved to Sunderland, I knew I would eventually go back to City. Not this time.

I sat on the train down to London contemplating what I'd left behind. I'd been severed sufficiently from the first team at City that it wasn't the players I was going to miss, even if they did form the most talented squad I'd ever been part of. It was Manchester that was hard to leave. I'm a northerner. I didn't even believe in London as a concept at that time – make of that what you will – but here I was, about to create a new life there. Where do I stay? What do I do? It's a very strange feeling when you're so attached to one place and then you turn up somewhere else with almost no notice. I didn't have a clue where to even begin. I spoke with Mark Hughes, agreed to join QPR and soon enough was on a train back up north to say my goodbyes to my family and to pick up Lucy and enough stuff to get us through the first week.

We'd been booked in to stay at the Heathrow Airport Radisson, which wasn't far away from the club's training ground, Harlington. When I arrived at the facility for the first time, I realised why they'd held the initial meeting with me at Loftus Road. The fields we could use flooded every time it rained and were bone-dry if it didn't. The buildings were almost all portacabins. The gym was dirty and run-down, and one of the treadmills had years' worth of bottles and dust fighting for space under it. It was not in good shape.

I wouldn't call it a scam, but having new players go to the stadium to sign their contracts was definitely a strategy. Not that Loftus Road provided significantly more glamour. At the Etihad you'd either drive your car – or have it driven – underneath the stadium before a match, and it was from there you'd leave at the end of the game. It was a new ground, built in a lot of space in east Manchester. There was none of that in south-west London. QPR's stadium was built almost a century before Manchester City's current home, and it's surrounded on all sides by houses, apartment blocks and a school which would provide the players' car park on matchdays. Well, some matchdays, because for certain midweek games school was still on, so we couldn't use it.

It didn't really feel like a Premier League club. The executive boxes – of which they were sufficiently proud to have them as the contract-signing location for new players – didn't have any seats outside, because it was so tight. During my time there they renovated the dressing rooms and at one point switched which one the home team was in. The new one was still quite small, to the extent they ran out of space when installing the toilets. The urinals were essentially in the main part of the dressing room, right next to where the manager would give his team talks. People could be having a wee, or worse, at the most inopportune time. Two of the team, Shaun Derry and Fitz Hall, used to intentionally throw up before they went out to play, so the rest of the players could be getting ready and having pre-match talks, hearing people retch literally 2ft away. We ended up switching back to the original dressing room later on.

Once we were outside, the seats were so close to the pitch that even without fans there was a sense of claustrophobia. But the hostility of Loftus Road was, for a player riding on its coat-tails, a huge benefit. If things were going well, the supporters would have our back and it was a great place to play. They would back us to the end, as if we could do no wrong. But we had to earn it, and if I or the team were going through a tough time, we had to be strong, because we didn't want that hostility aimed at us, especially as the small enclosed stands meant it was very loud. I'd never have thought 18,000 people could generate the same atmosphere as the much bigger stadiums, but it was impressive, and some of the most exciting moments I had with a home crowd were in that stadium.

It wasn't just the setting that was alien: so was the situation

I found myself in with my new team. I'd joined mid-season, so there was little time to settle in, and the team was involved in a relegation battle. That meant I was joining a fractious environment, with games coming thick and fast. Nobody was of a mind to welcome me, because they needed to tell me to get my stuff ready, as it was going to be an intense few weeks and months. That made it much easier to change focus from a club where I'd been cast out and ignored for months, to one which required me to play straight away. In that setting I didn't worry about whether I could still perform or not, because I was looking forward so much to getting my chance again. My thoughts were dominated by 'I want to play'. I was available and the manager wanted me to be in the side, so I had to go out and prove myself to my new teammates. All footballers will tell you those first few days are crucial: you start from zero and must immediately manage relationships with people who might need convincing. They're checking on your personality, your habits, your ability in training. It's true that you never get a second chance to make a first impression.

Mark Hughes had only arrived at QPR two weeks before me, so as much as I was grateful for a familiar face, I imagine he would have been too. As a new manager, he would have had to figure out quickly who's who and which players would be of value to him. He wanted me to join him at his new club, and he trusted me. How different to what I'd just come from. However, while the respect Mark and I had for each other hadn't changed and we were able to pick up from where we left off at City, our relationship was a little different at QPR. No longer was I the academy graduate, the young player to whom Mark had given an opportunity. I'd loved being the youth product, as it had forged a bond between me and Manchester City, but there are significant negatives to being the academy guy. You might fall under the banner of 'being happy to be here', someone who won't upset the apple cart because of their relationship with the club. That tag is often applied to those who have been with a team the longest, yet whose feelings are most easily ignored.

But now it was irrelevant that I had been a ball boy, cleaned boots and made my debut at seventeen. Now I was the player who had faced competition at City, one who had been signed to play for the club and inserted into the pecking order higher than those who were already there. I was the player who would be given time, because of how and when I had arrived. Mark had changed my status, and I appreciated that.

The burden that Mark faced at QPR was different to what he'd had at City, but it was no less intense. There's pressure to succeed, and then there's significant pressure not to fail. The goal at that point was to carry the QPR ship to safety, but with the money that had already been spent by the club's new majority shareholder and the potential that with survival he'd provide more, there were a lot of eyes on Mark. Normally he'd spend time working on the infrastructure of a club, improving the place of work, but there was none of that this time. All he could do was try to freshen up the tactics and get his team organised. Training was similar to how it had been under him at City, with his coaching team of Mark Bowen, Eddie Niedzwiecki and Kevin Hitchcock. There was also still a pressing need to win, but unlike at City, now we were the underdogs in almost every game.

Two days after I arrived, we lost one. The FA Cup might not

have been the priority, but being beaten at home by local rivals Chelsea was nevertheless an unpopular result. I was named as a sub and didn't come on. The following Wednesday I made my QPR debut in a 2–2 Premier League draw at Aston Villa. We'd been 2–0 up after less than half an hour, but relinquishing that lead was typical of a team that hadn't won away from home since November. The three games after that I played every minute, which meant I'd already doubled my game time from half a season at City, but we lost each time. The last of those games was another defeat to a local rival, Fulham. Results like that don't help a new manager, or a new player for that matter, endear themselves to a fanbase. What would be of more value than derbies, though, were matches against our relegation rivals, and we had one coming up against Bolton. They'd been in the bottom three almost all season, while we were hovering just above. Twenty minutes into the game my fellow defender Clint Hill headed the ball across the line, but the goal wasn't given. It was in, by 2ft at least. But this was before goal-line technology, and after the goalkeeper Ádám Bogdán clawed it away the referee waved play on. We ended up losing 2–1 to a late goal, and the contentious nature of the defeat made it feel like a big moment in deciding who would go down. We replaced Bolton in the relegation zone and had a stack of tough fixtures to come, starting with our next game, at home to Liverpool.

QPR 3, Liverpool 2 is a match that has gone down as one of QPR's most iconic games, but it was one of the worst I've ever played. I was horrendous, absolutely horrendous. People still want to talk about it and watch it back, but it's one of only a few games in my career I'd happily scrub from the internet. I'd like to strike it from my mind completely, and that's such a shame because I should be able to enjoy that feeling of Jamie Mackie's injury-time winner and the memory of the noise that accompanied it. We had been 2–0 down with thirteen minutes to go.

What I can still appreciate is that it gave us a springboard, particularly at home, for the rest of the season. We followed it up by winning all four of our remaining games at Loftus Road, including against both Arsenal and Spurs. Those victories were vital because our away form was just as consistent: defeat after defeat for the rest of the season. The most important win was the last one, against Stoke. If we lost that we'd go into the last match in the relegation zone, needing both to win and to hope other results went our way. It was intense, but Djibril Cissé, who had been signed five days after me on transfer deadline day in January, scored a goal in the eighty-ninth minute that would keep QPR in the Premier League. We won 1–0, and our fate remained in our hands. It was massive, and we heavily celebrated the win. It's rarely talked about because of what happened next, but it was exactly what happened next that proved how essential it was.

Next was our final game of the season, at Manchester City.

• • •

I had a lot to think about on the train to Manchester from London. The win over Stoke had given us momentum, but our safety had by no means been secured. We were seventeenth in the Premier League, one place above the bottom three, with Bolton two points behind. A late goal in Bolton's previous match had helped us as much as ours against Stoke, and now the bare minimum was they had to win their final game – ironically against Stoke. If they did and we lost at Manchester City, we'd be relegated, but at least for us there was more than one way to survive. This did not help my nerves. At times I can lean towards pessimism, and that day I was travelling up to a game that could go wrong for me both professionally and personally. I was going back to play my old club for the first time; I could be relegated by people I used to call my peers in front of a crowd who used to support me and a manager I despised. I was adamant that was going to happen, as I was convinced it would send me lower that I'd ever been. It would be pure everything going wrong.

I never thought I'd play at the Etihad wearing different colours, that I'd arrive and turn right instead of left, into the away dressing room. I didn't even know what it looked like. That had always been for 'them'. Now, I was 'them'. It was all I could think about in the days leading up to the game. I'd train hard, and then afterwards my mind would be on nothing else. On that train up to Manchester, I was more nervous than I'd ever been before in my whole career.

The rest of the journey was weird too. I was travelling for an away game, at home. I was to be playing against people I knew in an environment I knew, so I had to keep reminding myself I'd be in the away team. On a normal game day, I never paid attention to my surroundings when we were making our way to the stadium from the hotel, but I noticed all the familiar landmarks as we went over the Mancunian Way flyover towards Ancoats and onto Ashton New Road. I'm home. No, I'm not, I'm away. I'm away! The whole thing was confused further when we reached the stadium. In theory, I entered as the enemy, but every face was a person happy to see me, and me them. On security, at the front desk, each member of staff said hello with a wide smile. Even the City players. It felt like a homecoming, and yet I was wearing the colours of a different team. I even got a tiny clap from the City fans who were already in the stadium when I went out for the warm-up. The whole club was in high spirits; they would win their first ever Premier League title if they beat a team seventeenth in the table. It seemed likely. We hadn't won away from home in nearly six months; theirs was the best home record in the league. City were also bang in form; they'd clawed back an eight-point deficit on Manchester United in just five games, winning each of them to set up what was expected to be an inevitable, and smooth, coronation. During the warm-up, I went through the same routine I always had at that stadium. I picked out my mum in the crowd, though this time she was at the opposite end, part of the away support in the south stand. Lucy and some friends were also amongst the QPR fans, and I waved at them all apprehensively. Then the game started. Here we go. It was absolutely terrifying.

On any other occasion, I would have appreciated the nerves that started to develop amongst the crowd as Manchester United took the lead in their game at Sunderland and our match remained goal-less. There would have been plenty of Blues who leant in to the 'typical City' trope, one that presumed failure, predicted the worst. Being on the verge of a league title was, at the time, a unique pressure for them. After the adrenaline of the opening few minutes had faded, the songs started to die out and the anxiety levels grew. Still, that nervousness disappeared almost entirely six minutes before half-time, when

Pablo Zabaleta gave City the lead. You could see how much it alleviated the tension in the way they celebrated. Had it been 0–0 at the break, the atmosphere would have been very different, but now they were ahead against a team who'd not made them defend that much. They were probably thinking they'd just have to accept that the win might not be as beautiful as the occasion warranted. There was no reason for them to think otherwise.

Our dressing room was a lot less relaxed. Bolton had also scored six minutes before half-time, but then again just before the break, and were 2–1 up at Stoke. If things stayed as they were, we would be relegated. Mark Hughes knew we had to change plan and attack a bit more. These were to be the last forty-five minutes of the season, and we resolved not to leave anything out there. Just try to compete, because unless something happened we were going down. We had to take it to them, but we didn't have control of the match so we just shifted a little higher up the pitch, so as not to leave ourselves too vulnerable. City would tear us apart if we gave them the chance. It was one hell of a fifteen minutes to try to figure things out, with so much on the line. It had an impact in three minutes: Djibril Cissé took advantage of a mistake by Joleon Lescott to equalise. Everything changed. City were no longer winning the league, and because of our superior goal difference Bolton would be relegated, even if they won. Djibril wouldn't have been in a position to pounce if we hadn't changed our mentality at half-time; he'd have been stuck 10 or 15 yards deeper.

Then the new approach bore further fruit: Armand Traoré, attacking much more from left back, crossed to another player who'd been asked to play higher up the pitch, Jamie Mackie, to give us a 2–1 lead. There were just under twenty-five minutes to go. I didn't know how to celebrate the goals, unsure of how it would look as a former City player. I tried to be respectful. I remembered I had been irritated when Paul Dickov had once scored for Leicester against City and did a whole knee slide. I'd thought he was the worst. But knowing him as I do now, I understand why he did it. He thought it important to celebrate his personal achievement, and he's right, but at the time I didn't appreciate that. All I did was a quiet fist bump while congratulating the scorers each time. Just a tiny little fist bump.

Nobody would have predicted that QPR would have a 2–1 lead at Manchester City. None of us knew what to do next. We couldn't carry on playing on the front foot; we had too much to hold on to. So, we dropped off, and that's when it started to get a bit crazy. What followed was around twenty minutes of the worst football City had played that season. Their structure, their style of play, everything that defined who they were and how successful they'd been went out the window. We'd stopped offering anything going forward, so it became attack against defence, and the attack wasn't doing a very good job. So much so that had it been a training ground exercise, it would probably have been stopped by an unhappy coach. And boy, was the coach unhappy. I was playing right back and spent the second half on the side of the two dugouts watching Roberto Mancini lose the plot. It's tough for a team that is trying to score against one that's set itself up in a block, where there's no space to pass into. You try to do a one-two with a teammate when the person you're supposed to play around just stays where they are! So, the City team was taking turns shooting from distance, completely disregarding all those passing drills Mancini had spent endless hours attempting to perfect on the training pitch. He was furious, swearing at his players, unleashing the kind of personal attacks I'd heard myself before. Insults were flying everywhere, with Mancini telling his team that they were letting him down. But this was the problem with his way of doing things, with trying to dictate every last passage of play. He didn't have enough of an appreciation that there was another team involved and that they would have a say in the events of the game too. And here was a QPR team full of desire, and desperation, and a set of circumstances that meant it's not a normal game of football. It was a battle, and there were not going to be any forty-pass moves to provide the perfect goal. Our commitment was to try everything we could to stay up; the City players seemed to understand that, but the manager didn't.

Mancini was losing his mind until the ninety-second minute, which is the point at which I started to think I might lose mine. Edin Džeko had come on as a substitute, and it was my job to mark him at set-pieces. City had a corner, which David Silva swung in from the right-hand side. Edin was fresher and got the leap on me. There's still a picture at the stadium of him scoring the equaliser with me underneath him, getting dunked on. It was 2–2, and I felt responsible. Everybody knows that someone's to blame when the opposition gets a goal from a corner, and my man had scored. It was my fault. The clock was on our side and a draw was enough, but I couldn't shake that weight off my shoulders. City now only needed one goal to win the title, their first for forty-four years.

The crowd was re-energised, ready for one big push. Around a minute after Džeko's goal, Samir Nasri let the ball go out of play, thinking it would be a throw-in for City.

It wasn't.

A real momentum-sapper. Seconds were drifting away.

The throw-in was on my side, so I would be taking it, but the ball had gone out around 20 yards further up the pitch from where I was standing.

I could have walked.

Every other player in the world would have done. I also wasn't on a yellow card, so perhaps should have taken the risk. But something stopped me from deliberately time-wasting.

That thought of Paul Dickov again.

I'd promised when I saw him winding up his former club's supporters that I wouldn't ever do that.

Never. It's not me.

I could have taken thirty seconds to go and get the ball, but I was scared of being booed by City fans, so I did something just a bit quicker than a walk: a little canter. It's so dumb, but that's who I was at the time. I was coming to terms with a whole new part of my life, and each day I was away from City, trying to figure out who I was. I was completely unsure of how to behave when playing against them for the first time.

So, I cantered.

I didn't dwell for long once I'd reached the ball either. I motioned for Jay Bothroyd to take up a position down the line, and I threw it in his direction. He got blocked off and then didn't press the City player who picked it up, which was fair enough considering how defensively we were playing. But now we were on the back foot again. City had possession, and I had given it to them.

Another mistake.

Sometimes the player who's responsible for their team conceding isn't the one who's closest to the scorer or standing nearest the goal. You know if it's you. I could have walked, but I cantered, and now City were coming straight at us. I ran back into position, but the ball never came down my side again. I couldn't affect anything as I helplessly watched the attack develop, from Nigel de Jong's pass forward, to Mario Balotelli's sliding through-ball.

To *someone* scoring a goal.

QPR players all around me fell to the floor, thinking we were relegated.

I put my hands on my head, thinking I was responsible.

Engulfing us was one of the loudest noises I'd ever heard. I dragged my head up, looked around me and everyone was celebrating.

Everyone.

The far end from where I was standing, lit by bright sunshine, was dancing as one. My mum, wife and friends were amongst them, part of a mass of bodies in which you couldn't tell who supported who. I turned to the QPR bench, and they too were hugging and wheeling each other around. The moment we'd conceded a goal that we thought had sent us down, the full-time whistle was blown in a game that provided the result that kept us up.

At the Britannia Stadium, it had finished Stoke 2, Bolton 2.

The home side had equalised with thirteen minutes to go and had held on to prevent Bolton getting the goal that would have saved them. What became immediately clear to me was that I had just been responsible for the most irrelevant goal a team I played for had ever conceded. For Manchester City without doubt the most important, but for QPR and me meaningless. We would have been safe with or without it. As the ball went in, I thought I'd cost our team a place in the Premier League and I was the lowest of the low.

Seconds later, on top of the world.

Another few moments and the game was over. Had it lasted any longer I guarantee it would have been the worst football you've ever seen. Someone could have just rolled the ball into the centre circle and left it there while all the players sat on the grass and had a little kumbaya session together.

It was truly incredible to see a stadium where the joy is shared by everyone, but only the Manchester City fans piled onto the pitch at the final whistle. I'd always wondered whether it would happen, or if City had become a bit too serious to have a pitch invasion. You tended only to see them at lower league grounds, but this one was full-blown and showed how much it meant to the supporters. It brought me out of my bubble for a moment and allowed me to think of my former teammates and how pleased I was for them. I considered trying to find Joe Hart but quickly realised I would have to fight through hundreds of City fans to get to him. Some of them who were barging past realised it was me and stopped.

'We've done it! We've done it!' they screamed at me.

'Yes, we have!' I replied. 'We've stayed up!'

There were opened beers in the dressing room as we returned. No jumping around, just a huge sense of relief. Then, after a while, an invitation was extended for us to join City in their dressing room, and Shaun Wright-Phillips encouraged me to accept it so we could go and congratulate them. It was a chance to see the difference between staying in the Premier League and winning it. We had beer; they had champagne, and it was sprayed liberally all around. I was particularly ecstatic for Joe Hart, who's a really good friend, and also Joleon Lescott and Micah Richards. And I was happy for all the players, because even though my feelings for Roberto Mancini were extreme, I'm pretty sure there were others who, although they might have been playing, felt a similar way. Whether it was because of Mancini or in spite of him, what that team did was work exceptionally hard for each other.

They'd won the Premier League in an insane way, but they deserved it. Nothing had been easy for them that season. I knew because I'd been there for half of it. I'd watched them through pre-season, training and games, and if people ask me now about the best players I've worked with, a lot of them would come from that era. Not just because of their talent on the field but because of their personalities off it. That's why there was no jealousy on my part. I hadn't been part of it, I didn't feel like I'd won a league title, but I did feel privileged that I'd seen two contrasting halves of a Premier League season. Five months with a team fighting at the top, five months with one escaping the drop – and I'd seen the time, effort and stress that goes into both. The outcomes we were both celebrating also meant I avoided being the answer to a pub-quiz question: name a player who played for a team that won the Premier League and was also relegated from the Premier League in the same season. Well, not me, thankfully.

• • •

Once I'd seen my old teammates in their dressing room, I didn't hang around. Six weeks of time off had begun, and I wanted to get home. My teammates would have to wait for the bus to take them to the station, but luckily for me, home was only about a fifteen-minute drive away, so I rushed out of the stadium. I'd always tried to avoid the traffic if I could, and here was a unique opportunity to do so again. 40,000 people who would normally be flooding out at the final whistle were still inside, waiting for their team to receive the Premier League trophy. The problem was, the QPR fans were being kept in too, and amongst them was my lift home. After the presentation, the City supporters starting piling out.

'We've done it! We've done it!'

'Yes, we have. We've stayed up.'

Drunk on joy (or something else), I genuinely think some of them thought I was still a City player. A measure of how recently I'd left, perhaps, but they appeared to be including me in their 'we'. No, mate, I'd think to myself, I don't know if you noticed but for ninety minutes I was just doing the opposite of what you wanted. By that point, I just wanted to start my holiday. Lucy was eventually able to get out and take us all home. My immediate intention was to eat as much food as humanly possible, and late afternoon that Sunday I began to do exactly that in the sunshine of our back garden. Somebody had given me a QPR T-shirt which said 'Keep Calm, We Are Staying Up'. I put it on and my feet up. Thank goodness it was all over. I was home, and the sun was out. It was time to have some fun.

•   •   •

Two days and an extraordinary amount of food later, I turned on Sky Sports News. The goal that won Manchester City the Premier League was being played, complete with Martin Tyler's famous commentary.

'Aguerooooooooooo…!'

It was the first time I knew who had scored. I hadn't seen it, or him wheeling away spinning his shirt above his head. In my mind, it had just been *someone*.

'Oh,' I thought. 'How about that? Sergio scored.'

I must have been the last person on Planet Earth to know, when I'd been fewer than 10 yards away.

Chapter 14

Amid all the delirium in the QPR dressing room that day, there was one person missing. Part of the relief we experienced was because from the tenth minute of the second half onwards, we'd been playing with ten men. The score was 1–1 at the time, enough to keep us in the Premier League. As Carlos Tevez tried to make a run behind me into our penalty area, Joey Barton elbowed him in the head. As I turned around to get back into position, I saw Tevez go down. I hadn't seen the contact and nor had Mike Dean the referee, but the linesman had. Joey was sent off, a straight red card. But he wasn't done. As he walked away from the melee of players surrounding Dean, he kicked Sergio Aguero in the back of the leg. Now a new group were pleading with the referee on behalf of their QPR teammate. I wasn't one of them, because he'd been my teammate before and I knew what he was capable of.

Joey Barton was part of the generation at the Manchester City Academy that sat between me and Shaun Wright-Phillips. Shaun was the pin-up who had preceded him, and Joey's story was very different. He was the underdog. He worked impressively hard and had to take risks to win a contract at City. That then set him on a path taking the opportunities that dedication offered. His belief was that you can achieve anything if you're single-minded, because after not being as highly fancied at the academy his endeavour had got his foot in the door. He would revel in his role as the 100 per cent hard worker, accepting nothing less, but it led to a sense of entitlement when it came to his place in the team. Unlike Shaun, Joey was never great with those younger than him coming through from the academy, particularly if they played in his position. Marc Laird and Stevie Ireland, both midfielders, were bullied by Joey. He kicked them in training all the time, trying to establish himself as the alpha and prove they were of lesser standing. He knew who to target and always backed out of arguments with people he couldn't physically dominate – I would have been quite happy if he'd try to mix it with me, for example. Nobody who may have been kicked by him ever kicked him back, because Joey wouldn't start it with somebody who might. And if they did, it got very ugly.

At City's Christmas party in Manchester in 2004, Jamie Tandy fought back. It was my first party having broken through to the first team, and the theme was fancy dress. Joey came as Jimmy Savile (this was before Savile became the centre of the child-abuse scandal); Jamie was dressed as a sailor. For reasons that remain unclear but at the very most I imagine would have amounted to 'banter', Joey tried to burn Jamie's costume. Light it on fire. Later that night, Jamie tried to do the same to Joey. Joey was good at giving it out but not taking it, so he took the cigar that was part of his Savile outfit and put it out on Jamie's eyelid. Joey was fined six weeks' wages, while Jamie, who was twenty at the time, left City the following summer. He hadn't started it and he certainly didn't finish it, but Jamie Tandy came off worse from the whole encounter, both in terms of his career and physically – he lost sight in the eye for a time and is still scarred.

Joey is two years older than Jamie and both were midfielders, but age wasn't a barrier to Joey escalating a situation in the most violent way with someone in his position. Ousmane Dabo joined Manchester City in 2006 and was one of the nicest men going. He wouldn't hurt a fly, but Joey repeatedly hurt him. For the whole of his first season at the club, Joey would kick him in training. Literally every day, because Ousmane played in his position. He was a lot older, but Joey deemed him to be weaker, and by now he'd risen to being a regular starter under Stuart Pearce, so he had capital to spend. And spend it he would, regularly. The manager not only turned a blind eye to Joey's behaviour but allowed himself to be manipulated by it too. Joey and I were both in the team for a Premier League match against Aston Villa in late April 2007, and at half-time we were 1–0 down. Joey had missed a penalty, but it was something else he'd been doing in the first half that caught my eye. He kept on going over to talk to Stuart Pearce on the touchline. Once would have been fair enough, but he did it a few times. Then when we got into the dressing room, Stuart told me I was being taken off. I was confused, as while the team hadn't played well I wasn't the worst out there, and certainly not worse than Joey. Then I remembered the frequent conversations. I was convinced Joey had repeatedly suggested I should be substituted and Stuart had caved. 'Psycho' appeared to have let a 24-year-old member of his team dictate a tactical switch. The following Tuesday I had it confirmed by Joey himself, who came over to me at the beginning of the training session to say sorry.

Too late, I thought.

Get stuffed, I told him.

At that moment I decided that the way he'd treated me meant that from then on it would be a working relationship only between us, and I wouldn't engage with him on any other level. I don't know if my rejection of his apology put him in a bad mood, but at the end of that session he did something horrific. After yet another day of being kicked, Ousmane Dabo had had enough. He fouled him back. Joey took against this immediately, although initially only verbally. Then, as we walked off the training pitch there was a verbal altercation that made me turn around just in time to see Joey running up to Ousmane from behind. He threw a punch that landed on the side of Ousmane's head. Blindsided him. Ousmane was stunned and fell to the floor. Joey wasn't done. He grabbed hold of Ousmane's head and carried on hitting him. Over and over again, now in the face, until he was almost unconscious. As appalling as this was, not everyone was outraged. Some of the players even stood by Joey's side as the attack was taking place. That was the influence he had. After a whole season of being kicked, Ousmane kicking back just once tipped Joey over the edge, and like Jamie Tandy he now had serious injuries to his eye, as well as to his nose and lip. He pressed charges and Joey eventually pled guilty to assault, which resulted in a four-month suspended prison sentence.

Joey is one of probably only four or five players I've come across who once they've become angry during a game have lashed out with real intent then and there. Usually if you're triggered, you wait until you're in the tunnel, away from the cameras and prying eyes. The majority of fights on a football pitch aren't genuine; they're performances that are as fake as WWE wrestling. A skirmish between players is about the most token thing you'll see during a game – an outlet for built-up frustration and little more. I've been guilty of getting into the referee's face if I'm irritated, or squaring up to another player, but it wasn't real for me because I knew nothing was going to happen. The referee's not going to change his mind, and I wasn't really going to fight my opponent. If it escalates to the extent there's any physical contact, it's pushing and shoving and very rarely anything like a real punch, mainly because almost all footballers aren't very good at punching. Plus, there'll always be several players trying to break it up and pull the aggressors away from each other. It makes the melee appear far worse than it is, and in most instances it's a performative act for the fans. There are occasions when it's authentic – standing up for a teammate, for example, is the right thing to do – but the majority involved in so-called fights know they'll be thought of as 'showing passion'. Still, to my eye often it appears to be a pretty pathetic attempt to do so. But if somebody chases down an opponent and starts kicking them on the pitch, that's a reflection of that player's personality and how they potentially have a screw loose.

Considering the ban Joey Barton served following the Jamie Tandy incident and another eight-match suspension following a fight with Richard Dunne and a teenage Everton fan during a pre-season trip to Thailand, after he assaulted Ousmane Dabo he was told not to play for the rest of that season. There were two games left. Not sacked, not immediately sold. There was a sense despite all these issues that the club should stick with one of its own, an academy product who had beaten the odds to make the team. Apparently beating up his own teammates wasn't enough to change that. It was a narrative that influenced the fans, and one Joey was happy to perpetuate.

In December 2006, Joey was sent off against Bolton. We'd had a game plan which he'd selfishly decided to sack off, and we were losing 2–0 late on. With three minutes to go he went on a long run, and just as he got inside the penalty area he lost the ball to Abdoulaye Faye. He should have then put the defender under pressure, pressing him towards the corner in an attempt to win the ball back, but instead Joey jumped at him in a really aggressive manner, diving in miles away from the ball. After receiving a straight red card, instead of heading down the tunnel he sat on the advertising boards next to the pitch, receiving the applause of the crowd. I remember thinking, he's broken away from the plan and made things worse for his team, and yet he's managed to make himself the hero of the piece. He had always been cast as a fighter, but fighting in all these ways suggested he'd lost sight of the original reason. He was determined, yes, but he was leaning so much on the need for self-confidence that he became cocooned in his own version of events, convinced that his opinion was the only valid view. He would look down on people who weren't matching his actions and couldn't conceive of people wanting to do things in a different manner. Joey thought kicking someone in training was a necessary part of illustrating club standards, of showing the way things needed to be done to succeed. If he was right, he would have raised the game of more players than he did. But instead, he often had the opposite effect.

One away game at Newcastle in 2005, Stuart Pearce wanted to bring Stevie Ireland on to play in the No. 10 role, as we were 1–0 down and needed a goal. As soon as Stevie ran onto the pitch, Joey went over and told him he was going to play as a 10; Stevie could be an 8, just behind him. Joey said he'd win the game for us. He didn't. We lost 1–0. But he had assumed the kind of power that allowed him to make executive decisions about what he and other teammates did. It was partly down to his own sense of self-regard but also because of the permissive nature of Stuart Pearce's relationship with him. Joey made the wrong decision that day, but he wasn't called out for it after the game.

The Dabo attack should have been enough on its own, but instead it acted as the final straw. Perhaps it was the fact the police were involved or maybe because Stuart Pearce was sacked at the end of that season, but Joey was sold to Newcastle. He needed to leave because of the things he'd done, but it was also necessary for the rest of the squad finally to be able to be themselves. Stevie Ireland might have had a better start to his career if he wasn't shackled by Joey's treatment of him, and Michael Johnson's opportunities were enhanced by Joey moving on just before he broke through to the first team. Joey lasted as long as he did at Manchester City because of who the manager was, and I don't believe it would have happened under Sven-Göran Eriksson or Mark Hughes. And Roberto Mancini didn't like a misplaced pass within his team, so he certainly wouldn't have put up with what Stuart Pearce did.

But the other reason Joey stayed until the summer of 2007 is that he was a good player. Sometimes people bully because of insecurities buried deep down, but Joey was the opposite of insecure. He knew he was decent enough to stay in the City team, and just before he left he'd been called up, on merit, to the

England squad. He genuinely believes he's better than others because he doesn't understand their value, and for him to like you, you have to earn his trust. The only problem is, in order to do that you have to think exactly how he does, and I didn't like that. I preferred to be welcoming to everybody in a team, and we had very different opinions on how to approach things. He had friends within the squad, and I was happy to compliment him if he played well, but his personality was not for me. We were re-acquainted when I joined QPR, and he had changed slightly, but he was just a different version of what I'd known at City. Foundationally he was the same person, and still if you weren't on board with his thought process, he could turn hostile.

After we got promoted back to the Premier League in 2014, Harry Redknapp decided he wanted to play a 3–4–3 formation for the season, with two defensive midfielders, or 6s. Joey just said flatly, to the manager in front of all the players, that it wasn't going to work. So, he sabotaged it for three weeks straight. He was adamant that the shape would only work with one 6, because he'd seen Chile play that way at the World Cup, and he made that decision because it was what he personally believed, but it affected everyone. We never got a chance to find out if it would have been successful, because Joey thought his voice was more important than the manager's. Harry Redknapp was no Stuart Pearce, but as Joey was more established at the club in that moment he felt his personality was bigger than his boss's, and he was good at selling that story to those in the dressing room and the stands.

Another time, he simply wouldn't join in with the strength and conditioning sessions each Tuesday, proclaiming it was the kind of work you just didn't need in football. Instead, he would just go out on the training pitch and smash a few balls into the net.

'This is all you need for S&C!' he'd say, while the rest of us watched him, baffled.

I've no idea where he got that from, but because it was his opinion he thought it was the only one worth considering. He was the only person volleying a load of goals while everyone else was in the gym, but he didn't mind. He thought himself 100 per cent right, even if 99 per cent of people saw it differently.

What he didn't realise was the effect he was having on his teammates. He once described two Chilean players at QPR as 'bad eggs' to the rest of the squad. They were good guys who simply weren't playing that well at the time, but Joey was blissfully unaware of the irony that he was the only one making people feel unwelcome. He wasn't great for the collective even though he believed he was, and sometimes a team's accomplishment came despite him rather than because of him. He said in his autobiography that the only reason QPR got promoted in 2014 was because he brought in a sports psychologist, which changed everything. How is that tangible? That same season we were playing a five-a-side round-robin tournament in training on Thursdays, one that had a very different vibe to Sven's at Manchester City, as the setting was much more informal. There were four teams, and Joey was on mine along with Adel Taarabt. Adel had a shot at goal during one match against a team including Bobby Zamora, who stopped it on the line with his hand. He was not the goalkeeper, so obviously it was against the rules, but given the context Bobby was just having a bit of a joke. Joey protested and insisted that we should have a penalty. It was duly given; Adel took it and missed. Joey stormed off the field claiming the whole thing was a disgrace and that Bobby should have been sent off. Following his tantrum, we had to finish the last five minutes of the game a man down, and we lost. The punishment was a long run that none of us wanted to do, but as the rest of the team set off Joey sat to the side, still trying to find people to complain to. Harry Redknapp didn't do anything about his grievances, and he certainly didn't make Joey join us in the run. Then, just before the game on the following Saturday, Joey as captain was delivering a team talk. He started telling us how we're all a band of brothers and should stick together. As soon as he'd finished speaking, we all looked around at each other thinking, this guy! At times like this, we could never take him as seriously as he took himself.

He's spent his adult life talking up his abilities and attempting to crush those who either doubted him or tried to get in his way. He is not, as I think he genuinely believes, one of the best players to ever play the game. He was a capable footballer, but given the value he placed on himself, can he say he was the defining reason for success at any of his clubs? Is his greatest achievement his one England cap, or perhaps finishing eighth in the Premier League, which he did at City with me? For all the tough mentality, the hard work that won him a career and his subsequent conviction in his own ability, is the return on that a reputation as one of the greatest midfielders the Premier League has ever seen? No. He's just another player, like 80 per cent of the rest of us. What set him apart was not his talent but his behaviour. He was a bully. A bully with a tendency towards both physical and mental aggression, but one who could play football. Too many people let the former go because of the latter. And until he was put in his place, that wasn't going to change.

• • •

Joey has spent the years since that red card at the Etihad in May 2012 trying to explain why he elbowed Carlos Tevez and kicked Sergio Aguero. He claims, like with Ousmane Dabo, that it wasn't him who started it. It was Tevez who lashed out at him first. Aguero was complaining about him to the referee, and Joey wasn't having it. Apparently, he was trying to even things up after being sent off. It was for the team. None of this was evident or offered up as an excuse at the time. He was not remorseful about significantly increasing our chances of being relegated that day and went straight to sit on the bus, from where I've since heard he complained about the fact the rest of the QPR team were celebrating finishing seventeenth in the Premier League. To that I'd say, how could you not apologise? How could you do that to your team, consider yourself free from blame and, worse, display so much self-righteousness? Also, we were happy about staying up, not our position. Remaining in the Premier League is the prize for many of those seventeen teams that do each year, but for some of my teammates that was the highest they'd ever been in the football pyramid, and they'd guaranteed the chance to play at Old Trafford, Anfield and all the other grounds for another year. Why not celebrate that?

It's fine for Joey to have his own perspective on it. Maybe he didn't want to celebrate, but when he joined QPR they weren't eighth in the table looking to finish in the top six. They were in the Premier League and the goal was to stay up, and yet Joey put that in serious jeopardy for no legitimate reason. Seriously, why? That's all I could think with fifty-five minutes gone at the Etihad. He was one of our best players, and he'd decided to let his team down comprehensively at the time it mattered most. So why wasn't I one of those surrounding the referee, protesting his innocence in the way I would have for almost anyone else? It's because it was Joey Barton. That's why.

Chapter 15

Having survived in 2012, QPR immediately started taking a series of steps that meant they wouldn't a year later. Six months before I'd joined the club, Malaysian businessman Tony Fernandes had become the majority shareholder. He's a nice guy whose heart is in the right place, and he really wanted the club to do well. He bought into us and made us feel great, and he was certainly more visible than any of the owners I'd known up to that point in my career. At Manchester City I'd seen Sheikh Mansour once and felt like if I blinked wrong I'd be let go. Tony was a much more constant presence, both in person and on social media. Somewhere in between might have been better for me. I find the more frequently a person of authority speaks, the less weight it carries. Tony would communicate directly with fans on Twitter, and especially when the team wasn't doing very well. I didn't love that, because I'd rather not read critiques of the players from the owner's social media accounts. He's eased off as time has gone on, perhaps regretting how revealing he was, particularly because of how many eyes were already on us at that moment.

I preferred to go under the radar as a player, but for QPR that was never possible because of the list of famous names that had invested in the club and how that had increased exposure and expectation. Tony had bought out former Formula One boss Bernie Ecclestone's share in 2011, while in 2007 QPR was by some measure the richest club in the world, with a 20 per cent stake owned by then fifth wealthiest man on earth Lakshmi Mittal. Our west London rivals Chelsea were the previous holders of that title, and Manchester City next after QPR. But in the Premier League that kind of attention makes people root against you. When things go wrong there is little sympathy, and QPR weren't doing many things right at that time. Tony engaging so readily with people online added fuel to the fire.

Tony Fernandes had made his money owning the very successful airline company AirAsia. So, it was no surprise that our pre-season tour in 2012 was to Malaysia and Thailand. It was a great opportunity to visit part of the world I'd never been to before, but in terms of preparing for the new season it was one of the worst possible trips. It seemed like there were more AirAsia flights than training sessions, and sometimes there'd be both on the same day. There must have been at least twelve flights in two weeks. I understand how it was important for a club like QPR to go on a PR drive in an important market, and one our owner knew very well, but we didn't get very much work done. We also didn't lose a game that pre-season, which considering how we started the season proper shows how little those results can sometimes mean.

That summer there was also huge turnover in the squad. Sixteen players left, and the club signed twelve to replace them. This was the beginning of what proved to be a flawed strategy.

I'd come from a club that had gone through a similar process of trying to grow after an influx of investment, and while Manchester City's owners spent a lot of money on players, they made it clear that this needed to be combined with an upgrade to the club's infrastructure. Now, City are almost unrecognisable from top to bottom. QPR just became unrecognisable on the field. There's little structural evidence that the club ever spent time in the Premier League. Despite Mark Hughes's attempts to improve the QPR training ground aesthetically as much as he could, all the club's money was being spent on the workforce. Goalkeeper Júlio César came from Inter Milan, Esteban Granero from Real Madrid and José Bosingwa from Chelsea, where he'd just won the Champions League. Bosingwa and César were two of quite a few free transfers, so they would have been on high wages. Coming so close to being relegated the season before, and the desire both to secure itself in the Premier League and to improve its standing amongst rivals in west London, the club was prompted to buy into the idea that it had to go for it. It's easy to say in hindsight that perhaps a more conservative approach, to build incrementally, might have been better, but QPR felt it was the right moment to pursue that strategy.

For almost every club, the market dictates the timing of transfers, and it relies on nobody knowing what's going to happen in six months' or a year's time. These were good players, ones who might be unavailable or too expensive in the future. The difficulty in this approach is that it can create a divide between those who are freshly arriving at a club and those who are already there. The huge turnover meant that by the time I'd been at QPR for eighteen months, I was one of the players who'd been there the longest! To be successful, a new signing needs to make an effort to gain understanding of what, and who, the club they're joining represents. The fan base, the area, the rivalries, the history. Not many would be in a position to find that out before arriving, and I wouldn't expect them to either, so it comes with commitment and time. I got the impression some of those QPR signed in 2012/13, while being talented players and good guys, didn't prioritise those things. A lot of players before and after them would have done the same thing: found a foothold in the Premier League, used it as a stepping stone to a bigger club while being paid better than they would be elsewhere, in a city they liked.

I'd never got it as a Mancunian, but there's a big desire to be in London, especially for some foreign players. Not every one of them was going to be signed by Chelsea or Arsenal, so there was a pool for the likes of QPR to dip in to. But in doing so, the club was more likely to find players who were incompatible with what QPR needed. They wanted sustainability and success, but the players were thinking about money and location. That's probably why they didn't show new signings the training ground, either! Seriously, though, if a player comes from Inter, Real or Chelsea and sees Harlington, they immediately start to think they're missing out on something compared to what they've experienced before and might like to again in the future.

Esteban Granero, I must say, was not like that. Despite coming from Real Madrid (and only staying for a season), he never seemed that fussed about money. I don't think a lot of the others would have signed for QPR if they'd been offered lower wages, though. As a result they were emotionally disengaged, and when things start to go bad they weren't quite as motivated to put them right. Stéphane Mbia, who'd signed on transfer deadline day as part of a deal that sent Joey Barton on loan to Marseille, tweeted Joey that season to ask if they could swap back. Stéphane was funny, but he completely misread the room at a time when we were struggling, and it did not go down well. José Bosingwa was already on the back foot with the fans, having been a Chelsea player, so the moment he started to display even a hint of apathy about his new club's plight, he got it in the neck. We did go through periods when we produced some good football and everyone was on board, but when things were on fire some players knew the mess wouldn't stick to them, because they were just at QPR for the short term. It was easy for them to leave because of who they were and who might want them. They could come to QPR, struggle, and yet it wouldn't change their trajectory. Those of us who felt differently had a sense of being bailed on when our backs were against the wall.

I knew I was there for the long haul. With the team still in the Premier League I had no intention of leaving, and so Lucy and I made plans to settle in London. When we moved down originally, we'd got a six-month lease on a place in Richmond, and when that ran out in August we bought a house. I was in, this was my commitment. I was determined to try to be successful at QPR, and in September we moved to Claygate, a few miles south-west of London, into a house that was big enough to start a family. We were all-in. I had decided QPR was my future.

• • •

The momentum of our final-day escape hadn't swayed the bookmakers, because we were amongst the favourites to go down again as the new season started. And it started very badly, with a 5–0 defeat at home to Swansea. It was still very early, and there were plenty of opportunities for us to make it right, but let's say there were a few alarm bells. Winning your first game doesn't necessarily set the tone for the whole campaign, but it does get the monkey off your back. The pressure from outside eventually starts to bleed into the club and the team, with the losses counting up and up. We still haven't won, we still haven't won. Six, seven, eight games. Some performances were good, some indifferent, only a few were bad, but we didn't win any of our opening sixteen Premier League fixtures. That's almost half a season. Our dramatic survival was supposed to help us kick on, but we were going backwards, and it cost the manager his job.

Mark Hughes was sacked while I was on compassionate leave following the death of my mother. Despite several tweets suggesting he wouldn't, Tony Fernandes made the change after a defeat to Southampton. The next day, two things happened. Harry Redknapp was appointed as the new boss, and QPR played a game at Manchester United, so I was able to make a short visit to the hotel to say hello to the team. I was in the midst of organising my mum's funeral, so it was clear I wouldn't be available for a while yet. Less than a week later, Harry called me.

'I'm thinking about playing you at Wigan next Saturday, can you come back to train this week? I need you to be ready.'

I didn't know what to do. We were about to lay my mum to rest, but I was still scarred by being unavailable at the start of Roberto Mancini's time at Manchester City. I didn't want to get off on the wrong foot with another manager. I needed to go back.

'OK... I'll do it.'

The funeral was on the Friday. I returned to work on the following Monday. The distraction of the daily sessions helped me a little, and I trained well enough through to the end of the week. We travelled to the hotel in Wigan, and on the morning of the game Harry puts up the starting eleven. I'm not in it. Then the subs are announced. I'm not one of those, either. Harry Redknapp had made me leave my family forty-eight hours after my mother's funeral to go back down south because he was considering playing me but had then left me out of the whole squad. It is the lowest I've ever felt in my life. The train journey to Wigan had given me a chance to get my mind right, to come to terms with the fact this was the moment I'd have to restart everything without my mum alongside me. And then he left me out. What was he doing? What was the purpose of it? The Mancini situation had been reversed. Now, my new boss was getting off on the worst foot with me.

For someone known as a great man-manager, Harry couldn't have given a more contradictory first impression. The feeling at QPR was that bringing him to the club was something of a coup, given his reputation in the game and the fact he'd been linked with the England job only a few months previously. Away from the cameras it was clear Harry didn't share that positivity. He was gloomy, and when things didn't go well in training – sessions he'd rarely, if ever, lead himself – you could see him shaking his head and kicking the ground, almost as if he was embarrassed by his team. We were on a catastrophic losing run; surely the great motivator would be trying to gee up his players, inspiring them to get out of the situation? But he cut a miserable figure, the opposite to what we'd been told to expect. The week after that Wigan game he did pick me, and we won for the first time that season. Helpfully for the mood around the club, it was against Fulham. It took us off the bottom of the table for the first time in a month, but we'd soon be back there despite a second win against our other local rivals Chelsea. Those are big games in west London, and we hoped the wins would be a springboard, but there were to be only two more in the league that season.

I didn't play in either, because it was during a six-week period when Harry Redknapp was ignoring me. We'd been knocked out of the FA Cup in January, and that meant we had a free weekend the following month, when those left in the competition were playing their fifth-round ties. Given the weather in England in February, the club decided to take the team out to Dubai for a week of training. With the prospect of his players burning the candle at both ends, Harry had a rule: no drinking. He hated it and made sure we knew this was a non-negotiable while we were away. That was no stress for me as I don't drink anyway, and when the rest of the team snuck out past curfew they didn't demand I go out with them. I also wasn't going to stop them. However, at training the next day a few players were still drunk. Not hungover; drunk. One in particular had a horrendous time, probably the worst training session I've seen anybody have. And Harry knew why. Even though they knew it was a bugbear of his, some of his players had been drinking. He was furious but took it out on the wrong person. Me.

'Don't have a go at me, I've not done anything wrong!' I shouted back.

Harry started to criticise me personally, insisting it was my fault that the session was compromised. It took a lot for me to challenge him, but I was exasperated.

'Why are you trying to blame me for this?' I said. 'I'm just doing my job.'

From that moment until the beginning of April, he didn't

speak to me. For a month and a half we'd pass each other in the corridor and he wouldn't say anything. We'd be in a lift together and he'd ignore me. Not a word for six weeks. There were four games in that time, and each time I was a substitute he never called on. Prior to that I'd played ninety minutes in all but three Premier League games under Harry. Now, he was giving me the silent treatment based on a completely false accusation. Even more than that, I would have been on Harry's side in Dubai. It's not like I benefited from how those players behaved. If you want to go and drink, go and drink, whatever. But maybe don't do it if it affects your work and others around you. I was embarrassed by the training session.

I don't like the taste of alcohol, so I just don't bother with it. I'm lucky I was a player in the modern era, because as a non-drinker I might not have fared so well in times gone by. Things are different now in football, particularly at the highest level. There's more scrutiny on what players do. When I was first coming through it might have been normal to see footballers out after a game, but modern professionals can't be seen to be doing that. They are one Instagram story or tweet away from their squeaky-clean image going down the pan, whereas in the last century footballers being drinkers *was* their brand. Players now realise they have to be marketable, some globally, and they fear the consequences of having that undermined. It means that if there's any drinking it's most likely to happen at a team party, where players don't have to be quite so cautious. Even managers used to encourage it within their squads as a way of generating team spirit. That may well still happen further down the football pyramid, but my experience is that there is no longer a 'drinking culture' in elite English football.

Although I was treated differently on nights out, I was never fully an outsider. Perhaps I didn't get invited out as regularly as others, but that doesn't really matter to me. I'd never want anyone to feel guilty about drinking around me, and if I'm having a good time I can last until three in the morning. I'll enjoy myself just as much, plus I'll remember it and have a free car-ride home too. Some people have said, look at you, you're such a pro, you're a saint! It's nothing to do with that. I eat chocolate. I eat biscuits. I'll eat two packs of chocolate digestives in ten minutes. That is not the done thing from a professional standpoint. It's not that I take my job more seriously, it's simpler than that. You might not like chocolate digestives; I don't like alcohol.

I was initially a bit surprised that Harry Redknapp wasn't one of those managers who thought drinking was a useful team-building tool. In fact, he was the only one I worked with who was 100 per cent against it. He didn't even want his players to drink socially or in moderation. Some managers will understand the reach of their powers and encourage their team to be careful, but Harry was all-in on his No. 1 rule. He was more bothered about players drinking than being late for training every day. That's why I was so angry when he misjudged my character, and I became even more so with his punishment. Had he frozen me out because he still thought I broke the rules in Dubai or because I'd answered him back when he picked on me? I am not a disruptive person, and yet I was living the Mancini nightmare all over again. Everyone around me knew who I was, so why did the man in power seem so oblivious? Making me the bad guy when there were clearly people who'd violated his rules was one thing, but I didn't see the field until the second Fulham game that season, on 1 April.

I'd been available the whole time, but it took us being 2–0 down after just over twenty minutes at the home of our rivals for Harry Redknapp to break his long silence.

'Nedum. Go and get warm. I need you.'

After six weeks of not uttering a word to me, that's what he said. He'd left me on the bench for four games, ignored me like a jilted teenager, and now he needed me. I couldn't believe the nerve of the man. He expected me to dutifully respond to his request after how he'd treated me, because it was what *he* needed. A personal plea to help him in a time of need. Man-manager and motivator he was not.

•   •   •

What Harry Redknapp is good at is recruitment. He was engaging enough with prospective new signings to make them want to come and play for him. Four players came in during the January transfer window in 2013: Loïc Rémy, Christopher Samba and Jermaine Jenas all cost a bit of money, while Andros Townsend joined on loan. There was a bit of a bump in our form, but only in terms of avoiding defeats with draws. Those two wins in March – against Southampton and Sunderland – would be our last. The next match after Sunderland was away at Aston Villa, providing the first defeat of seven from our last nine games and the death of any momentum we'd built up. We were 1–0 up and playing well but conceded just before half-time and eventually lost 3–2. It felt like the balloon had been fully deflated. Any suggestion of cohesion vanished and was replaced by hostility.

It got to the point that Harry's three assistants took twenty minutes of a training session each, but they'd contradict each other. It was an absolute shambles, all of them telling us different things because they weren't getting on. Harry's message wasn't particularly nuanced either. He had a reputation for at least wanting to play good football, but that had long been shelved in favour of whatever might help the team win.

'Get it to Bobby! Get it to Bobby!' was the constant cry from the touchline when one of his defenders had the ball.

Lump it up to Bobby Zamora, and then try to come underneath him to pick up the second ball. That was the tactic. It meant some players started to lose interest, and that led to fans calling them out, in turn making them even less bothered. It got really sour for José Bosingwa, who was responsible for that mood-killing equaliser at Aston Villa and in December had refused to sit on the bench after being dropped from the first team. Supporters were chucking dogs' abuse at him at the final home game of the season, although he didn't care. Stéphane Mbia was a little hurt, though, when he received the same treatment after saying more than once that he wanted to leave the club. But conflict between players and fans, especially when one of the players isn't concerned what the fans think, doesn't put the rest of the team in the best position.

The wheels had well and truly fallen off, and fittingly the season ended with a whimper. A goal-less draw at Reading at the end of April relegated both teams. One of us needed to win to maintain a chance of staying up, and live on TV we both failed. We lost the remaining three games after that and finished bottom of the table, fourteen points from safety. The postmortems all made reference to our start to the season, those sixteen games without a win. We had started with a sense of optimism that we were a progressive football club with money to spend and new players to excite the fans. It goes to show the Premier League is far too competitive just to reward teams that have recruited player X or Y. We had an identity that was too mixed, with people like Clint Hill, Shaun Derry and Jamie Mackie alongside Stéphane Mbia and José Bosingwa. Two sets of players expecting two different outcomes: one fresh from a relegation battle and prepared to fight another one; the other brought in to make the club upwardly mobile. When you're winning it's easy to find common ground, but when you're losing, and consistently, that kind of a squad becomes fractured. The ideas for how to turn things around are too diverse, and the divide grows. For some players, showing character and personality in adversity is to get on the ball, take it under pressure and make the right decisions, playing their way out of trouble. But others might think the exact same qualities are displayed through simplicity and taking no chances. They won't worry about playing out from the back; to them it's about winning headers, second balls, each player's duel with their opponent. It's about getting it to Bobby.

Each approach is great if everybody does it, but when it's half and half it's of no value whatsoever. A player looks for a pass and won't find one; another comes short and has the ball passed over their shoulder. As a consequence, QPR had no identity, and, worst of all, there was no leadership from the manager. The extreme situation forced players to revert to what came naturally, and there was no guidance, no deciding which of the survival methods we should adopt. It was a complete mess.

Perhaps Harry Redknapp always knew he had the insurance of the first half of the season not being his responsibility, and I don't blame him for thinking that. He wasn't the manager, they weren't his results, he may well not have wanted the players either. I appreciate it would have been a difficult environment for him to come into, and it became even more toxic, but he was supposed to be a motivator. It turned out he had the opposite effect on lots of people, myself included, because he was nothing like the cheery manager we were told to expect by others who had worked with him and his profile in the media. And that's why Harry was an impostor. He created a narrative that meant any success was his, but none of the blame. If he had lost his job then, there would have been people saying it was unfair. It'd be the players at fault, the recruitment, the previous manager – even though he's been sacked enough times throughout his career to suggest it can't always be that. This was a guy we had been excited about. He was going to cultivate the workforce and inspire us into becoming a great team. Instead, he seemed to hate being at QPR. An image of him during training, literally a couple of weeks after he'd taken charge, with his hands in his pockets and head bowed, will stick with me for ever. He was kicking the ground as if it was a loose piece of gravel in a prison yard, and being our manager was his sentence.

Chapter 16

'**D**on't worry, we'll get you out. You'll get a move.'

It was my agent on the phone. It was the run-in, and QPR were struggling. Relegation felt more inevitable with each passing weekend. He'd called a number of times with the same message.

'You don't want to play in the Championship, so we'll sort something out.'

I'd been with the Stellar Agency since it became clear my future lay away from Manchester City, and my mum had selected one of their senior agents to work with her in securing a move. She had always taken the lead on all my contract negotiations and the loan deal with Sunderland, but she'd never found me a new club before. I'm sure she could have done it alone, but after shopping the market she landed on the agent from Stellar. She trusted him, and he was certainly charismatic; she felt he had the right connections to get a deal over the line and find the best future for me. It was a very rare error of judgement on her part. I never fully got on with him, and it was the summer after QPR were relegated that I decided I didn't want to entrust any more of my career to his agency. On 4 August 2013, another call: 'Nedum, I'm not going to be able to get you a move.' The tune had changed completely. 'I know how the market works, and for centre backs there's not really a chance that anything will happen.'

That's weird, I thought. The transfer window is open for nearly another month, so why are you telling me this now? I understood that I wasn't an agent and perhaps shouldn't question the assurances of somebody more knowledgeable than me, but nevertheless I was disappointed. I hadn't asked to leave QPR, but I still felt like a Premier League player and assumed there'd be at least some level of demand for those young enough to retain future value. QPR might have wanted to sell me anyway. Either way, there was an expectation in my mind that I would move on. I hadn't joined the club to play in the Championship, and not to disrespect it, but it wasn't a division I was interested in experiencing. Had I been, potential loan moves as a much younger player could have given me a taste of the second tier, but I was lucky to start my career at the top level, so why wouldn't I choose to stay there for as long as possible?

Now I was being told the market was preventing that from happening, when the market was open for another three weeks or more. This is why it had been a mistake joining a big agency. Those companies representing the most famous players don't tend to be the best agents for a lot of their other clients. It turns out Stellar had decided there wasn't a demand for me because they had prioritised the other centre backs on their books. If they've got ten of them and there aren't ten opportunities, it's almost like they have to pit us against each other. I think two centre backs represented by Stellar moved that summer, so the market wasn't dead, they just made the choice of who those two were based on their judgement and not necessarily on the person who most wanted to go or was the best fit for the interested club. That judgement is based on money.

Most of the conversations I'd had with my agent were about money, which immediately created a conflict as that wasn't what motivated me. It so happened that 4 August was the day they received their commission for my original move to QPR, and while they may not have been related it seems a little too coincidental. I realised that to them I was a figure on a balance sheet, not a human being with ambitions. They were happy if I brought them value, and they didn't need to move me to make money.

There was no binding contract with Stellar, my mum had made sure of that, so I ditched them and went back to my first agent, Peter Morrison. I've known Peter since I was a sixteen-year-old playing at the City academy. As soon as we went full-time, the vultures immediately started circling, walking along the touch-line during games, speaking to the parents about whether their kids had representation yet. Peter, on behalf of his agency run by Peter Harrison, was one of those to throw his hat into the ring for me. He's only five years older than me, so he held a junior role in the company and that's part of the reason my mum thought he'd be best. This one she got absolutely right. Either officially or unofficially, Peter represented me for my whole career, and when we each got married we were the other's best man. He understands what drives me as a person. I think that's the goal for most football players: to have somebody who both represents them and looks out for their best interests above just transfers and contracts. They'll protect you from nonsense and big you up when others might not, because you're more than just a number on a balance sheet. When Stellar wanted me to join QPR, Peter had recommended a move to Everton even though it would have made me, and therefore him, less money. He knew it would have been a better decision for what I wanted at the time. He tried to chase the best move, not the biggest figure. If you get the right sort of relationship with an agent, they won't bother about squeezing as much as possible out of it financially, because they understand they're providing a service. Others might be doing themselves a service while pretending it's for the player.

I think my mum chose Stellar for the QPR move because she felt that Peter's junior position within his agency had started to work against him. It proved to be a mistake, but for whatever reason that's what she thought at the time. Still, leaving Stellar was easy. There's no one I trust more than Peter. He's a good guy with good intentions. On a night out when we were younger, Peter would be blind drunk and I'd be stone-cold sober, but we'd still get along. He cares for me and my family, and we've always respected each other, even when we've disagreed. If I turned down some of his advice he'd try to understand, and if he thought I was wrong he'd try to teach me why. We've always talked about more than football, and I could reach out to speak to him about things that lay beyond the professional realm. From the very beginning he was a mentor, guiding me through the transition from academy to first team, going above and beyond his role as an agent. He was, and remains, one of my best friends.

I choose the word 'remains' deliberately. In February 2016, Peter went quiet for a few days. Eventually, he raised his head and told me he'd been involved in a car crash. He'd lost control in bad weather on a motorway and hit two Highways England officers who'd been at the side of the road. One had died. The other survived but was paralysed from the chest down. Peter was distraught about what had happened, and we both knew that what he'd done was unequivocally bad, but he insisted to me that he didn't expect or deserve to go to prison. Deserving is very subjective in any case, even in a court of law. During his trial it emerged that earlier in the journey he'd been texting while driving, with the last message sent a minute and a half before he swerved off the road. He'd also been speeding. However, at the time of the accident he was doing neither, and from what I understand the traffic officers were at that location because earlier in the day there was a similar incident of a car slipping in the wet and windy conditions. Those mitigating circumstances were enough for me not to be angry with him, given that I and many others have been guilty of going a little above the speed limit or looking at our phones while driving, but they weren't enough in court. Peter pleaded guilty to causing death by careless driving but denied death by dangerous driving. Nevertheless, he was found guilty of the more serious charge and was given a seven-year jail sentence. That was extended to nine years after an appeal was lodged claiming the original sentence was too lenient.

I felt bad for him, but I felt worse for the victims. It meant I couldn't openly support him during the case, as it would have been disrespectful to the family of Adam Gibb, who died, and to Paul Holroyd, who was paralysed. They objectively deserved to have some level of justice. But the reason it was never a test of our friendship is because, given the facts as I understand them, I was happy to back Peter to his face and advocate on his behalf in private. If he had been texting or speeding at the time he lost control, if that was the reason for the crash, I think he knows I would go after him. He did make mistakes along that journey, and it made me want to look him in the eye and shout at him, but to call him out for that would make me a hypocrite. I've been lucky that, like millions of others, I've not been caught out; he was, and it happened on the same trip that a man lost his life and another his mobility. I believe Peter has gone behind bars as punishment for those two things together, even though in my opinion they happened separately. Although I don't agree with the severity of the sentence, I do understand the point of view of the victims and their families.

So, Peter remains one of my best friends, but there were plenty of people who deserted him. As soon as word started going around about what had happened, certain players were quick to jump ship. The industry is so poisonous that there would have been agents seizing on the situation to nudge Peter's clients to leave him and join them, claiming it was justified. They tried it with me, but along with others, including the company for which he works, I trust and believe in him. It was an easy decision for me. He's still my guy, and the job he had will still be waiting for him when he comes back.

• • •

Having been told by Stellar that my future lay at QPR, my mentality switched to starting the new season in the Championship. I will say to the bitter end that wherever I was, whatever the situation, I was committed. For the pre-season that followed, I needed to be. It was another tough one. The reserves were one day ahead of us in the training programme and had their session just before we took to the field, so each time we went in for training we could see what was coming our way the next day. If we thought it was hard, all we had to do was look over to the other pitch, where each day it was getting harder and harder for the reserves. There was a lot of running. The first week we might as well have been track stars. Even the second, which at least involved a ball, there was still so much running. Then, after we'd been to play two games in Austria, pre-season changed completely.

Harry Redknapp needed knee surgery, and to cover some of the period he was incapacitated he added former England manager Steve McClaren to his coaching staff. We barely saw Harry for the next few weeks, and while he was away Steve was basically in charge. I'm sure Harry was involved in passing on instructions from afar, but Steve spent the rest of pre-season focusing on getting us to play. And it worked; we won all but two of the league games he was at the club for, with some of the best football I've ever been a part of. We had a great defensive record, but at the same time we were completing 600 passes each game. I thought Steve was very good and explained things well. He also had a completely different attitude with his players.

We lost to Swindon in the League Cup, by which time Harry was back from his surgery, and I was responsible for one of their goals. I'd been playing out from the back, as requested, but I'd made a mistake to allow them to seal the win with a second goal in injury time. Back in the dressing room, two contrasting reactions: Harry was very angry about the goal, while Steve, although he wasn't happy, accepted how it came about because I was following instructions and showing the right intent. He understood it would sometimes go wrong if defenders tried to take the ball out from the back, and instead of criticising me to the extent I feared attempting it again, he left me feeling encouraged that I was doing the correct thing. It was that approach that allowed the team to feel free in those first few weeks, because for Steve it was all about the style of play. It helped us start the season very well, which veteran watchers of the Championship will tell you is vital. Without traction at the start, it's almost inevitable you'll fall short. Steve left at the end of September 2013 to manage Derby, who we'd see in the final match of our season. In the time between him leaving and QPR qualifying for the playoffs we had a couple of rocky patches and ended up hanging on a bit, but we eventually got to face Derby partly because of the start that team's new manager had given us.

What Harry Redknapp had given us was a stacked squad. After relegation there was a feeling the club needed to reset in some ways, and there was another overhaul in the playing staff. Nine came in, eighteen went out (including one retirement), and Harry reshaped the team for the Championship. This was his greatest skill. It was sensible to offload the likes of Loïc Rémy, Park Ji-Sung, José Bosingwa and Stéphane Mbia, and their replacements were just what the club needed. The defence and midfield were shored up with Danny Simpson, Karl Henry and Gary O'Neil, while up top Charlie Austin came in from Burnley, to be supplied by loan signings Tom Carroll and Niko Kranjčar. I was also reunited with two of my former teammates, with Richard Dunne signing from Aston Villa and Joey Barton returning from his loan at Marseille.

Those deals inspired two contrasting emotions. Richard's signing was one of the biggest coups of the whole season, and he proved it right up until the final game. Joey coming back, I found a little less inspirational. He had spent most of his year in

France being very vocal on social media about how badly QPR were doing. He really didn't like Mark Hughes, wasn't having him even 1 per cent, so barraged him with negative tweets. How much better we would have been with him in the team I don't know, but all the while we were plunging towards relegation, his stock was rising, simply because he wasn't associated with our struggles. Now that Harry was the manager, Joey had a clean slate and decided he was in for a penny, in for a pound. Harry saw fit to return the captain's armband to him, even though the last time he'd worn it he'd kicked Sergio Aguero. Joey, though, remained a good player, and in midfield with Karl and Niko, behind Bobby Zamora and Charlie and ahead of Richard, Danny and Clint Hill, he was one of the many senior players QPR could call on for the Championship battle.

I landed the first blow of that battle. We beat Sheffield Wednesday 2–1 at Loftus Road on the opening day of the season, and I scored the equaliser five minutes before half-time, flicking in Junior Hoilett's shot. Funnily enough, I also got the first goal of QPR's season in 2016. It came in the fourth minute against Leeds, rather than the fortieth, but when you don't score that many it sticks in your mind! That's also not to suggest I found the Championship easier, but it did provide a different challenge, and that first match against Sheffield Wednesday showed me that straight away. I was used to seeing everything through the eyes of a Premier League player taking on Premier League teams. That affects your decision-making, particularly when you're in possession. The opposition at the top level are very good at luring you into traps by giving the impression there's space to make a pass and then stealing the ball away when you attempt to play it into the gap. I went into my first ever match in the Championship with this cautiousness built into my game. I'd spotted a teammate beyond the opposition striker, some 5 yards further up the pitch. He was open, but I thought it must be a ploy. I tried it, nonetheless, and put my head down to pass the ball, half expecting that when I looked up the striker would have nabbed it and I'd be back defending again. But he hadn't. In fact, once the ball had gone past him to my teammate, it was obvious the striker hadn't even known there was a player in the space behind him. Very quickly I learned that while there are good players in the Championship, it's those little details that prevent the majority of them making it to the Premier League.

Later in the season, in a game we were leading, we were hit on the break. Their counter-attack ended with the striker only needing to tap in at the back post, but he ballooned it over the bar. Having spent the previous eighteen months fighting at the bottom of the Premier League and being punished by clinical players, suddenly it felt like I might get more leeway. Perhaps strikers in the Championship don't score with every chance and defenders might not concede every time they make a mistake.

The kind of defending you do is also different in the Championship, particularly at centre back. In the Premier League there are tons of games in which you don't really have that many one-on-one battles with strikers. Some teams don't even put one up against you directly, and with the fluidity a lot of them have, goals tend to come from a more varied source anyway. A division below, even though the players might not be quite as good, I spent more time defending against them. There were more crosses and throw-ins coming into the box, and usually at least one striker trying to break through the middle. I was engaging in individual battles all the time, because tactically it's more direct and physically it's more combative. There's less reluctance to spin a ball down the channel or hit it long for a flick-on. I was heading balls endlessly, in open play and set-pieces, and sometimes I'd have to make more clearances than passes.

That was the job in the Championship, where you'd get eaten alive if you didn't stand up and be counted, but it made it no less enjoyable. For me, defending is about the end more than the means. I wanted to go into a game making it as hard as possible for whoever I was up against. In the Premier League, that might have required me to read the game well; I had to be alert for ninety minutes, knowing exactly where those dinky No. 10s were as they tried to exploit little pockets of space. In the Championship, I might have had to run the channels more, and it was more physically demanding. I relish both challenges and like that the art of defending is so varied; I don't mind which route gets me to the goal of stopping my opponents from scoring one. Even in training I liked upsetting the strikers on my own team. They'd be frustrated when they played against me because I wouldn't give them anything. The more times I got in their way, the more their heads would go down. I really enjoyed it when that happened in games; some strikers just want to have their way, but I'd always say, 'Nah, not today.'

At the other end of the pitch, I loved having players who I knew could score at any point. There was an expectation rather than a hope that we would get at least a goal in every game, and that adds value to what defenders do as well. There's true purpose to throwing yourself in the way of a shot, putting your body on the line, if it keeps the scoreline goal-less and you're pretty sure Charlie Austin is going to score at some point. We won by the odd goal sixteen times in that first season in the Championship, including twice, crucially, in the playoffs. Just in the first two months with Steve McClaren as the head honcho, there were four 1–0 victories in a row. So even though we had the best players in the division and we were really controlling games, defending was key.

The Championship is so competitive, and a lot of people prefer it because it is a purer version of the game: a battle between two teams for three points, where there might be some nice football to watch but it's less likely to be tactical. I've always been happy to play the ball out from the back and enjoyed the fact that Steve McClaren encouraged it in those early weeks, but if I'm not in possession, give me someone to stop and I'm all the happier for it. When Steve left for Derby, Harry initially attempted to keep the changes he'd made, but soon enough he was content to embrace the more chaotic nature of the Championship. It was understandable, as our good start had made way for the kind of inconsistency that makes the division so unpredictable. If you don't fall prey to that tradition, you'll fly. In the second half of the season, Leicester City went on an unbeaten run of twenty league games, and it was demoralising to look at our phones after each match to find they'd won, again and again. Burnley weren't dropping many points in second place either, so it got to a point where we just had to make sure we stayed in the playoff places. There were enough teams threatening our position in the top six that it wasn't about style of play but staying in the hunt.

The January transfer window saw Harry bring in more players on loan, and by the time it closed we had eight temporary signings, even though we were only allowed five in any match-day squad. They were reinforcements for the new goal: getting to the Premier League, by whatever means necessary. It was about winning, and Harry was at the forefront of that. It was not a place for the nice football and principles that Steve McClaren had instilled, even though that's how he'd helped his Derby team to improve considerably, to the extent they were also heading for the playoffs.

They finished third, five points above QPR, and scored more goals than any other team in the Championship. But because we were fourth, our playoff semi-final was against fifth-placed Wigan. The end-of-season tournament involving four teams fighting for one Premier League place is another reason fans find the division so enticing. Like them, I'd watched the play-offs over the years and enjoyed them. Now I was about to be in them for the first time, it felt like one hell of a lottery. If we made it through our semi-final there wouldn't just be the riches of the top flight on the line, it would also provide the first trip to Wembley of my career. We also knew that if we failed, we'd be forced to have the shortest off-season in the history of foot-ball. The playoff final is usually the final weekend of May, and Championship clubs start their pre-season towards the end of June. It only amounts to around three weeks of holiday and is genuinely a reason why some teams don't mind missing out on the playoffs. The belief can be that if you don't finish top two, don't limp into the top six. Second is the same as seventh if you want any certainty of what's happening next season and when it's going to start.

For QPR, though, one year removed from relegation, there

was more than just the longer break to fight for. It was for us, as it has been for so many others, close to being a financial imperative that we go back up as soon as possible. The reason for that – a loaded squad with high-quality, relatively highly paid players – was the same reason I felt we were good enough to be promoted, even though our form hadn't been great going into that first game against Wigan. Perhaps unsurprisingly, we weren't brilliant at the DW Stadium, in a 0–0 draw.

It was all to play for in the second leg at Loftus Road, which produced one of the most memorable nights of my life. We arrived on the bus to what appeared to be thousands of fans waiting outside. That flare-lit ride into the stadium was the stuff footballers' dreams are made of. It felt awesome. The atmosphere was bolstered further when we went a goal down. The crowd's reaction was incredible as they willed us to get back into the game. We did, in an improved second half during which Bobby Zamora came on and made a huge difference. He played one of the best games I've ever seen him have, bullying Wigan's centre back Rob Kiernan, absolutely destroying him. The QPR supporters sensed what I could, as this was one of the few times I've been on the field knowing we were going to win even though we weren't leading at the time. I loved having players in my team who I knew could get a goal, and I was pretty sure Charlie Austin was going to score at some point. He did, in extra time, to send us to the final. It was him who had equalised from the penalty spot too. Moments later I did something I'd only seen on TV before. Something I couldn't ever have imagined doing and which only added to what the fans had already made an outstanding evening. I was on the pitch, holding a banner that said, 'We're going to Wembley!'

• • •

The horrendous, gut-wrenching feeling I'd had for less than thirty seconds at the Etihad in May 2012 returned for more than thirty minutes in May 2014 at Wembley. We were playing Derby, who Steve McClaren had taken from fourteenth to the playoff final. The kind of football he'd asked of us, he was now getting from his new team, who were the better side for large parts of the game. With sixty minutes on the clock, I gave the ball away, and Johnny Russell was through on the edge of the penalty area. Gary O'Neil decided being a man down was better than being a goal down, and he fouled Russell. He was shown a straight red card, and I hung my head. The thought of having cost my team hovered over me for the rest of the game, and again it involved a possible place in the Premier League. At least two years prior it immediately hadn't mattered. This time, I was bailed out as late as the eighty-ninth minute by two players who hadn't been universally popular with QPR fans and yet who took the club to the Premier League.

It was a miracle we had anyone forward, because with ten men we'd been under huge pressure, but Junior Hoilett tackled Jake Buxton down in the corner and crossed into the box. Then, another Derby mistake: Richard Keogh miscontrolled the ball. Bobby pounced. He'd been the recipient of some unfair criticism after he joined QPR in January of the season we'd been relegated. He was never fully fit, blighted by a really bad hip injury, but he had still put himself out there to try to help the team. It's the kind of thing I think people should get credit for, but instead fans got on him because he wasn't performing to his best. From a character standpoint, I'd rather have players who are 50 per cent and want to be there than 100 per cent and don't. That's why he and Junior are two of my guys.

My view was stunning. Around 40 yards away, I was looking directly at the goal, behind which the QPR supporters had filled half of Wembley. As Bobby hit the ball with his left foot into the left-hand side of the goal, almost every person I could see jumped up. It was late, and likely undeserved, but so, so important. I sprinted to the corner to celebrate, going particularly nuts because it felt so special that the goal had been provided by two of the people I was closest to in that team. It was 1–0 with one minute of normal time to go, plus any injury time. We had to shut up shop. Derby had spent the whole game slicing us open, but their desperation played into our hands. Suddenly they had to abandon the football that suited them and resort to what suited us. With the clock running down, they couldn't play it out from the back; instead it was all down the channel and long balls into the box. Since the turn of the year, that had been our game. That had been my game. That had been Harry's game. The final five minutes were in some ways less stressful than the previous thirty, and I was happy to head away from danger as many balls as they were willing to send my way. Richard Dunne was at centre back alongside me and put in one of the most impressive performances I'd ever witnessed. He had needed to partly because of the circumstances I'd helped create. Just like May 2012 it had been my fault, and just like May 2012 I had got away with it.

When the final whistle sounded, I was one of the furthest away from Bobby Zamora, but I was the first to reach him. We didn't hug, I hugged him. I was so relieved: I hadn't cost the team, and he had got us promoted. It was the first time in my career I realised the value of the Premier League; we'd had to play forty-nine games to get back there again, to be a feature game on Sky Sports, to be part of the conversation on *Match of the Day*. I understood how you had to earn the right to play in the Premier League, at Old Trafford, at Anfield, at all the other grounds. You can start your career in the top flight if you're lucky enough to be at one of those twenty clubs, but for everyone else in the footballing pyramid it's the pinnacle to which you aspire. That season I'd seen what it takes to get there: the running in pre-season; replacing the style of the first half of the season with the grit of the second; playing the last half an hour of the playoff final with ten men. Just ask Derby. They fell just short that day, and they haven't been in the Premier League since. As I jumped on Bobby and the Derby players fell to the ground, two things occurred to me. The first was that my knee hurt; it had swollen significantly after being battered and bruised for ten months straight. The second was that it was 100 per cent worth it, because there was another banner on the pitch for me to hold. It said, 'We Are Going Up!'

Chapter 17

Amaia Onuoha was conceived in pre-season and born during the run-in of the 2013/14 season. A footballer's family planning. I was an excited and engaged father-to-be from the moment I found out Lucy was pregnant. We marked each week with a little celebration, and I read up on the baby's size at every stage. What I hadn't prepared for was the speed of the birth. On 6 April 2014, Lucy complained of having a sore back, and only four or five hours later she had brought a child into the world. Six days after that I scored against Nottingham Forest in a 5–2 win, celebrating with a thumb in my mouth to mark the occasion. By the end of April, I was named QPR's player of the month, all after very little sleep.

Real life matters more to me than football. My mum's passing had confirmed this, and Amaia arriving drove it home. The final six years of my career, I didn't hang on to so much emotionally, because as soon as I stepped through the door at home my daughter had no idea what I'd been through and cared even less. The life-and-death feeling around my job died a little bit as we brought a life into the world, and father came before footballer.

If I had to be awake to do night feeds instead of getting the requisite ten hours of sleep before a game, I'd do it. I was tired, but I adjusted, and I don't believe it's any coincidence I played some of my best football in the final two months of that season, when I was having the least sleep of my life. Being with my daughter at any time of day or night was more important, and it made me happier than resting in the other room with earplugs in. It's definitely true that the game can be a lot easier if you feel good and everything's settled at home.

I became a dad for the first time at twenty-seven, but that wasn't the catalyst for me becoming a more sensible person. I'd started preparing for retirement at twenty-five, when I joined QPR. The dressing room was, on average, older than any I'd been in before, with several players in their thirties. I remember once overhearing a conversation involving Bobby Zamora, Luke Young and Andy Johnson, in which two were complaining about their bad hips and the other a bad knee. You could tell they were fighting every single day to be able to perform to the best of their abilities, while also realising that level was nowhere near its peak. At the other end of the age spectrum, the talk was all about watches and cars; for Bobby, Luke and Andy it was about investments and property. The three of them wouldn't think about buying a watch; they would consider investing in a watch company. I recognised I should have the same approach, by now, in my mid-twenties, and so I got a financial adviser. It seems a bit premature, but before I reached what should be the best years of my career, I had cleared the debt in my houses and focused on building towards retirement. It meant I could start preparing for the rest of my life, about which I actually got more excited with each passing year. Amaia was a huge part of that then, as my other two children Teia and Ruben became later. I increasingly loved the thought of days off, because they would be spent with my family. Football is a great game and being a player is a great job, but you're never quite sure when it's going to end. You don't even always know how much you'll earn from it or what value people will place on you. When I was twenty-eight, the accepted peak of a player's career, my agent was in talks with Sam Allard-yce at West Ham. He told Peter I was already too old and signed 27-year-old Angelo Ogbonna instead.

Harry Redknapp was apparently also thinking about retire-ment. After the playoff final he said he didn't fancy another year in the Championship if we'd lost. It also didn't reflect well on the faith he had in his team that he went on to tell the media: 'With ten minutes to go I was thinking, "What golf club should I join this year – should I play here or there?" and then sud-denly Bobby ruined it all.' I didn't appreciate the joke and would suggest this is an example of many a true word being spoken in jest. We busted our collective guts to keep QPR in the game, so perhaps the manager should have been on the touchline think-ing about how best to help us win. He also annoyed me a little by bringing in two centre backs that summer. Rio Ferdinand joined on a free from Manchester United, while Steven Caulker was signed from Cardiff. It felt like every season in my career had started with my club buying new centre backs. Rio was part of a plan to play three at the back, so there was a place either side of him to fill, with Caulker, Clint Hill, Richard Dunne and myself all fighting for them. Having played at right back and in the middle, I thought I'd suit the position on the right of three centre backs, as I was just as comfortable dealing with threats in the centre as out wide. However, I got the impression about two thirds of the way through pre-season that I was not going to be in the team. Once again I had to lean on the conviction that if I didn't start the season, history showed I would often end it.

As it turned out, we played three at the back in the first two games of the season, and that was about it. Rio played only twelve times in total, with his availability affected in part by his first wife Rebecca's breast cancer diagnosis. By the end of November, I'd become a fairly regular starter in a back four, playing as much on the right as in the middle, but things weren't going well for the team. We'd been in the Premier League's bottom two for approaching two months, and I hadn't helped; five minutes into my first league start of the season at West Ham, I'd scored an own goal. I'd made it that far in my career without one, but a corner came off my knee about 4 yards out. So dumb. I'm annoyed I'm even mentioning it, because you can sometimes get away with it if you're not at a big club or if it's not the only goal of a game. Most own goals just hit you, so there's nothing you can do about them, and even though at the time it feels like everyone's watching you, I reckon most people I know have forgotten about it. And now I'm reminding them. So dumb.

It might be easier to recall our two games against Arsenal that season. In the first, on Boxing Day, their striker Olivier Giroud headbutted me. He was angry after he and I went for the same ball, which ended up going harmlessly beyond us both, and he stormed back towards me. He stuck his head into mine, and I dropped like a stone. He was shown a red card; I was hammered for my reaction in the post-match punditry. Obviously I shouldn't have gone down, but it was an instinctive reaction to being so surprised. I thought the only thing to do was to try to highlight that I'd been headbutted. The physical version of 'Hang on a minute, did you see that?!' It's like if an attacker's in the penalty area and a defender makes contact with them. If they don't go down, they're told they should have, but if they do, they did so too easily. It's a no-win situation. I almost immediately got straight back up to complain to the referee. I couldn't understand why he'd done it, and as it turned out nor could Olivier's teammates, who admitted to me afterwards that he'd let them down. Indeed, he apologised to me himself the next time we played Arsenal the following March, a match in which I genuinely hurt my head.

Steven Caulker and I both went up for a header together and clashed in the air. I felt a bit of pain but couldn't work out what had happened. People were freaking out around me, but I was adamant I could carry on. The physios looked at me like I was a psycho. It wasn't until I'd been taken off and into the dressing room that I realised a large flap of skin was hanging off my cheek under my left eye. It was quite a gash, and too big for the club doctor to close himself, so I had to get a friend to take me to hospital. The first one we went to was closed. At the second, I waited an hour before being told I needed a cosmetic surgeon to fix the wound. At around midnight, at a third hospital, I eventually had my face stitched up, by which time a picture my friend had taken of me at the stadium had come out. I'd sent it to Shaun Wright-Phillips by way of explaining my whereabouts, and he'd put it on Instagram. It had been a bad day, but at least my luck improved after that, because my scar is hidden beautifully by the shape of my cheekbone.

That happened a month and a day after Harry Redknapp left QPR. We'd won three games in the four weeks before Christmas 2014, but three defeats in a row in January had left us second from bottom. Harry officially resigned, blaming the need for knee-replacement surgery. There were also suggestions he was annoyed with the club's lack of activity in the transfer window, but I imagine he just jumped before he was pushed. He'd been there for more than two years and was facing a second relegation from the Premier League, but this time it was his team. There were no get-out-of-jail-free cards relating to the previous manager or players he hadn't signed or him coming in part-way through a season. He was fully responsible for a side that wasn't doing much better than two years previously, and that's why the extra scrutiny came his way. The squad wasn't as toxic as in 2013, but the mix still wasn't quite right. The players who had made the side so stacked in the Championship were of Premier League quality, but those who made up the rest of the squad, while being good enough to play for QPR, lacked the experience that helps you through tough times in the top flight. We had a good bunch of characters, and that's why we got promoted, but sometimes you have to understand the dark arts of football to be a winner, and that's how you survive.

My relationship with Harry Redknapp had improved enough for me to feel sympathy for him. His own appreciation of the job also appeared to have increased, as the turf-kicking, depressed figure of the beginning had been replaced by one more on board with the collective. That helped him understand his players and who he could trust, while we felt there wasn't so much separation between us and the coaching staff. He'd been at QPR long enough for the 'they' to become 'we', and he was engaged; the losses seemed to genuinely hurt him. And even though I'm not sure he fully knew me 100 per cent, he had at least been through a lot more with me and could see I was somebody he could believe in. Two years on from the false accusations in Dubai, he now knew I wasn't a disruptive player, and if he picked me for ninety minutes or brought me on for ten seconds, my intent to make an impact was always going to be the same. The way things had started it could have been an absolute catastrophe, but a relegation and a promotion together had established some trust between us. Mind you, until the very end he shaped his own narrative through the more charismatic interviews he gave to the media, who were sometimes a little too happy to go along with it.

Like Stuart Pearce putting a goalkeeper up front or Phil Brown giving his half-time team talk on the pitch, some managers seem to have at least half an eye on how the story will be told afterwards. These are, at their core, egotistical acts. But it works often enough for those managers to keep doing it. How the players are affected is not necessarily high up on the list of priorities. If the Hull team had performed brilliantly in the second half of that game at Manchester City on Boxing Day 2008, I guarantee the players would have felt their improvement was in spite of Phil Brown's public dressing down, not because of it. But that's not how the story would have been told. I get the impression he did it for the fans, and for the cameras, but most of all for Phil Brown. There are other examples of managers thinking these kinds of media-conscious displays bring out the best in players, but it only shows how little they know about their own team and the opposition. We footballers are very standard in our thought processes, and most of these quirky ideas serve no benefit long term, especially if the manager's gamble doesn't pay off. We don't want game-playing from managers looking to enhance their own storylines, we want honesty.

It's also true of words as well as actions. Roberto Mancini was completely different in front of the cameras than with the Manchester City players. It seemed to us like he was a media darling, wearing his scarf on the touchline and dropping jokes into press conferences. I can tell you he wasn't cracking any with us while we were grinding away in training. When footballers see headlines or quotes about ourselves, we often don't know the context or how the question was posed. We don't know if, like José Mourinho and Sir Alex Ferguson have done in the past, they've gone into a press conference with something to say regardless of what they're asked. In that case, I admit they might be helping us, trying to distract the media from a poor performance or protecting an individual who was responsible for a bad result. But if a manager is asked a question specifically about a player, he has a choice, and that's when I want him to be honest. If I objectively haven't done well, say so, and then commit to being better next week.

Don't do what Harry Redknapp used to do. He'd come into the dressing room after a defeat and be quite calm, saying it was a shame, but then he'd go out and hammer us in front of the media. We were criticised out in the open significantly more often than in private, and my perception was that he was trying to create distance between himself and the failures of his team. If ever something went wrong, it was the players' fault; if anything went right, it was due to him. He would rarely say the latter directly, but it was the result of a long-term strategy to mould the narrative in his favour. Players could very quickly just not be good enough – but when things improved, look how much he's getting out of those players he's only just reminded you are no good.

Twice now Harry Redknapp had been in charge of a QPR side struggling in the Premier League, with the extra pressure meaning all eyes were on us. If we lost, we'd plunge further into crisis, while winning would only be a plaster covering the mess beneath. Nothing positive could happen, and that's when you don't need your manager, the most regular spokesperson for your club, giving you more heat through the press. I understand it's tough to manage a group of people, particularly because there's often such a mix of nationalities, personalities and motivations, so perhaps that's why, for some, there's such a focus on self-preservation above all else. When things get tough, some managers become really laissez-faire. They're concentrating on getting their ducks in a row and all set for their next job. They indulge in a series of mini-manipulations to ensure their reputation isn't damaged too much by leaving a difficult situation. I've had times either leading up to a transfer window or towards the end of one when managers did things like deliberately not filling the allocation of subs for a game to make the point that the squad needs strengthening. It's the same when they make eleven changes for a League Cup game, which they then lose, leading to claims that the back-up players aren't good enough. But what you don't see is that those players – who are sometimes already on the outside of the team, unliked or untrusted by the manager – have been given one day of training to prepare for the match, when there'd normally be three or four. Then they're told they should have been good enough to win the game, when in fact they've just been used in a Machiavellian plot to try to get more money for new players, some of whom may well replace them. At no point would the manager have been honest with either the players or the media. It's building blocks for the bigger picture. Imagine if they'd said in the one training session: we're deliberately under-preparing for this match, because it doesn't matter.

Instead, when Harry Redknapp made eleven changes in this context and the team lost, he claimed the result was proof he had been right to ignore those players' pleas to get more game time.

'Some of you guys have been trying to knock on my door saying, "Why aren't I playing?"' he'd say. 'Well, look at that performance. That's your answer!'

I would be thinking, he literally set the team up to fail. No prep, eleven changes, different approach. He'd basically sent out eleven strangers trying to win a cup tie. It might have been a player's only chance to impress, and with defeat their season would be done, their confidence shattered. Even if the team had won against those odds, it's not likely a player would keep their place for the league at the weekend. That's not a great foundation for success in any game, so what did Harry expect? I came to realise what he expected through his media messaging, but I just wanted an honest boss. You tend to find out more about a manager's character when things aren't going well. They reveal whether they're in it for themselves or the team. The ones who think about the group can often find ways to lead their side out of a hole, while the others lose the faith of their players very quickly.

With that said, I wasn't angry that Harry left in what appeared to be an act of self-preservation. Whether it was indeed because of his knee or because he didn't get the players he wanted in the January transfer window, or even because he realised he couldn't provide the spark to ignite a change in fortunes for QPR – he'd decided it was time to go. He'd been managing for a long time, so who am I to begrudge an older man for calling it quits? We weren't good enough, and I think he sensed that.

• • •

Chris Ramsey, who'd been working in the QPR Academy, was asked to step in on a temporary basis when Harry Redknapp left. Two games and ten days later, he was given the job until the end of the season, partly because the second of those matches was at Sunderland and brought our first three points away from home. Chris came in and immediately read from the same first page of the new manager's manifesto: he told us we weren't fit enough. He worked alongside Les Ferdinand, the club's director of football, and they were both very demanding from the get-go as they attempted to deliver a new set of principles. Chris believed in coaching core skills, and each time we arrived for a training session there'd be ten balls on the side of the pitch, which he'd want us to pick up and start practising with. We'd get into pairs and do headers, volleys and chest control exercises. He'd brought those drills from the academy, so they were geared towards ten- to fourteen-year-olds, not senior professionals. Picture the scene each morning: pairing up with 34-year-old Bobby Zamora to practise techniques he'd first learned more than two decades earlier. We did it, though. That's the thing: we did it, out of respect to the new manager. We followed his instructions, but there was a sense he was treating adults like the children he was previously responsible for, and it meant we weren't ever fully engaged with the tasks he set.

These principles also appeared to be non-negotiable, and that's why we were relegated in such emphatic style. We went into the third last game of the season at Manchester City hanging by a thread, and I'd been suspended. I'd been sent off in the previous match at Liverpool, which, given the red card I got all those years before was rescinded, led to the first ban of my career. The first yellow card I got at Anfield was one I disagreed with; it was for pulling Martin Škrtel down in the box. The second I couldn't argue with. With Liverpool about to break on us after we'd lost possession, I took out Jordon Ibe. As the referee went to his pocket, Liverpool's Dejan Lovren sprinted over shouting that I was a disgrace and should be sent off. I had been happy to accept my fate, but Lovren got right under my skin. I was furious and thought about reacting. But that's where me and a certain teammate differed. I decided kicking an opponent wasn't the right move and walked off, remaining annoyed with Lovren and the first yellow card. I'd miss the next game, which just like in 2012 we went into with our Premier League status on the line.

Chris Ramsey was convinced the team should press Manchester City, and I watched as they dutifully did just that, and how it failed so spectacularly. As each goal went in, those who knew where I was sitting kept turning around to see my reaction. There's one, there's two. Three, four. We lost 6–0, but it could have been ten. Chris's principle was to press, but in practice you have to be a very good team to try that against City. We weren't, and they slaughtered us. It was horrible to witness, and it had a long-term effect on the players, setting the tone for how they viewed the manager. His determination to instil his values failed to give any consideration for the quality of both his team and the one they were playing. We had tried to go toe-to-toe with Manchester City at the Etihad, knowing that if we lost, we were down. Survival should have been the only principle.

I was better able to deal with relegation the second time, partly because I wasn't on the pitch when it happened but also because we knew we were done before that day at the Etihad. In a season like that you go from competing to existing before you go down mathematically. Your name on the Premier League table changes to red, and you start thinking of next season. It's such a tough league. Teams enter it with a sense of belief and desire and faith in their preparation, but you have to execute for such long periods of time to succeed. Some of those down the bottom aren't there because they're not working hard. They might be struggling to score or conceding too easily, but not every team is able to address their issues within the space of a season. QPR had good players, and we tried and tried to find inspiration, but it didn't work. Two years previously, we had been good enough to avoid relegation. There had been more quality, but no cohesion. In 2015, we got what we deserved based on who we were and how we played. It was a shame because we'd earned the right to be back in the Premier League only to fail again. It was less toxic than 2013, and the mix was slightly better, but all that did was increase the level of hope that was eventually dashed. So much was different, but the outcome was the same.

Chapter 18

As I walked off the pitch at Loftus Road on 13 September 2016, I knew. It was our second consecutive season in the Championship under our third manager in less than a year, and the game had finished QPR 0, Newcastle 6. It was the moment I accepted we were going to be stuck there for a while yet. There had been times in my career when my team was apocalyptically bad, but this wasn't one of them. Newcastle were just a lot better than us. A lot better, man for man. Maybe we should have kept them down to four, but in terms of taking the game to them we had no chance. That wasn't us. The realisation of who we were hit me: a team in mid-table trying to get a little bit higher, trying to avoid going a little bit lower. We weren't going to threaten either top six or bottom three. Newcastle were the team dreaming of promotion, and they went up as champions that season. We were nowhere near it, and I couldn't really get too angry.

That wasn't everybody's reaction.

'You're a terrible captain! You can't lead anything!'

One particular QPR fan hammered me relentlessly. Loftus Road could sometimes be the best place to play, but not always. I imagine I was being singled out because I was by now the team's skipper, the public face, the spokesperson – or the scapegoat. Chris Ramsey had made me captain after we were relegated in 2015, when it was clear the ambitions were going to be very different. He wanted somebody to lead a much younger team, which because of significant financial problems that led to a brief threat of not being allowed even to compete in the Championship, was likely to stay that way. The first time we were relegated the talk was of promotion; now it was of rebuilding. The recruitment strategy had changed completely from the early days under Tony Fernandes. While those contending for a place in the Premier League were spending £6 million or £7 million on players, we were shopping for bargains in Leagues One and Two.

It took a while for those new ambitions to filter through to the fans, who retained the same ambitions as two years previously and sent pelters my way. I once went up to that supporter who called me a terrible captain to say how much I disagreed with him. I was doing all I could to integrate new players and encourage them to follow the manager's message. If we'd been told to balance on our left legs for sixty minutes or run around doing 360-degree windmills, I'd do it and ask the rest of the players to do it too. The squad was one with in-built inconsistencies. We were average. Never too hot or too cold, and at least not getting battered 6–0 too often.

'We're doing our best. I'm trying. We're all trying. We're not quitting.'

It was all I could do. That angry fan might not have realised it, but I had: we would be stuck in the Championship for a while yet.

As well as being made captain, I signed a new contract in 2015. I had one year left on my original deal and agreed to restructure it so I was paid the same amount, but over the next three years. With Amaia now just over a year old, my priority was job security. The length of the contract mattered; the money did not. I was happy with where I was and for whom I was playing. There's an assumption that money trumps all for footballers, that if you're being paid well you can never be unhappy. That's absolutely not the case. I wouldn't ever want to be in a place only for business. If you can't call it home, you'll never stay for long, and it affects your commitment. I had been in the perfect situation at Manchester City, because I was home. There were plenty who joined the club and complained about the weather, but that was just a way of showing how uncomfortable they were changing their lifestyles – and I concede they may well have also come from somewhere where the weather was incredible, certainly comparatively. They no longer felt at home, and yet if they were costing the club a lot of money, they weren't allowed to complain, they were expected to deliver. If you're expensive, you can't ever be bad, you have to be great. It's a shame, because a player's value can work against them, particularly if they're not settled. There were plenty, particularly in London, who didn't enjoy the experience and as a consequence found it tough to train well on a daily basis. Then they would find themselves out of the team, and before they knew it they were struggling professionally as well as personally while being a million miles away from home. Then it doesn't matter how much you're being paid. It's a situation I wouldn't wish on any player.

I had been a relatively cheap purchase when I signed for QPR in 2012. It was the only time I was ever bought or sold in my career, and they met the buy-out clause in my Manchester City contract, which was £2,750,000. In theory, I've cost more in transfer fees than Lionel Messi! My initial contract paid me very well, but while securing my future, it held me back too. When QPR were relegated the first time, I was on Premier League wages, and that worked against me. A player's salary might indicate their worth to their current club, but it also helps to form the perception of other clubs. An interested party will determine how expensive a player might be based on their current wage, and mine put people off because they assumed I'd want the same or more from them. I didn't, but most clubs don't get far enough down the line with a player or their agent to find that out. That first QPR deal set me up for life, but it also locked me into the club almost whatever the circumstances.

•   •   •

My second season in the Championship started with Chris Ramsey looking for an assistant. He'd been given the manager job full-time despite our relegation and eventually settled on a surprising choice. Chris had talked about needing an experienced man to support him but went with somebody who'd only ever been the one in charge, including once before at QPR: Neil Warnock. He'd never been a beta to anyone's alpha, and it took a bit of time getting used to seeing them together at training sessions. Chris would still be the one barking orders, so we could imagine him as a No. 1, but we couldn't see Neil as a No. 2. While he would never undermine the manager directly, it was an interesting decision to have someone so suited to stepping in if things didn't work out with Chris.

It took three weeks for that to happen. When Neil came back to QPR, officially as a first-team adviser, he said he wasn't interested in full-time management any more (although he's still working as I write some five years on), but even as an assistant he worked the players as if he was the boss. He was a motivator, and not just in the manner he's famous for. Neil's time as de facto assistant and then interim manager was less than two months in total, so perhaps not long enough for us to witness the full-blown, full-throttle Warnock experience, but I did catch a glimpse of it in other ways. Chris Ramsey barely picked Junior Hoilett for the first two months of that season. After the manager had pinned the squad up on the dressing room wall before one game and left, Neil sidled up to Junior.

'I can't believe you're not playing,' he said. 'If I was the manager, you'd definitely play. 100 per cent. I love wingers.'

He wasn't undermining Chris as such, but he would use any means necessary to try to cultivate beneficial relationships. Having planted that seed with Junior, he must have also done it with the manager, because after Neil arrived at the club Junior came on as a sub to make his first three league appearances of the season. The third of those was a defeat to Derby that cost Chris his job. Then, Junior started for every game he was available while Neil was interim manager, and the seeds flowered a year later when Neil made Junior his first signing as Cardiff manager. It was a brief window into how Neil Warnock operated and confirmed that he wasn't particularly suitable for any role other than the main man.

He was only that for four games, always aware that he was a temporary appointment. After a month, QPR made Jimmy Floyd Hasselbaink the new permanent manager. He got the job after doing very well with Burton Albion and was the fifth boss I'd had since joining the club fewer than four years previously. I was grateful that I had some stability in my own life and could provide some on the pitch during all these changes at the club. Each of Chris, Neil and Jimmy had me as captain and picked me regularly, so new managers coming in didn't really affect me that much. At no point were we really involved in a relegation battle – the kind of situation that could prompt more seismic changes – and my aspirations of getting back to the Premier League were fizzling out too, so with everything settled at home I was happy to let my priorities adjust accordingly.

I also really liked Jimmy. I remembered him as a player, including from games against me, and he brought with him Dave Oldfield, a former midfielder who'd spent a year at Manchester City during his own playing career. Like many managers before him, Jimmy was quite strict from the jump, but he was also consistent. He had completely different methods from those most English players would be used to, particularly in the more traditional environment of the Championship. We'd be told to come in on the Sunday after a Saturday game, but not just for a normal warm-down. Jimmy would have the team doing much more intensive fitness work, which helped us get ready for the next match quicker. The English model tends to include a day off on Sunday and a light session on Monday, maybe with a bit of time on the exercise bike and a massage. Not with Jimmy. He wasn't having us popping into the gym and going on a foam roller; he'd tell us to get our boots on and go outside for a run, even if the rain was lashing down. Doing this the day after a game was nowhere near common outside the Premier League or for players who might have normally been allowed to down tools for a day and a half. It was active recovery involving hard work, and by Tuesday it meant we were ready either for another game or, if not, for a tougher physical session.

Those would include competitions to see who could run the most or, more accurately, to avoid being the player who'd run the least, as the stats would go up on a board half an hour after training was over. It was demanding, and there was a lot of resistance at the start, but I bought into it. I had got to the point in my career where I had come to realise why managers do certain things. Even Roberto Mancini taught me that what your boss says goes, even if how he says it causes conflict. Mancini was the coach, I was the player, and we were not on the same level. It was a brutal way of learning that lesson, but it nevertheless helped me to trust decisions that future managers made, because I was more open to the benefits. If we spent a session on a Tuesday focusing on apparently random long diagonal passes, I was more open-minded, and lo and behold we'd do it again on the Friday because it was a tactic designed for the weekend's opposition and the manager didn't want to introduce it for the first time on the day before the game. I was experienced enough to see the plan and accepted that most coaches don't just make stuff up on the spot.

I had no reason to push back, even if I didn't immediately agree with everything we did under Jimmy, because he gave me the opportunity to be involved from the start. If there was a problem, I could visit the manager's office and ask questions. He certainly wouldn't stand for open indiscipline, even from senior players. One training session Jimmy had planned an 11 v 11 game, and before it started he was attempting to give out some instructions. Jamie Mackie was talking over him, perhaps thinking Jimmy couldn't hear. At this point, Jamie was a very popular figure in the dressing room and with the fans, beloved by the staff and therefore blessed with all the leverage in the world. Jimmy told him to be quiet, but Jamie kept talking. Then Jimmy just lost it with him. He told him to shut the f**k up and go inside, hammering him in front of everyone. It was an important moment and made me stand a little bit taller, because if the manager's doing this to someone of Jamie's standing, nobody else was going to try to push it with him. Everybody's going to be in the same boat, rather than those with seniority getting extra leeway. This was his consistency with the players, and I enjoyed working for him. However, in the end, he proved a little too consistent with how he got us to play. We were solid, but we didn't win enough games. That 6–0 defeat to Newcastle was a couple of months before he was sacked, by which time we were seventeenth in the Championship.

Jimmy was a good guy to be coached by, and I thought his time at QPR was cut short a little early. He didn't have either the best or the worst record. I'm sure there's an added pressure on black managers because there have been so few of them in the English game; and once they're in the job it feels like for a black man things need to go *really* well for it to seem like it's just gone OK. There's also a conversation to be had about getting jobs on merit, and in terms of permanent bosses I'd had two black managers in a row but two completely different experiences with each of them. I don't think Chris Ramsey would have been promoted from the academy if Les Ferdinand wasn't director of football with a voice on the club's board. Meanwhile, Jimmy Floyd Hasselbaink was a famous black player, which often allows a candidate to bypass any bias, and he'd also been a great success at Burton. The contrast continued in their personalities. Jimmy had grown up amongst gangs on the outskirts of Amsterdam and once spent three months at a youth detention facility. He's said that football took him away from a possible life of crime and addiction, but he retains that edge; I think if you pissed him off, he'd fight you. I found more of a connection with Jimmy as there was something about him that felt closer to who I was. I respected him, and his mutual respect was worth having. He'd earned his playing career and had worked hard after it ended to get the chance at QPR. That's a black story that should be championed.

Chris, on the other hand, was a typical old-fashioned Londoner who once complained about some spiced Asian food the dietician had provided pre-match as having 'too much flavour'. The players thought it was much nicer than what we normally got, but he dismissed it as being like a takeaway and before the next game we had boiled chicken breasts. It was like chewing cardboard; I was disgusted by it! Chris, in my opinion, also didn't make the most of the professional opportunity that came his way. Even though he had softened his approach by the end of his time in charge, eventually understanding how his principles were difficult to put in place in senior football, there were still things that suggested he wasn't ready to take advantage of what was essentially his big break. He was initially appointed to be a Premier League manager, one of only ten black coaches in that league up to 2021, and while the team was in a situation almost nobody could have got us out of, I don't think he failed only because it was nigh-on impossible to succeed. In the match when we were relegated in 2015, I remember seeing the two managers standing in their technical areas: Manchester City's Manuel

Pellegrini in his beautifully cut slim-fit club suit; and Chris a few feet away with a hoodie jacket tied around his waist and Gola trainers. I admit it's superficial, but if it is the case that black managers are unfairly judged by different standards, it didn't help in changing any preconceptions. He didn't look the part.

It was the same behind the scenes. On the bus heading to a game and then also while the players were getting changed in the dressing room, he'd whip out his iPad, put his headphones on and watch *EastEnders*. The players would listen to music, privately or together on a speaker, but the top guy was just sitting in the corner catching up with the latest episode of his favourite soap. It was approaching parody, a man playing the role of manager despite not being at all suited to it. Again, things like that shouldn't matter. If a manager is doing his job successfully, why not take a few minutes out to chill out? Nobody was disrespectful enough to stop him doing it, but it affected our perception of him nonetheless, and that's why I'd recommend others don't watch *EastEnders* on a matchday if they want to be taken seriously. Can you imagine any other Premier League manager doing the same thing?

I support black managers getting opportunities, but equally I want them to be capable. Don't give a black man a job just because he exists; picking somebody who's definitely not good enough from the get-go might tick a box, but it misses the point. There are some who are more than talented who don't get the chance because a club or owner or chief executive is too scared to take a leap of faith on a candidate who doesn't have the same experience as a similarly qualified white man. This is where a paradox bites: how do you get the requisite experience if nobody's giving it to you in the first place? I'd like to see more black managers in the football pyramid, so that then at least you can see if they are good enough, as opposed to deciding they aren't without giving them a shot.

• • •

I'd had two interactions with Ian Holloway before he became the next man to take charge of QPR. The first was in person, just after Christmas 2010, when I was on loan at Sunderland and Holloway's Blackpool had travelled to the Stadium of Light. I was playing right back down the touchline next to the dugouts, and I was fouled.

'That's a dive!' He said as I tumbled over. I looked up, confused. Dripping with sarcasm, he continued. 'Oh, I can see where you've come from.'

He had decided I was play-acting, thinking myself big-time because of who, and how successful, my parent club was. I was not impressed. Who did he think he was, having a go at me, talking to me like I'm an idiot? I didn't know him, he didn't know me, and I certainly didn't find him funny.

The second occasion was when he was working for Sky Sports, and he gave me the man-of-the-match award for a game on which he'd commentated. I never got that many, so my view of him immediately changed. Of course Ian Holloway was a good guy, because he's obviously such a fine judge of character and performance!

Outside my own experiences of him, everyone was familiar with the madman Ian Holloway. But he didn't get the call from QPR in late 2016 because of his eccentricity. There was a sense of doom and gloom when Jimmy Floyd Hasselbaink was sacked, as we'd been less than entertaining to watch. What the club needed was an injection of energy to put some bums back on seats at Loftus Road. Apart from all the drama of promotions and relegations, the QPR fans had also had some flair players to enjoy watching, and the memory of the likes of Adel Taarabt scoring twenty goals a season and doing ten times as many nutmegs was fresh enough to be missed. The spark had gone, and so the club set about reigniting it with a familiar face. Ian loved QPR, had managed the club once before and was also a former player. The initial signs were good, with a huge buzz at his first game in charge, a sell-out against Norwich that we won 2–1. The message to the players reflected his enthusiasm too. He and his assistant Marc Bircham – another former player and coach at QPR – talked about bringing our club back and how they were going to make it exciting again. It was probably the most passionate introduction I've seen. He spoke about how proud he was to be back, like a fan who had been put in charge. Despite it all being delivered in his heavy Bristolian accent, you had to take him seriously because it was clear he meant it.

Then, in one of our first training sessions, he said he wanted the players to stick around afterwards because he wanted to show us something that illustrated what kind of a manager he was going to be, and what the club meant to him. Everyone trooped upstairs to the canteen – the staff and the first and reserve teams – and sat down. Ian made us watch the movie *Coach Carter*. The one where Samuel L. Jackson is a high-school basketball coach who insists on his players getting good grades. I hadn't seen it before, so I at least paid attention, especially considering I wanted to be on my best behaviour for a new manager. But this was at 1.30 p.m. Peak post-training nap time for footballers. Some of them were shattered, falling asleep around me, completely oblivious to the point the film, and the manager, was trying to make. It was about working for each other, Ian said as it finished. Like the kids in the movie, we were going to do a metaphorical version of 'suicides' – a gruelling running drill – because of what QPR meant to us all. It was an admittedly passionate message, albeit one not necessarily delivered in the most efficient way. It didn't quite answer the question I'd been asking myself about who the new boss was, but at least I stayed awake long enough to see the end of the film.

The win over Norwich was a dangerous one, because a victory in a manager's first match in charge can often prove to be a false dawn. That was emphatically the case under Ian Holloway, because we lost our next six Championship games. But there remained a positive atmosphere around the club, and the vibe was probably the best I felt during my whole time at QPR. The energy was different, and so was the football. Ian promised to bring in a progressive new style, with multiple systems focused on attacking. For all his idiosyncrasies – he would always dance before games, even when returning to his former club Millwall for the first time since leaving on bad terms; their fans had gathered at the stadium early as it was a night game, and Ian just pranced around at the front of the bus, baiting them – it was his tactical innovations that caught my eye most, even as he taught them to us in typical Ian Holloway fashion. During his first pre-season with us, he was desperately trying to explain to our forward players what he wanted them to do when in possession. The principle was that there would only ever be three people up against the opposition defence; never four or two, always three. The winger on either side would be on the outside shoulder of the full backs, and the striker between the two centre backs. That was it, a simple but non-negotiable tactic to make sure the opposing back four was pinned back, providing an overload in another part of the pitch. But our front line consistently failed to grasp the idea. The striker would drop short, or the No. 10 would push too far forward, or a winger would come inside. Ian would video each training session and we'd hear him watching it back, cursing his players' inability to follow simple instructions. He eventually gave up, using one of his many analogies.

'You know what this is like?'

It would always begin the same way.

'This is like I've just built myself a new swimming pool, and I've spent the day filling it up with water. I then go to bed, wake up the next morning and find the pool empty, and I've got to fill it up again.'

He got so frustrated, and it always stuck with me because it made me realise the difference between top-level players and some of those he was trying to coach in the Championship. Not every one of them is good at taking on instructions, and Ian was pulling his hair out as he discovered the same issues every single day. The players didn't have the ability to understand what the problem was and then communicate between themselves how to fix it, and all Ian could do was scream, 'Aaaaaaarrrgggh!' every time he watched it back on tape.

He remained undeterred, though. There were times when he put the team up on two sheets of paper because there were two different formations he wanted us to play: one with the ball, and one without, when a central midfielder dropped back to make a third centre half. On another occasion I was playing right back, but the team shape he'd drawn was lopsided, because when we were out of possession he wanted me to play as a third central defender while the left back stayed forward. Manchester City fans will recognise these ideas, knowing that Pep Guardiola does that with his team. Well, Ian Holloway was doing it in the Championship at the same time, if not before, albeit with different levels of success. It's the kind of tactical thinking that people can miss with Ian, because he's known more for being that crazy manager with a West Country twang. Even his players sometimes missed the method in his madness. One of his plans was to ask the left centre back to play a diagonal pass to the right winger, but it was a ball he had no intention of his player winning. The winger, usually smaller than the defender he's challenging with, would constantly complain.

'Why are you playing a ball in the air to me when the left back's massive?' he'd ask. 'I've got no chance to win that header!'

But Ian's idea was for the winger only to jostle for it, because as the ball was travelling, the right back and right central midfielder would sprint up to support him, ready to pick up the loose ball. Why was it loose? Because the left back couldn't control his header under pressure from our right winger. Then we would at least have territory, and the chance for possession too, with three of our players against one of theirs. There was a benefit to the tactical things he was doing, but because they were different to the norm, not everyone fully understood. This is the distinction between 'eccentric' and the 'quirky' I encountered with Stuart Pearce. I could describe to you what Ian's tactics were, and how he wanted them to work. I couldn't with Stuart, and I think his quirkiness was part of an overcompensation for lack of tactical intelligence.

There was a downside to Ian's obsession with QPR. He would

get exceptionally disappointed when things didn't go well. It wasn't just his job he was thinking about but the bigger picture. He tried to instil that purpose into his players, but nobody was going to love QPR as much as him. We did care, and he did help us feel like it was more than a workplace, but players have an in-built hesitancy; you might love your club, but at any moment they might decide they don't love you any more and send you on your way. It's rare for us to fall so deeply, because we know how quickly things can go wrong.

· · ·

Ian Holloway was my final manager in English football. The last of eleven. A shame none of them were goalkeepers, as they'd have made a good team. Barring the move from Roberto Mancini at Manchester City to Mark Hughes at QPR, each one was brought into the club I was at to change or rebuild. I'd had all those restarts and very little continuity. Every time, the previous person was deemed not good enough and was replaced with another who wanted to teach new principles and, of course, make us fitter. The range of personalities and styles of play they brought into my career was remarkable, and even though each one was very different, I think it's given me a diversity of thought and understanding about what works and an exposure to so many different ideas. I've had man-managers, motivators, the quirky and the eccentric. I've had the obsessive and the stylish and a guy who kicked the ground a lot.

It kept me on my toes, always knowing it might not go my way under the next man in. I had to adapt, and even though I had my fair share of injuries, I played consistently under a lot of managers, which means a lot of managers trusted me. That's why I'm happy to consider myself a good player. If you have the same boss picking you for fifteen years, how do you know it isn't just him who likes you? The consensus amongst almost all the managers I had was that I should be selected in their team, and perhaps I should give myself a little credit for that.

Chapter 19

I got up from the table and stormed out of the meeting room.

'I'm done,' I thought to myself. 'I can't tolerate that.'

Les Ferdinand had just fined me half a week's wages and presented it as if he was doing me a favour. It was April 2018, and I'd been sent off in the previous game against Hull. We were 4–0 down in the final minute of normal time, my teammate Josh Scowen fouled one of their players, and it was a bad one. As he got up, shoulders slumped, he was shown a yellow card. At the same time, Hull's Markus Henriksen came over and pushed Josh. If the fouled player had sought some sort of retribution I could have understood it, but this was a third party weighing in. Already annoyed because we were getting battered, I wasn't having this at all, so I barged Henriksen in the chest. I was sticking up for my teammate, as I'd been told to do for the entire fifteen years of my professional career, and with my blow delivered I turned round and started to jog back into position to deal with the free kick. I didn't get very far. The referee showed me a red card. He considered it violent conduct, while I had thought I was acting on principle. Ian Holloway understood what I'd done and backed me in the press after the game. Privately he told me he'd try his best to make sure I didn't get fined a week's wages, which you'd normally expect for being sent off. I certainly didn't think I should be punished. I was Josh's captain, and it was part of my job to stand up for him. On the Monday morning, Ian was alongside Les and one other as I explained myself, saying I did what I did and I wouldn't change it.

'They wanted to fine you two weeks' wages, you know?' Les was the director of football, and the 'they' was the board. A board he was on. 'But I convinced them to give you just half a week.'

My head went. Massively. I'd begun to think the club was a little too happy to fine players, almost as if it was a way of raising money, and now I was being told my punishment was less than 'they' had wanted in a way that suggested I should be grateful. You can debate whether it was a red card or not, but Les was the latest in a long line of people to complain about a failing team not laying a scratch on the opposition and never sticking up for each other. And yet when I did exactly that, he wanted to fine me as if it's a favour. He's a former player, he should have understood the situation I found myself in like the manager had done. I could have minded my own business when Henriksen came steaming in, but what would Les have said then? Just half a week. It was ringing in my head as I walked out without saying a word.

Outside that meeting room, the end of my time at QPR was a much more positive experience. The three-match ban for being sent off at Hull meant I only played once more for the team, in the final home game of the season. I came on as a second-half sub against Birmingham, and we won 3–1. During the traditional post-match lap of honour, with the vast majority of the fans still in the stadium, there was one sound that followed me the whole way round.

'CHIIIIIEEEEEEEEFFFF!'

The nickname I'd never used to introduce myself was now being adopted by thousands to identify me. It felt like a coming of age, as if I had become that person who means so much to my culture, and I was incredibly proud. My daughter Teia had been born in 2017, and along with Amaia and Lucy, she was in the stands watching. With my contract up and the club deciding not to exercise an option for another year, I was walking away, but I knew that I was doing so as a success. I'd played more games than some of those considered icons at the club, like Rodney Marsh, Ray Wilkins and Terry Venables. More than Les Ferdinand. Those 224 appearances also put me higher in the list than some of my more legendary peers like Clint Hill and Jamie Mackie. It was unfortunate that the three seasons I was captain were pretty much the lamest in QPR's recent history, as we finished twelfth, eighteenth and sixteenth in the Championship, but despite missing around ten weeks of that 2017/18 season, I was voted the players' player of the year. I think they understood me and knew what I stood for. Hopefully they also thought I was good to them on and off the field, playing well and leading by example. I'd always felt trusted by my teammates, but this was them acknowledging me too. I was exceptionally proud.

At the age of thirty-one, I found myself out of contract for the first time in my career. I'd loved my life down south, but we found the time we could give our friends from up north more and more limited. The first club I heard was interested in me was Burnley, which suited my ambitions to move back to Manchester, but that very quickly disappeared. As the transfer window progressed, I got a few more little bites. Sheffield United were an option, as were Rangers, who'd just appointed Steven Gerrard as manager. I was kind of interested but wondered why it wasn't catching my imagination. I looked at my family and saw two daughters, a four-year-old and a one-year-old. I realised we had a life that could be moved anywhere. The clubs that were coming in for me and the money on the table weren't inspiring enough to keep me in the UK, so it wasn't just Europe that I started to consider but the whole of the world. The continent was a difficult sell because of my age, but at the end of June something piqued my interest. Wayne Rooney signed for DC United in Major League Soccer (MLS). Once the idea of going to America got into my head, it never left.

• • •

In pursuing one goal, I had to give up on another. After leaving QPR I'd decided to try to get in touch with Jay-Jay Okocha, the Nigerian legend who'd spent part of his career at Bolton. I'd watched him from the bench in one of my first games in the Manchester City squad in 2004, and he was not only still close with the Nigerian national team but also friends with my uncle, a surgeon who lived in Bolton. I wanted to see if I could get a chance to play for Nigeria, because if I didn't in the final stretch of my career I would miss out on something that by then

I wanted, and needed, to do. Berti Vogts was the first to get in touch about playing for my country of birth. He had been the Nigeria manager for the 2008 Africa Cup of Nations (AFCON) and had called me a couple of times, but it hadn't felt right as I was still playing for the England Under-21s. The second opportunity arose four years later, when things had gone sour at Manchester City under Roberto Mancini. I turned it down again but for a different reason. I was at a really low ebb and as far on the back foot as you could possibly imagine with my manager. It would have been impossible to leave during the Premier League season, potentially for a month, when I had absolutely no standing at a club that was trying to get rid of me. I wasn't playing, and if I went away I'd likely have nothing whatsoever to come back to. Even if I'd gone to AFCON and played well, I was advised it would only open doors abroad, and that wasn't something I wanted. Because my club situation meant everything to me at that point, I insisted that while it was an honour to be asked, I just couldn't do it.

I resented that I had to make the choice based on the conflict that exists between the Premier League and the Cup of Nations. Having a tournament in January and February might not be to English football's liking, but not every country's calendar matches that of the Premier League, and it's frustrating that tournaments that happen during that season are labelled disruptive. When it comes to England and other British nations, it's called international duty. It's an honour to represent your country. For other nations on other continents, who might call up a player for six weeks for a competition that's essentially exactly the same as the European Championship, all the talk is about how the clubs are being deprived of their players and how AFCON should conform to the Premier League. AFCON and the Euro should be perceived as equals, and they're not. The imbalance forced me to choose the Premier League over Nigeria, and it cost me.

The assumption in Nigeria was that I never wanted to play for them, and that's why I didn't get another call for the remainder of my career. I did once have a guy come and give me his card, which identified him as an electrician, but he insisted he could get me into the Nigeria team. It was a little off-putting, because using a person who knows someone who knows someone else didn't feel like the right way to go about getting an international call-up. This was not the same as trying to speak to someone with direct influence, like Jay-Jay Okocha. But if Nigeria had got in touch in a more proper manner at any other time than they did, it would have been an easy decision. I would have said yes. It's a shame that over the years there have been plenty of managers who might have tried again, but I imagine they would have received guidance that I wasn't available. It was a misunderstanding, but I admit it's an understandable one. There have been tons of players come and go, some better than me, others not, but still, nobody called.

The thought of getting in touch with Jay-Jay went away when we landed on the idea of moving to the US. Travelling to one country only to leave my family there regularly to go to another would have been too much, so I decided to call it a day on my international ambitions. My family's future would be dictated by the next destination in my club career, and that was the priority. I don't regret how it ended, or never even really started, with

Nigeria, but I do wish I had played international football at a senior level. It would have been nice to say that I did, but I think I'll be fine. I didn't lose my identity because I never played for the national team, and I still want Nigeria to do well. Even if England, where I've lived most of my life, are playing Nigeria, I'm kind of rooting for Nigeria. That's where more people like me exist, and it's part of me that I'm very proud of. I don't go shoving it down people's throats, but that history matters to me, and I have no intention of trying to get rid of it. I'm part of British culture, and my kids were born here, but I'm looking forward to the point when I can take them to the country of my birth, to show them the part of their history they haven't seen yet. My two daughters could get married and lose their surname, and in one or two generations something that ties them to their Nigerian heritage might be gone. That history meant everything to my parents, and it does now to me too. I'm a Nigerian person who was raised in England, and throughout my life the customs and standards of the former have given me a different experience to most of those people in the latter. I would have liked to have reflected that by wearing a Super Eagles shirt during my career.

• • •

Deciding I wanted to join a club in America's MLS was one thing; making it happen was another entirely. Peter Morrison had been sent to jail in early 2018, but I was still represented by his agency. I told them what I'd like to do, and they said they'd look into it. As time went by, there wasn't a lot of traction. I spent the summer training on my own, and realising that I didn't really miss football, I became even more sure that not only was I making the decision to move to the USA for the right reasons, but it would be the last place I'd play in my career. Others might have been panicking, looking for anywhere to sign just so they could be back in time for the new season, but I'd got a taste of life without the game, and I quite liked it.

My last appearance for QPR had been in April, but as May, June, and July passed, still nothing was happening. The agency kept telling me the summer transfer window is a difficult time to move to MLS because it's halfway through their season, and my stars would need to align to make it happen. They kept saying the same thing, the stars needed to align. I waited and waited; I even watched some MLS on TV to become more familiar with it, just in case my stars aligned. They did, but via a different route.

When I had been sponsored by Umbro, my main contact at the company was Andrew Mashiter. He was a big Manchester City fan who'd become a friend and had since set up his own agency, with mostly cricketers and track and field athletes as his clients. I bumped into him and mentioned I was trying to go to MLS, so he asked if I'd like him to see what he could do. Sure, I thought, why not? There were apparently dead ends everywhere else. Andrew then set off on a journey essentially cold-calling every single MLS club. He was relentless. He learned about how teams put 'discovery rights' on potential signings, which allows them to have first option on a player. If you're on their 'discovery list', other clubs can only sign you if that original team doesn't want to, and they have to pay a fee as well. Then, you can only join a club if they have a spot available for an international player. That left four teams: Orlando City, Houston Dynamo, LAFC and Real Salt Lake. Orlando seemed like the most sensible option, as it was on the east coast and therefore closer to home. Plus they were getting battered every week, so might need reinforcements. Andy spoke to them, and the answer was they were OK for now.

That was a mind-bender. But a team that's losing 4 or 5–0 all the time doesn't need to get better, because in the MLS structure finishing bottom doesn't really matter. The mentality is, there's always next year. That threw me off a bit because I'd spent my whole career thinking there was only this year, and I'd seen so many players come and go because of how clubs have to get it right, right now. My agents insisted they too were speaking with clubs, and by the time August rolled around they called to say they'd drawn a blank. By now, though, Andy Mashiter had talked to another one of the four clubs with an international spot free, Real Salt Lake, and they'd offered me a deal. It had arrived the night before my agents told me they wouldn't be able to find anything. A man who'd never done a football deal before, let alone worked in MLS, had got me an offer for the rest of the season and two years more.

I didn't know anything about Salt Lake City, but I had been told of all the MLS clubs, avoid RSL. Don't go there, they said, it's weird. Well, they couldn't have been more wrong. Lucy and I had seen the *Book of Mormon* musical, but I didn't immediately associate it with the place even though they mention it endlessly in the songs. It's proof I don't hold on to the finer details of lyrics! I didn't know much about Mormonism and how the religion is centred in Salt Lake, though I remembered there's a temple just outside Preston that I would have driven past countless times. I did know there'd been a Winter Olympics there, but these were just pieces; Google filled in the rest of the jigsaw. I immediately set about searching for bits of information, looking at maps to get a feel for where to live, what to do and where the training ground and stadium were. The internet does not do any of that justice.

After the negotiations with RSL, they asked me to fly out to Utah and train with them for a couple of days. I travelled over with Andy and met the coach and the staff, and saw the training ground and stadium in person for the first time. I was blown away. Salt Lake City sits in a basin with the famous Great Salt Lake to the north-west, Utah Lake to the south and mountains east and west. You can see the Oquirrh Mountains from the training ground, while if you sit in the main stand of the Rio Tinto Stadium, your view is the field, the seats on the opposite side and the Wasatch Range stretching along the horizon. That's where I was standing when Andy took a call. It was LAFC making a rival offer. They wanted to bring me in for the remainder of the season with the option for one more year. Surely to go to Los Angeles would have been the obvious thing for a British player to do, so I could sample the lifestyle. Why would I not go to LA, or maybe New York? Keep to the coasts and have a good time. But it didn't appeal to me, or Lucy. We were moving the whole family over and wanted the right destination for the kids too. RSL were also offering me one year more, which would be triggered if I played twenty-four games in season two. Did I really want to go to LA for six weeks and then not be sure of staying? That offer, plus the immediate impression that Salt Lake was a place I could see my family settling, made me even more excited about joining RSL. I returned to Manchester, and while I waited for a work visa to arrive did some more googling. I tried to learn the name of every player in the squad so that when I joined them I would be hitting the ground running. I watched their games, saw issues, spoke to the coaches about it and promised to help solve them. Two days before Lucy's birthday, I got a text saying I could pick up my passport; the next, I was on a flight.

It was September, and I went back to Utah on my own for the rest of the 2018 MLS season. When I arrived, my homework paid off; I could say, 'Hello, Damir. Hello, Brooks. Hello, Nick. Hello, Albert.' That last one was a cheat, as I'd known Albert Rusnák from when he was at the Manchester City Academy. He had helped me during my two-day trial and was the only player I knew before joining the team. I think I got a lot of respect from the jump for familiarising myself with the other players, especially when a new arrival the next year didn't do the same. He failed to buy into the culture or the place at all, and he left two seasons later barely knowing any of his teammates' names. They had been written on plaques above each locker the whole time!

Having not played for so long, I had a mini pre-season in real time. The team was coming towards the end of the regular season, with six games left before the playoffs. I missed the first two and made my debut in the third, coming on for two minutes at the end of a 1–1 draw with Sporting Kansas City. Personally it was a strange period, being alone for the first time in so long, but it gave me the chance to take in the city as if I was a tourist. In fact, for my entire two-and-a-bit years in the USA I behaved like one. There's enough space in the MLS schedule to explore the country between games, and often at least a day in a new city if you've travelled for an away match. I used to arrive at the hotel, pull out my phone and see what's around. It never got old taking a scheduled flight to a city like Chicago, where I could sightsee with some per diem expenses in my pocket. No being whisked away off a chartered or private plane or being sectioned off in the front two carriages of a train. I could take it all in, and from my perspective the whole thing was just spectacular.

My first ninety minutes for Real Salt Lake was in the penultimate game of the regular season, so I was up to speed in time for the playoffs. The head coach Mike Petke had allowed me to establish myself within training, while the fitness coaches had to make sure I was able to play a whole game at 4,500ft above sea level, and that takes a while. As I was preparing for the trial in August I had learned about the city's altitude, so I had it in my mind when I started the first session. I was playing normally and thought it was fine. Then it hit me. What had just happened to my soul? Why do I feel like this? It's hard, particularly when it comes out of the blue. My entire career had been at sea level, and now I was floored while everyone around me was acclimatised to it. Even warming up at 4,500ft knocks you down. I'd look at my teammates and see how easy there were finding it, chatting away. I was just trying to get through some stretches without getting tired. Still, if I ever did something a bit nuts, I could blame it on the altitude.

The others told me I'd get used to it in time and that once I was on board I'd be fine, understanding that it wasn't a personal weakness but a strength of the city and the team. And once you're accustomed to it, you appreciate the benefits the altitude brings. Away teams would struggle when they came to play us, particularly in the summer when the air is extra dry and it's 30 to 40 degrees Celsius. Our home form from June to August was mythical. Teams would come and start off well, but about seventy minutes in they'd just die. That's when our runners would kick in and break the spirit of the opposition. It was like clockwork, the same point in every game; just as the play started to stretch our guys were going end to end, back and forth, whereas the other team went one way or the other, never both. If they couldn't run forward, they'd be penned in for the last twenty minutes; if they tried attacking, they couldn't run back, and we'd find overloads all over the pitch. It was absolutely incredible, and a brilliant feeling to know we had such an advantage at our disposal.

RSL's final game of the 2018 regular season wasn't in the last week of fixtures. The schedule was lopsided because of the number of teams in MLS at the time, so having lost 3–0 to the Portland Timbers in a match that, had we won, would have qualified both teams for the playoffs, we had to sit and watch as the league's 'Decision Day' took place without us. I decided that going to a driving range was the best way to spend my time while all the games were being played, including the one that would dictate whether we had a place in the post-season or not. I would keep an eye on LA Galaxy against the Houston Dynamo via my phone, knowing that the Galaxy were likely to win and put us out of the playoffs. They were 2–0 up by half-time, and I started to plan my journey home, checking out flights for the next day on the Skyscanner app. Houston hadn't had a good season; it was surely all done. I hit a few more balls and had another look at my phone. 2–1. Still, I thought, away teams don't often win in MLS because of the distances they have to go. It's not going to happen. 2–2, then 2–3 in the space of six minutes. I'm glad I never hit go on those flights, but in just opening my mind to the possibility of going home and how excited I'd be to see my family, I was a bit frustrated that Houston won the game, sending the Galaxy out and us through. If I'd just concentrated on the golf and not Skyscanner, I would have been fine!

I was only briefly annoyed, because the playoffs are everything in MLS. The relief of reaching the post-season quickly made way for anticipation, and I immediately got how it's not exclusively about final league position in the USA but whether that position gives you a place in the playoffs. My instinct would have normally been to wonder about all the joy at finishing sixth, thirteen points behind the leaders in the Western Conference. There were eight points between us and our qualifying round opponents LAFC. We were huge underdogs, and not just because we were the away side. Even though every team in the playoffs has an equal chance in theory, there's a reason we made it as the sixth-best team in the conference and not the third, as Los Angeles were. The LAFC playoff game was just my second start for RSL and one of the best games I had for them, helping me to create some early standing with my teammates. We won 3–2, and despite only having been there for about six weeks, I could already feel how significant the victory was. In the quarter-finals, though, the bracket bit. We drew the home leg against Sporting Kansas City but lost the second game 4–2, and our season was over.

• • •

Only at this point in November did the temperature start to cool. I'd worn shorts almost every day since arriving two months before. Remarkable scenes. When I went over for my first full season, this time with Lucy, the girls and our new-born son Ruben, shorts would not have cut it. Salt Lake City was under a foot of snow, and as we arrived at our rented house in Cottonwood Heights, our neighbour was slicing through it with a snowblower.

'Welcome to Utah!' I said to Lucy. The snow was high enough to almost bury the kids, and all I'd told her was how often I'd been wearing shorts.

Thankfully, Lucy felt the same as me. This was an adventure, like a long-term holiday. We were in a country where we'd loved to take trips in the past, and the thought of living there trumped any hesitation we might have had. I could have stayed in England for another three years but played another 150 games like the previous 350. We had moved to the USA because the number of games I would play didn't interest me as much as the experiences we'd have, and Lucy was up for broadening our horizons too. We knew it wasn't permanent, and we didn't sell or even put our house in Manchester up for rent because of that, but I felt lucky to be with my family in this completely different place and couldn't wait to show them around. I hadn't been in a position the previous summer to choose from a whole host of next steps, so to end up at RSL when the right kind of interest hadn't been there in the UK felt like a privilege, and I wanted to share that with them. We were also still benefiting from that first contract I signed at QPR. My RSL deal paid me the lowest wage since I was a teenager at Manchester City, and likely a lot less than I would have earned in the UK, but the other side of it was that I was doing something I really wanted to do. I still felt like a Premier League player, but no Premier League club had wanted me and that reality had pushed me to find a different solution. If I had been close-minded it would have been a disaster, but it wasn't long before I knew I'd made the right decision. It would be probably the most enjoyable stretch of my career, and our family would have some of the best days, weeks, months and years of our lives.

The snow continued to hammer down as I started my first MLS pre-season, with a lesson on how differently people in the USA deal with the weather. One day we were due in Salt Lake City to get some physical screening done, and there had been a huge dump (of snow; that's honestly what they call it). Some 3ft had come down in three hours. A text arrived from the club's player liaison guy. I was convinced the screening would be called off, but instead he only advised me that I'd have to plan a little more time for my journey downtown. The whole infrastructure was geared up to cope, including the indoor facilities at the training ground. Every box was ticked. In England, there'd have been weeks of cancellations!

●　●　●

I'd barely had a chance to get a sense of the challenge MLS would provide in the first five games, so the learning curve came at the beginning of my second season. Almost every player was new to me, and it heightened my senses in those early games. The second match, our first at home in 2019, was against the Vancouver Whitecaps and one of their attackers was running at me. I had no idea how to respond: was he right- or left-footed? Which way would he go? He was bearing down on our penalty area, and I had to make a decision based on instinct instead of the kind of knowledge you build of players over time. In the Premier League or the Championship, you play against roughly the same people over and over again. You know which ones are better than others, what their tendencies are and how to stop them. I'd learned the names of my teammates, and now I had to do the same with all the opposition players. I felt like a seventeen-year-old at the beginning of my career again, having to prove myself. But when you reach a certain age, everything being new isn't as daunting as it was when you're younger. It was refreshing and I loved it.

There's such a variety of approaches in MLS that it's hard to describe the standard I faced. There are some clubs that get the recruitment spot on, which combined with a strong coaching staff can, like anywhere in the world, make a really good team. There tended to be around six of that nature who, barring disasters, were locked in to be part of the playoffs, even though MLS is supposed to be a league of 'parity'. Some found success by bringing in a small number of star players on huge wages and filling the rest of their squads with draft picks. These youngsters are good players but literally months out of college, where the soccer season is short. Weeks removed from being on campus, they might now be in a team with a Champions League winner.

It means that the gap between the best and worst on any MLS roster is wider than it is elsewhere, and the number of difference-makers is fewer than in other top leagues. That doesn't stop it being competitive; the cliché of no game being easy applies just as much in the USA, partly because the salary cap prevents there being teams full of either the best or the worst. There is an issue around motivation, though. With no relegation from the league, some play the game as if it's a hobby. There was so much jeopardy at QPR, for example, and if we didn't win, there would be serious consequences. That forced us to play under pressure. MLS operates with a closed-shop franchise system that is only added to with expansion teams, and like when Orlando said they didn't need me in 2018, there's no great fear of failure. Add to that the fact that it flies relatively under the radar in a country with four huge sporting institutions, and there won't be a ton of conversations about you if you're doing badly.

That also leads to a different set of expectations from the fans. In my first few weeks at RSL, I was on the bench for a home game against Portland, one of our big rivals in the Western Conference. We lost 4–1 and conceded some appalling goals. At the end of stoppage time, I looked around and saw that 10,000 people had remained applauding the team, and the players clapped back. I had expected a hailstorm of boos, as would have happened in England – and that's if anyone had even stayed to the end. If that's the attitude of the fans, who while being admirably supportive aren't totally bothered about a horrible performance against a rival, then you can understand how that filters through not only to the players but to the so-called front office too, where the club's future is being shaped. The English alternative is a double-edged sword; it can be very hostile, sometimes severely so, and

I wouldn't wish that upon anyone, but when there's not just a desire to succeed but a *need* to do so, that can bring greater satisfaction. Some of the best moments of my career came playing under the most pressure and against the best players, because I was motivated by the consequences of failure.

• • •

Zlatan Ibrahimović is undoubtedly one of those best players, and he was in MLS. Incredibly talented, a legend of the game and personality-wise the antithesis of me. He's very outspoken, and he got a lot of attention in the USA during his two seasons with LA Galaxy. I understand that he's scored a ton of goals, is a better footballer than I (or pretty much anyone in MLS) ever was, but I felt a lot of what he said was disrespectful. At one point in 2019, he referred to himself as a 'Ferrari among Fiats'. I get it, he's an icon. But someone with that level of stardom could have tried to grow the league rather than belittle it. He got away with it, though, precisely because he's a star. In American sports, and increasingly in the Premier League, a match will be billed as not between two teams but two individuals. Manchester City against Liverpool is Pep Guardiola against Jürgen Klopp, while in MLS it was Zlatan's LA Galaxy against Rooney's DC United, even though the latter two would literally never cross paths during the ninety minutes. The status of a game may well be elevated by those stars, but that doesn't mean it's meaningless without them. A *Clásico* between Real Madrid and Barcelona is still a *Clásico* now Cristiano Ronaldo and Lionel Messi aren't involved.

This was the message I tried to give the team ahead of our first game against the Galaxy in 2019. It might be that nobody else cared that Zlatan was so dismissive of our league, but I did, and I wanted them to.

'As good as he is as a player, we're going to be on the same field as him, and you're just as deserving of that opportunity as he is, so act as such,' I said.

One of my teammates said he found him funny. I said he should be angry, not amused.

'If he says something or does something you disagree with during the game, stand up for yourself. Don't be walked over by his legacy.'

It was understandable that they might be. Zlatan's reputation was tremendous. A lot of goals, wins and trophies. They were also wary having played against him twice the previous season, even though RSL had thumped the Galaxy 6–2 at home, because he'd got two goals in a 3–0 win in Los Angeles. He couldn't get them to the playoffs because of that Decision Day defeat to Houston, but he had scored twenty-two in twenty-seven appearances. There was even talk of double-teaming him. Instead, I spent a non-eventful first half single-teaming him, and having never played against him before it felt just like two players going about their business. No chat between us, and he only appeared half into the game. Then in the second half a pass was heading his way, and I turned and stood in front of him to block his run. As the ball went by, Zlatan grabbed my shoulder and dragged me to the floor. Bear in mind I have no relationship with this man. I didn't like some of the stuff he'd been saying, but at this point that was it. So I wasn't angry, I was confused.

'F***ing get up!' he yelled at me.

Now I was angry. I got up, and fuelled by everything I'd said to my teammates about not being bullied by anyone, I got in his face. It was time to back up my words, and so I threw a few ugly ones in his direction, almost nose to nose. It had escalated quickly. I had been happy not to know him and certainly hadn't gone into the game with any intention of having beef with him. We'd been playing fair, and now all of a sudden we're in each other's faces having this back and forth. Who did he think he was talking to? Why was he telling me to get up when he's the one who just pulled me down? For one of the few times in my career, the red mist fully kicked in. I was really mad. The referee split up our shouting match and booked Zlatan. He told me to move away and calm down. I did so, eventually, but the animosity remained. For the rest of the game everything he did poorly I laughed at him, and he did the same to me. It was bizarre, and I had a moment outside of myself: what's going on with my life? I thought, as I realised I was giggling at every bad touch by Zlatan Ibrahimović as if the Dignity Health Sports Park in Los Angeles was the Miles Platting school playground. By that point we'd equalised to make it 1–1, and as we grew in the game he started berating his players from the halfway line, offering no help and appearing to become more and more disinterested. But with twelve minutes to go, he got the winner.

'Oh, for God's sake,' I thought as I raised my head skywards. My eyes were closed, so I didn't see Zlatan behind me, getting in an aggressive last laugh. There's a famous picture of it, and it led to a lot of people asking me afterwards how I had stayed so calm. I stayed calm because I had no idea it was happening. If I'd seen it, I would not have been calm at all, because it was disrespectful.

At the time, I was annoyed because it was another example of how attackers only need a second to be great, even if they, as he was, are ineffectual for the rest of the game. Defenders need to be great for ninety minutes. That's why I was so frustrated after the game. I felt like we deserved to win, and that was more important to me than what happened with Zlatan.

As I walked off the field, something caught my eye to make me angry again. Sam Johnson, the RSL player who couldn't name his teammates, was asking our photographer Bobby to get a picture of him and Zlatan together. To his credit, Bobby said no. Zlatan had just scored the winner against our team. He had also thrown one of his RSL teammates to the floor during the game, but still Sam persisted. He asked the Galaxy photographer instead and got his picture. It was absolutely pathetic, like they were out on a work bonding trip together, and a reminder that some players in MLS just don't take the league seriously. In England, if Manchester City had a cup game against a non-league team, the opposition might love the City players and want to swap shirts at the end of the game, but I guarantee they wouldn't if City disrespected any of them. I would also expect the non-league team to go out and play as hard as possible, even if they're up against much better players, so why are some in MLS scared to do the same? Sam Johnson was an example of not meeting standards, and not because he was a poor player but because of his attitude and application. It should always be about the team, not selfies with the star names. So, I returned to the dressing room feeling massively insulted and in a very bad mood.

I walked through the door and sat down, irritated. These are deeply personal moments for a footballer. Almost without exception, I would always be deathly quiet in those first few minutes after a game, waiting for the manager to come in and speak. It's sacrosanct, and the dressing room is a no-go area for anyone other than the members of that team. My head was bowed when out of the corner of my eye I saw movement. It had only been five minutes since the final whistle, and Zlatan Ibrahimović had walked in.

'Have you calmed down yet?'

'Excuse me?' I replied, sitting up straight.

'Have you calmed down?'

I was triggered. He'd come into our dressing room at a time nobody should and was being all pally-pally, taking the mick out of me in front of my teammates. In a rage, I stood up and started telling him to shut his mouth and where to go. I don't really swear, but I sent all sorts of filth his way. The red mist had descended again, and it wouldn't lift until Zlatan left. What I didn't realise was that the whole thing had been caught on camera, filmed from behind Zlatan with me bare-chested and furious. I was double angry. In hindsight, maybe I should have been a little more careful, considering he's 6ft 5in. and a black belt in tae kwon do – fighting him might not have been the best idea. But in that moment I was all-in, fully committed, because he'd broken the unwritten rule of never coming in to the other team's dressing room straight after a game. Apparently, he had wanted to apologise, but he should have known how disappointed we were as a team, so joking around about me calming down wasn't the way to do it. I'd spoken to my teammates about standing up to him, so when it was me who was offended, I stood up. I wasn't going to let him treat me – or anyone else, for that matter – like that, and I think I got a lot of respect that day. I certainly received a lot of messages, and I remember a little spate of people around the league treating Zlatan differently for the following couple of weeks. LA Galaxy's Twitter feed on the day had a different take. They posted the picture with Zlatan and Sam Johnson with the quote, 'I make the haters become my fans.' Embarrassing.

We met again in September, in Salt Lake. I was thinking, this could go either way, we could have proper beef. I'd been hounded by the Zlatan hive on social media for months, and somehow they'd found my private Instagram account. People had been saying I was soft, a loser. But in fairness to him, he was sound in that second game. It was a regular battle with no laughing, and this time we both scored. His was the winner, again, but mine was the only goal I got for RSL and the last of my career. At the end, there was respect between us, and we shook hands. I preferred that outcome, because even though I still didn't like some of the things he'd been saying – the Ferrari and Fiats comment had come between our two games – we said, 'Well played' to each other on the final whistle, and off we went. All business, no drama. And certainly no pictures.

RSL finished third in the Western Conference in 2019, my highest finish in MLS, but it was only secured by beating Vancouver on the last day of the regular season. The first round of the playoffs was against Portland, a team I'd lost to every time. The game at the Rio Tinto was played through rain, sleet, snow and wind, but we prevailed 2–1 with a late winner from Jefferson Savarino. To get across the line against Portland was massive, and I really, really enjoyed it. The quarter-final was in Seattle against the Sounders just four days later. We didn't play at all. You can only get so far in MLS being solid and direct; at some point you need to move the ball around and at least try to play football. We didn't do that enough to get control of the game and lost 2–0. The season was over, and that was the closest I ever got to winning the MLS Cup.

And yet, I still retain one particularly fond memory from the end of the 2019 campaign that has nothing to do with victories or defeats. One of our neighbours in Cottonwood Heights would open up his garage every Friday, bring out a table with drinks and invite us all over. We'd gather with our kids, having popcorn. It was great fun and showed what an incredible place it was to live. As did the final home game of the 2019 regular season against Houston, because I needed forty tickets for the entire estate to come and watch. Parents, children, most of them attending their first soccer match. Asking the RSL player liaison for that many seats was one of the most enjoyable moments in my life, because they all genuinely wanted to come and support me. Half of them had masks of my face to wear to the match, and I could see them all sitting in the same corner as we beat the Dynamo 2–1. I still have the photos – the kind I'm happy to see taken on a matchday! It proved to be more significant than I could have ever imagined, because by the time the next year rolled around, it would be very hard for anyone at all to come and watch a game.

Chapter 2020

We were locked down, and I was sitting alongside Lucy on the sofa, crying. I had my earphones in and was watching horrified as all eight minutes, forty-six seconds played out on my phone. I didn't look away for one moment, even when the tears had filled my eyes. When it was over, I turned to Lucy.

'I've had enough. I can't take this any more.'

It was May 2020, and George Floyd, a black man, had been killed by a police officer in Minneapolis, Minnesota. The video showed Derek Chauvin kneeling on Floyd's neck for what was eventually revealed in court to be nine minutes, twenty-nine seconds, asphyxiating him. It was already a stressful time, because the Covid-19 pandemic had forced the shutdown of the MLS season after just two games. There had also been other high-profile murders of black people, like Ahmaud Arbery in February, and Breonna Taylor in March. I was fed up and told Lucy so. I opened up about my own experiences. How I perceive things. How I have to carry myself in public. How I have to live. She would have known, but I had to say it out loud.

• • •

I've spent my life worried about doing something wrong. Or something that's considered by others to be wrong. I am a 6ft 2in., physically imposing black man. People see me as a threat. Some cross the road to avoid me. With law enforcement, it's the opposite; they won't leave me alone. Security guards follow me through shops, police cars pull me over. Once, when leaving a photo shoot for Umbro with Joe Hart while at Manchester City, I got in my black Audi A3 and drove approximately 5 metres before I saw flashing lights.

'Where have you been?' the officer asked me.

'Just there,' I said, pointing to the building I'd left moments before. 'What's going on?'

'We have reason to believe this car has been involved in a robbery.'

He was close enough to have literally seen me walk to my car, get in and drive no distance at all. I'd been inside for two hours; had he been waiting the whole time to stop me? There's an inherent suspicion: they'll ask, 'What have you done?' and even if the answer is nothing they'll come back with, 'Well, you must have done *something*.' There have been so many occasions like this, and that's why I don't feel safe around the police. I'm concerned something's going to happen to me. I can understand how others get a sense of comfort when they see a uniform, but that's because most people never have real interactions with police officers. They're used to seeing them through the lens of a TV screen, which suggests that 99 per cent of the time they're heroes.

If I go to New York, I see NYPD merchandise for sale

everywhere. Why? It's a police force, not a sports team. I understand having pride in and identifying with something local – that's exactly what football fans do – but it unsettles me. Particularly in America, cops can be just everyday people who have been given greater authority, and there's a level of discrimination or bias that exists within a lot of everyday people. By definition there will be elements of that within football too, but fans – and players – aren't given badges and guns.

On a recent trip back to Salt Lake City, I was picked up by a driver, a white guy, who was talking about how he'd been to England. He said he hated London because it's 'full of thugs'. As soon as he said it, I knew what he was thinking. Then, 'Refugees are just raping everyone.' He didn't need to say specifically, but it was obvious what he meant. What's to stop this cab driver becoming a policeman? If those are his views, why would they change with a badge? It's naïve to believe that people who have power shed those discriminatory characteristics. Why become a police officer? Is it because you want the best for your neighbourhood, or is it because you want to stamp out some of those who in your mind are detrimental to it?

Then you add weapons to the mix. Because so many Americans have guns due to the second amendment, the police all have to be armed too. Like the guards in Montenegro who racially abused me. They wanted to show they had power and provoked a situation that allowed them to. Why do some people like to show they have more power than others, and is that why they have the job they have? It's obviously not the case for everybody; some people do genuinely join the police force to serve and make a difference. But others use a position of power to create an artificial hierarchy where they're above someone else, and if they see black people as a threat or the enemy, how does a good person guarantee they won't get into trouble? It doesn't depend on what I do, it depends on what they want to do, and I hate that.

Then there's the 'bad apples' argument. The one that says we shouldn't judge an entire police force by those few who are racist and perpetrate crimes themselves. Where was this reasoning after 9/11? Why did the Western world become nervous about getting on a plane with an Arab, or indeed anyone with brown skin, when there are tens, hundreds of millions of Muslim men, women and children who wouldn't consider, even for a second, doing what the terrorists did in New York and Washington? Those who support the bearing of arms in America insist guns aren't responsible for mass shootings; it's just a tiny minority of people who are to blame. Bad apples. But those same people might find *every single* black person a threat and discharge their weapons accordingly. It's warped and hypocritical, and another example of how TV and movies, particularly in the US, have an outsized influence. There are hundreds of programmes about police that champion the force as they hunt down Islamic extremist terrorists or criminal black men. This is how biases are built, with some people's only (theoretical) interactions with ethnically diverse communities being what they witness on television. They have been, more often than not, the baddies. If the viewer lives in an area that's predominantly white and middle class, when do they get the opportunity to talk to people different to them and change that perception? Without it, they will assume, based on their limited experience, that they have a rough idea of what a person who doesn't share their skin colour is like and make a judgement on them.

I've spent most of my life in a position where I'm perceived in a certain way without having any direct influence on it. A determination can be made about me based on what someone has been told by someone else. I'm two people removed from defining my own identity. We're not all the same, and I mean that both within the black community and more generally. I'm proud of who I am based on how I got here. I accept and appreciate that I'm black and my story is different, but it's just as important that I'm an individual within that context too. I want you to enjoy me for who I am and what I bring, because you can find another black person who was born in the same hospital on the same day as me and we will share nothing other than birthday and skin colour. We are different too. So don't say I'm the same as everybody else, don't look down upon me, and don't think that I'm not good enough just because I'm not the same as you.

This is what I told Lucy. I was sick and tired of having my own experiences, and those of other black people, questioned and often dismissed. I'd have my hair mocked, ask them to stop and be told I'm uptight. Think about that: the person who has been discriminated against needs to chill out, somehow making the abuser the victim. It's nonsense. The constant subliminal racism I had faced had given me a sort of PTSD. I'd been strangled keeping it all in. My career hadn't protected me from it on the field, nor off it. When I'm walking the streets in a city, the only time I might feel more secure than any other black man is when somebody identifies me as a footballer. The rest of the time I'm the same, and I'm still tracked when I go into shops even now, after nearly two decades of playing the game. When we moved into the gated community in Surrey during my years at QPR, I drove up the long driveway to the estate and everybody looked.

Who is this black guy and how has he got enough money to live here? their faces asked. It wasn't overt, but just because it's subconscious doesn't make it less disturbing. These are the implicit prejudices that exist within most people. Your views might be the same, it's just you're not using words to express them. Some people do the right thing and try to address them, to figure out why they feel how they feel. Others do not.

While waiting for a TRAX tram in Salt Lake City, a man on a bike approached Lucy, my sister Diuto, the kids and me. He rode closely past us, shouted something, then sped away. There was a short silence, which Diuto broke.

'Did you hear that?!' She was genuinely shocked.

'No?' It had happened quickly, and I'd missed it. 'What did he say?'

Diuto was hesitant, unsure whether she should repeat it. 'He said Hitler was right.'

I boiled over with rage, but the man was already 30 metres away. He'd not only been talking about my sister and me but also my children because they aren't white. I realised I was going to have to explain to them everything I had been going through myself, and have the kind of conversations no father should need to have. I will at some point need to tell them these things happen because of their race, even when people tell them it isn't. It might be better for them than it was for me and certainly for my parents, as they are growing up in a much more financially secure environment, but as the looks I got in Claygate show, even people from the same socio-economic background are judged by their skin tone.

Salt Lake is a more diverse place than this episode suggests. Like a lot of US states, Utah is progressive in its cities but not quite so much in rural areas. Overall, about 1.5 per cent of the state population is black, and that's underpinned by those in less affluent parts of Salt Lake City and those African American students attending one of the many colleges. Cottonwood Heights was an area that drew from all over; our neighbours were from San Francisco, and there were many more from other parts of California too, while black people existed in the city at large, even if you didn't see many. The place I'd encounter the most was the Brickyard Barbershop, which was run by Romone Vaughn. I loved the culture of a traditional barbershop, where I didn't have to recognise all the faces to enjoy the mood and could sit there for hours. Romone would provide music that was as good as the conversation, and I could just imagine the history of the place while having my hair cut. Move further north or south outside of the city, and you'll find smaller towns, where I would sometimes feel like the only black guy. It wasn't massively hostile, but I'm always acutely aware that when I'm the one person of colour in a room there's pressure on me to behave in a 'proper' manner. If I do something wrong, there'll be a knock-on effect the next time a black person goes there, as they might face a more prejudicial environment. It's weird to be a representative for your entire race while you're visiting a museum in St George, Utah. Lucy will often try to help by pointing out I'm not the *only* black person in a room, nodding towards another individual or family. I respond by saying, 'Well, that makes three people out of a hundred, then!' It highlights both the problem and the fortune we had to live where we did with the workplace environment I had and the school the kids were able to go to. All three were brilliant but partly sheltered us from a more unpleasant reality beyond.

George Floyd's murder brought all this to the surface for me and out into the open for millions of others. Black Lives Matter protests swept across America and the world, including in Salt Lake City. I didn't join them, for two reasons. Firstly, there was a pandemic and I wanted to avoid the possibility of catching Covid; but secondly and more significantly, watching the demonstrations on TV, I saw how diverse it was. It wasn't a total black protest for a total black audience; it was a national and global issue, and that brought with it a real mix of protestors – which was both good and bad. Some were doing real damage, and while they might feel comfortable enough to flip over a car, for me as a black male, I'm worried about driving too fast. There was a lot of support for the movement, and I was glad that most people were trying their best to be heard without hurting anybody, but I was worried my experience would be different. I'd also seen some of the coverage, and a segment on Tucker Carlson's Fox News show has stuck with me ever since. It shows how in parts of America, opinions of a certain demographic aren't just formed by cop dramas on mainstream TV. Fox News is a right-wing news channel, one that talks to a predominantly white, older viewer. Tucker Carlson reported on the protests as if they were riots, focusing not on the massive majority who were peaceful but on the 'bad apples', if you will.

'This is what's going on,' he said, with his fake, quizzical frown. 'This is what's happening across the country.'

And then a phrase that chilled me.

'What happens when they come for you?'

What happens when *they* come for *you*. Who is 'they'? This is the most-watched cable news show, broadcast primetime every weeknight. That's a lot of people being whipped into a frenzy about the 'they'. For my last six weeks in Salt Lake, we moved to a place called Draper to tide us over until we returned home. The bins were housed just around the corner from our house, past a couple of neighbours. The guy next door always had his curtains open, with the TV constantly on Fox News. It made me worry. What might he be thinking about this black man who's moved in on his street? What might Fox News be telling him to think? For a British person not used to a country so divided by politics (even after Brexit), I thought it wasn't right that I felt that way. Someone having an extreme view at either end of the political scale will inevitably have an effect on other people who are just living their lives, to the extent that others might be nervous when putting the bins out. And that's a great shame, to say the least.

I imagine much to the dismay of people like Tucker Carlson, the BLM protests did change the conversation for the better. The video of Derek Chauvin with his knee on George Floyd's neck was so stark, so brutal, that instead of just asking, 'What did he do?', now it was also, 'Why did it happen?' It was the genesis for more people being prepared to believe the experiences of those other than themselves. And after I'd opened up to Lucy, I resolved to do something different too. I couldn't protest directly with the Black Lives Matter movement, but every time I speak about the issue of racism I can give a real sense of perspective and try to eliminate some of the bad actors, and I'm more than happy to say my piece. If it doesn't get said, then the issues brought to the fore by the protests might get pushed away as the quest for a return to 'normal' takes over. But in that 'normal' lots of people live a life they shouldn't have to.

So, as a consequence, I'm going to be saying and doing as much as I can. It's particularly important now, as racist opinions are being expressed more overtly and often under the cloak of anonymity on social media. I hate that people of colour might need me to speak out and need help to be taken seriously, when what they go through should need no advocate to be heard. But that's the nature of being the minority in any room. I've heard too many appalling jokes to count in dressing rooms throughout my career, with people from different ethnicities and the LGBTQ+ community as the punchline. It's outrageous, but it happens because these groups don't form the majority within those con-versations. And not only jokes, I've also heard views expressed within football clubs that would directly affect the lives of people in the minority; they were gay, black or Asian, and they wouldn't be hired because of it. In some ways I'm in a privileged position, because I've seen it and can speak out. I'd rather I didn't need to, but now that more people are understanding the reality of the situation, I'll try my best to make things better for everyone. But it can't just be me and others like me. It needs to be everyone. It's not enough just to have somebody from a group that's being discriminated against be the only voice that pushes back. That's the key thing: people must try to help others who don't look like them. I'm pushing for that, because for the longest time things haven't been as good as they've been made out to be. So, I'm going to use my influence on whatever platform to try to keep things honest. It's not all doom and gloom, but my two ques-tions will always be 'Why did it happen?' and then, 'Well, what can we do?'

• • •

Sport responded to the murder of George Floyd in its own way, and within MLS a black players' coalition was fully formed by the time the league held its MLS Is Back Tournament in Orlando. The restart was only possible after a new collective bargaining agreement (CBA) – the deal between an American sport's league and its players, without which essentially no games happen – was signed. The original CBA, agreed in February 2020, hadn't been ratified before the MLS shutdown in March, so the Covid-19 outbreak forced everybody back to the negotiating table. The MLS Is Back Tournament would have kept players in a bubble in Florida somewhere between thirty-four and fifty-eight days. I wasn't prepared to leave my family in Utah for that long in the middle of a pandemic, and opted not to go. Lucy and the kids were already in a foreign country and would have been alone, with nobody able to travel over from Manchester to help out. The players who were US nationals, particularly those with more relaxed attitudes to the virus, understandably didn't have the same concerns, and the tournament went ahead without me. A lot of them also couldn't afford not to go.

In April 2020, an email was sent to most of the staff at Real Salt Lake saying they were being furloughed, which in the USA meant they were being put on temporary leave without pay. It's different in the UK, where during the pandemic workers received a government-subsidised salary, optionally topped up by their employers. There was an overwhelmingly negative reaction to Premier League football clubs, some with vastly wealthy owners, instituting the scheme amongst the non-playing staff. In the USA, however, such decisions didn't face the same nationwide criticism, and RSL's then owner was the first in MLS to basically get rid of a lot of his workforce. Dell Loy Hansen, who is worth about $4 billion, made his money through real estate and spends it on sports teams, radio stations and rare coins. In 2019, he paid almost $4 million for a trade dollar from 1885. Apparently, it would have cost him a small percentage of that to keep his staff on during the pandemic. The fact he was a coin collector made me cynical; furloughing his staff made me upset. This was not my dude. I'm a person who considers the whole picture, and I try to see the importance of a cleaner in the same way I see the importance of a sweeper in a back three. What Hansen had done was harsh and didn't feel right.

I spoke with a few of those who'd lost their jobs. One was Ryan Hill, who produces my podcast with me, and another was Michelle Meinking, a nutritionist. Michelle helped me work out that around ninety people had gone from both the stadium and the training ground. We got the details of all ninety, reached out to them and asked for their addresses. With a little help from a couple of teammates, I sent every single one of them some money. It was an attempt to help them financially but also to alleviate some sadness. They didn't know if they'd ever get their jobs back and the pandemic was affecting everybody, so why were they being punished more than others, especially when the owner was a billionaire? The cheques were for $1,200 for the vast majority, and $500 for those who worked part time. I footed more than 85 per cent of the bill myself, against the wishes of my financial adviser. I asked him if I could afford it, considering it was the last year of my professional career and I was being paid less than ever before. I knew he'd say it wasn't sensible, but I also knew it was the right thing to do. Some of those to whom I was able to send money didn't ever come back to their old jobs, but one who did told me about how he'd been put on furlough at the same time as his wife, just as they'd had a child. He had health problems and said he couldn't thank me enough.

I was so glad to see the difference the money made, but it made me angrier towards Dell Loy Hansen. Sure, the rich were losing money because of the pandemic, but to those less fortunate their job is everything. It was my goal to help them during the summer while I couldn't play, and I think it created a good feeling at the club. I'm also proud that it's part of my legacy at RSL, especially considering I'm not from Salt Lake City. In fact, that was a big driver for me, because I'd come into their home at a time of need and in a relatively privileged position. What the owner did wasn't right, and I wanted to address it in whatever way I could. Michelle was brilliant and helped me a ton. I couldn't have done it without her commitment and her contacts. I'm also indebted to those teammates who helped and understand why some couldn't. One of the great things about any football club, and particularly RSL, is that the bulk of people who work there aren't highly paid players. You'll always meet some incredible people, working disproportionately hard based on how much they're earning compared to the footballers. It's one of the things that makes RSL what it is, and one of the reasons why I loved being there. I got a sense that I was surrounded by good people. Accompanying each cheque, there was a message that contained a bit of a white lie but was important nonetheless: 'Thank you, on behalf of all the players and staff at Real Salt Lake.'

• • •

The final season of my career resumed in late August 2020, and we stank. We won only four of the remaining games and missed the playoffs for the first time since I'd arrived at RSL. Crowds were either locked out, or, as in Utah, limited. The whole league was going through a very different experience, and it was a strange environment in which to play out my final weeks as a professional footballer. But I'm someone who is caught somewhere between principled and stubborn, so when I set the plan to retire in 2020, that wasn't going to change, even with the fractured final year. The contract offer from RSL was all I had wanted. At its end I would just be turning thirty-four, which I'd decided was a good age. I didn't fancy squeezing some quick money out of the years that followed.

The Rio Tinto Stadium was running at a reduced capacity of around 4,000 during the main part of the 2020 season. The last game of my career had fewer than 3,000 because there was a blizzard. I was unable to see the other side of the pitch, and it was the first time I played with an orange ball. We lost my final game in MLS 2–0 to Kansas City, the same team I'd played in my first, and they went on to win the Western Conference. There was an agreement with coach Freddy Juarez that I'd come off at sixty minutes. I checked the clock in each of the sixty-two that I lasted, thinking, 'This is it.' Then the moment came, and I walked off in an almost empty stadium, with the thick falling snow probably preventing most of those there from taking in my final seconds as a footballer. I could hear the applause and felt the love as I shook the hands of my teammates and hugged those I joined on the bench. I sat down and watched the last thirty minutes, beaming. It's all done, I thought. All done. In the dressing room afterwards, Freddy gave a speech. I liked him and appreciated that amongst the sadness of us not making the playoffs, he took a moment to thank me. After Aaron Herrera had spoken on behalf of the players, it was my turn.

'I want to thank everyone for all the help you've given me across the years. I hope that when you stop playing in the future, you feel what I feel in this moment. I am immensely proud to walk away on my own terms, to know that I am loved and re-spected by my teammates and the fans. It's a truly incredible feeling. I don't feel sad because I'm walking away; I feel happy because I've achieved everything I wanted to, and to be able to walk away like that is a genuine privilege.'

It would have been perfect if my family was able to be with me, but Lucy and the kids were prevented from coming into the dressing room by the pandemic. It had also stopped those in Manchester coming over to be with us. They had been there on the journey with me but couldn't witness the final part in person. They did stay up to watch on TV, and afterwards I received lots of messages saying, 'Congratulations on your retirement!' That's a hell of a feeling, reading that at the age of thirty-four, even though I'd set the date myself and had been looking forward to it. The spell without a club between QPR and signing for RSL had shown me how much I could enjoy life without football, and I was glad to be returning to that for good. I never thought I'd be content to end anything in failure – we'd not reached the playoffs, and I would end my professional career without a trophy – but I was content based on everything else that came with my time as a player. I was ecstatic that I'd had the oppor-tunity to play in MLS and to live in the US. When I returned to Cottonwood Heights for the first time a year after leaving RSL, it seemed like the whole neighbourhood, young and old, ran to the car to welcome me. I had wanted to make an impact on and off the field, and I think I did. I tried to be a good person and be seen as one. That was as important to me as being a good player. I could have won trophies, but silverware without the respect I felt from my teammates would have meant so much less. This is success to me: when I go back and those people make me feel like a king.

I left the Rio Tinto for the last time with a huge smile on my face. I walked out of the tunnel, along one side of the field, past the corner flag in the south-west of the stadium. I looked around to see the pitch covered in snow, the stands empty, trying to take it all in.

'I did this,' I said to myself. 'This was my home. I played here, lived the dream here.'

I turned towards the exit, freezing, and walked to where my car was parked. The first time I'd driven to a football stadium was to the sound of one of the D'Laryea twins' bootleg CDs, making my way through the council estates of east Manchester under slate-grey skies. Now as I sat in my car the music was streaming on my phone, and had there not been a blizzard the 11,000ft Twin Peaks of the Wasatch Range would have been right in front of me, filling my car's windscreen. Good job I had countless photos, obsessing sufficiently over the beauty of my commute to take as many in year three as I did on day three. I was so happy. Just so, so happy. I knew who I was, and I liked what I'd become. A boy from Nigeria and Manchester, via Sunderland and Surrey, had ended up living amongst the lakes and mountains in Utah, with nearly 450 games of professional football in between.

At the end of the journey home Lucy, who'd been there every step of the way, would be waiting with the kids. They'd put up banners to celebrate. After putting Amaia, Teia and Ruben to bed, Lucy and I just kicked back, full of joy and relief. I've not missed playing once because of all of them. I'd been fighting on the football field since the age of ten. Soon it would be time to fly home to Manchester and to the people I love. There, I'd start planning for the rest of my life, with a question. A question that's an incredible feeling for a 34-year-old.

'What's next?'

Timeline and Statistics

Chinedum Onuoha, born 12 November 1986

Mother: Dr Anthonia Ezinwanne Onuoha

Father: Martin Enyinnaya (E. M.) Onuoha

Sisters: Chioma (Diuto) Onuoha, born 1985; Chidinma (Chidi) Onuoha, born 1989; Lynda Chiamaka Onuoha, born 1995

Married in 2011 to Lucy Elizabeth Onuoha (née Halsall)

Children: Amaia Uzoma Onuoha, born 2014; Teia Chinyere Onuoha, born 2017; Ruben Obinna Onuoha, born 2018

TIMELINE

Summer 1997: joined Manchester City Academy

October 2004: Manchester City first-team debut

July 2010–May 2011: joined Sunderland on loan

June 2011–January 2012: returned to Manchester City

January 2012: joined Queens Park Rangers

June 2018: left QPR

September 2018: joined Real Salt Lake

November 2020: left RSL, retired

STATS

Sources: transfermarkt.co.uk; soccerbase.com; englandfootballonline.com

MANCHESTER CITY

Debut (competitive): 27 October 2004 (v Arsenal, League Cup)

Appearances: 116 (95 Premier League; 6 FA Cup; 8 League Cup; 7 UEFA Cup, including 1 qualification)

Goals: 5 (3 PL; 1 FA Cup; 1 UEFA Cup)

SUNDERLAND

Debut: 14 August 2010 (v Birmingham, PL)

Appearances: 32 (31 PL; 1 League Cup)

Goals: 1 (1 PL)

QUEENS PARK RANGERS

Debut: 1 February 2012 (v Aston Villa, PL)

Appearances: 224 (62 PL; 148 Championship, including 3 playoffs; 7 FA Cup; 7 League Cup)

Goals: 8 (7 Championship; 1 League Cup)

REAL SALT LAKE

Debut: 30 September 2018 (v Sporting Kansas City)

Appearances: 50 (44 MLS; 5 MLS Cup playoffs; 1 US Open Cup)

Goals: 1 (1 MLS)

CLUB CAREER

Appearances: 422

Goals: 15

Assists: 11

Yellow cards: 31

Red cards: 4 (3 straight red, one of which rescinded; 1 2x yellow card)

ENGLAND U-20s

Debut: 8 February 2005 (v Russia)

Appearances: 1 (1 friendly)

Goals: 1 (1 friendly)

ENGLAND U-21s

Debut: 11 October 2005 (v Poland)

Appearances: 22 (7 UEFA U-21 European Championship; 7 UEFA U-21 European Championship qualifying; 8 U-21 friendlies)

Goals: 2 (1 UEFA Euro; 1 UEFA Euro qualifying)

INTERNATIONAL CAREER

Appearances: 23

Goals: 3

Yellow cards: 2

TOTAL

Appearances: 445

Goals: 18

Assists: 11

Yellow cards: 33

Red cards: 4 (3 straight red, one of which rescinded; 1 2x yellow card)